Plays By Eugene O'Neill: Early Full-Length Plays

Broadway Play Publishing Inc
New York
BroadwayPlayPub.com

First published by B P P I: December 2000
I S B N: 978-0-88145-181-8

Book design: Marie Donovan
Copy editing: Sue Gilad
Typeface: Palatino

CONTENTS

BEYOND THE HORIZON 1
THE EMPEROR JONES 91
ANNA CHRISTIE 119

special thanks to

The Best Plays of 1919–1920 and the Year Book of the Drama in America, edited by Burns Mantle, ©1920, Small, Maynard & Company

Contour in Time: The Plays of Eugene O'Neill by Travis Bogard, ©1972, Oxford University Press

O'Neill by Arthur & Barbara Gelb, ©1960, 1962, 1973, Harper & Row

O'Neill: Son and Artist by Louis Sheaffer, ©1973, Little Brown

The Provincetown: A Story of the Theatre by Helen Deutsch and Stella Hanau, ©1931, Farrar & Rinehart

BEYOND THE HORIZON

To Agnes

ORIGINAL PRODUCTION

BEYOND THE HORIZON was first presented at a special matinee performance at the Morosco Theater on 2 February 1920, produced by John D Williams. The cast was:

ROBERT MAYO	Richard Bennett
ANDREW MAYO	Robert Kelly
RUTH ATKINS	Elsie Rizer
CAPTAIN DICK SCOTT	Sidney Macy
KATE MAYO	Mary Jeffery
JAMES MAYO	Erville Alderson
MRS ATKINS	Louise Closser Hale
MARY	Elfin Finn
BEN	George Hadden
DOCTOR FAWCETT	George Riddell

This production moved to the Little Theater, opening on 9 March 1920.

CHARACTERS

JAMES MAYO, *a farmer*
KATE MAYO, *his wife*
CAPTAIN DICK SCOTT, *of the bark* Sunda, *her brother*
ANDREW MAYO *and*
ROBERT MAYO, *sons of* JAMES MAYO
RUTH ATKINS
MRS ATKINS, *her widowed mother*
MARY
BEN, *a farm hand*
DOCTOR FAWCETT

The "right" and "left" of the stage directions are the audience's.

ACT ONE

Scene One

(A section of country highway. The road runs diagonally from the left, forward, to the right, rear, and can be seen in the distance winding toward the horizon like a pale ribbon between the low, rolling hills with their freshly plowed fields clearly divided from each other, checkerboard fashion, by the lines of stone walls and rough snake fences.)

(The forward triangle cut off by the road is a section of a field from the dark earth of which myriad bright-green blades of fall-sown rye are sprouting. A straggling line of piled rocks, too low to be called a wall, separates this field from the road.)

(To the rear of the road is a ditch with a sloping, grassy bank on the far side. From the center of this an old, gnarled apple tree, just budding into leaf, strains its twisted branches heavenwards, black against the pallor of distance. A snake-fence sidles from left to right along the top of the bank, passing beneath the apple tree.)

(The hushed twilight of a day in May is just beginning. The horizon hills are still rimmed by a faint line of flame, and the sky above them glows with the crimson flush of the sunset. This fades gradually as the action of the scene progresses.)

(At the rise of the curtain, ROBERT MAYO is discovered sitting on the fence. He is a tall, slender young man of twenty-three. There is a touch of the poet about him expressed in his high forehead and wide, dark eyes. His features are delicate and refined, leaning to weakness in the mouth and chin. He is dressed in grey corduroy trousers pushed into high laced boots, and a blue flannel shirt with a bright colored tie. He is reading a book by the fading sunset light. He shuts this, keeping a finger in to mark the place, and turns his head toward the horizon, gazing out over the fields and hills. His lips move as if he were reciting something to himself.)

(His brother ANDREW comes along the road from the right, returning from his work in the fields. He is twenty-seven years old, an opposite type to ROBERT: husky, sun-bronzed, handsome in a large-featured, manly fashion—a son of the soil, intelligent in a shrewd way, but with nothing of the intellectual about him. He wears overalls, leather boots, a grey flannel shirt open at the neck, and a soft, mud-stained hat pushed back on his head. He stops to talk to ROBERT, leaning on the hoe he carries.)

ANDREW: *(Seeing ROBERT has not noticed his presence—in a loud shout.)* Hey there!

(ROBERT *turns with a start. Seeing who it is, he smiles.*)

ANDREW: Gosh, you do take the prize for day-dreaming! And I see you've toted one of the old books along with you. Want to bust your eyesight reading in this light?

ROBERT: *(Glancing at the book in his hand with a rather shamefaced air)* I wasn't reading—just then, Andy.

ANDREW: No, but you have been. Shucks, you never will get any sense, Rob. *(He crosses the ditch and sits on the fence near his brother.)* What is it this time—poetry, I'll bet. *(He reaches for the book.)* Let me see.

ROBERT: *(Handing it to him rather reluctantly)* Yes, it's poetry. Look out you don't get it full of dirt.

ANDREW: *(Glancing at his hands)* That isn't dirt—it's good clean earth; but I'll be careful of the old thing. I just wanted to take a peep at it. *(He turns over the pages.)*

ROBERT: *(Slyly)* Better look out for your eyesight, Andy.

ANDREW: Huh! If reading this stuff was the only way to get blind, I'd see forever. *(His eyes read something and he gives an exclamation of disgust.)* Hump! *(With a provoking grin at his brother he reads aloud in a doleful, sing-song voice.)* "I have loved wind and light and the bright sea. But holy and most sacred night, not as I love and have loved thee." *(He hands the book back.)* Here! Take it and bury it. Give me a good magazine any time.

ROBERT: *(With a trace of irritation)* The Farm Journal?

ANDREW: Sure; anything sensible. I suppose it's that year in college gave you a liking for that kind of stuff. I'm darn glad I stopped with High School, or maybe I'd been crazy too. *(He grins and slaps* ROBERT *on the back affectionately.)* Imagine me reading poetry and plowing at the same time. The team'd run away, I'll bet.

ROBERT: *(Laughing)* Or picture me plowing. That'd be worse.

ANDREW: *(Seriously)* Pa was right never to sick you onto the farm. You surely were never cut out for a farmer, that's a fact—even if you'd never been took sick. *(With concern)* Say, how'd you feel now, anyway? I've lost track of you. Seems as if I never did get a chance to have a talk alone with you these days, 'count of the work. But you're looking fine as silk.

ROBERT: Why, I feel great—never better.

ANDREW: That's bully. You've surely earned it. You certainly had enough sickness in the old days to last you the rest of your life.

ROBERT: A healthy animal like you, you brute, can hardly understand what I went through—althrough you saw it. You remember—sick one day, and well the next—always weak—never able to last through a whole term at school 'til I was years behind everyone my age—not able to get in any games—it was hell! These last few years of comparative health have been heaven to me.

ANDREW: I know; they must have been. *(After a pause)* You should have gone back to college last fall, like I know you wanted to. You're fitted for that sort of thing—just as I ain't.

ROBERT: You know why I didn't go back, Andy. Pa didn't like the idea, even if he didn't say so; and I know he wanted the money to use improving the farm. And besides, I had pretty much all I cared for in that one year. I'm not keen on being a student, just because you see me reading books all the time. What I want to do now is keep on moving so that I won't take root in any one place.

ANDREW: Well, the trip you're leaving on tomorrow will keep you moving all right. *(At this mention of the trip they both fall silent. There is a pause. Finally he goes on, awkwardly attempting to speak casually.)* Uncle says you'll be gone three years.

ROBERT: About that, he figures.

ANDREW: *(Moodily)* That's a long time.

ROBERT: Not so long when you come to consider it. You know the *Sunda* sails around the Horn for Yokohama first, and that's a long voyage on a sailing ship; and if we go to any of the other places Uncle Dick mentions—India, or Australia, or South Africa, or South America—they'll be long voyages, too.

ANDREW: You can have all those foreign parts for all of me. A trip to the port once in a while, or maybe down to New York a couple of times a year—that's all the travel I'm hankering after. *(He looks down the road to the right.)* Here comes Pa.

(The noise of a team of horses coming slowly down the road is heard, and a man's voice urging them on. A moment later JAMES MAYO *enters, driving the two weary horses which have been unhitched from the plow. He is his son* ANDREW *over again in body and face—an* ANDREW *sixty-five years old, with a short, square, white beard. He is dressed much the same as* ANDREW.*)*

MAYO: *(Checking his horses when he sees his sons)* Whoa there! Hello boys! What are you two doin' there roostin' on the fence like a pair of hens?

ROBERT: *(Laughing)* Oh, just talking things over, Pa.

ANDREW: *(With a sly wink)* Rob's tryin' to get me into reading poetry. He thinks my education's been neglected.

MAYO: *(Chuckling)* That's good! You kin go out and sing it to the stock at nights to put 'em to sleep. What's that he's got there—'nother book?

Good Lord, I thought you'd read every book there was in the world, Robert; and here you go and finds 'nother one!

ROBERT: *(With a smile)* There's still a few left, Pa.

ANDREW: He's learning a new poem about the "bright sea" so he'll be all prepared to recite when he gets on the boat tomorrow.

MAYO: *(A bit rebukingly)* He'll have plenty of time to be thinkin' 'bout the water in the next years. No need to bother 'bout it yet.

ROBERT: *(Gently)* I wasn't. That's just Andy's fooling.

MAYO: *(Changing the subject abruptly; turns to ANDREW)* How are things lookin' up to the hill lot, Andy?

ANDREW: *(Enthusiastically)* Fine as silk for this early in the year. Those oats seem to be coming along great.

MAYO: I'm most done plowin' up the old medder—figger I ought to have it all up by tomorrow noon; then you kin start in with the harrowin'.

ANDREW: Sure. I expect I'll be through up above by then. There ain't but a little left to do.

MAYO: *(To the restive team)* Whoa there! You'll get your supper soon enough, you hungry critters. *(Turning again to ANDREW)* It looks like a good year for us, son, with fair luck on the weather—even if it's hard tucker gettin' things started.

ANDREW: *(With a grin of satisfaction)* I can stand my share of the hard work, I guess—and then some.

MAYO: That's the way to talk, son. Work never done a man harm yet—leastways, not work done out in the open.

(ROBERT *has been trying to pretend an interest in their conversation, but he can't help showing that it bores him.* ANDREW *notices this.*)

ANDREW: But farming ain't poetry, is it, Rob?

(ROBERT *smiles but remains silent.*)

MAYO: *(Seriously)* There's more satisfaction in the earth than ever was in any book; and Robert'll find it out sooner or later. *(A twinkle comes into his eyes.)* When he's grown up and got some sense.

ROBERT: *(Whimsically)* I'm never going to grow up—if I can help it.

MAYO: Time'll tell. Well, I'll be movin' along home. Don't you two stay gossipin' too long. *(He winks at* ROBERT.*)* 'Specially you, Andy. Ruth and her Maw is comin' to supper, and you'd best be hurryin' to wash up and put on your best Sunday-go-to-mettin' clothes.

(He laughs. ROBERT'S *face contracts as if he were wincing at some pain, but he forces a smile.* ANDREW *grows confused and casts a quick side glance at his brother.)*

ANDREW: I'll be along in a minute, Pa.

MAYO: And you, Robert, don't you stay moonin' at the sky longer'n is needful. You'll get lots o' time for that the next three years you're out on the sea. Remember this is your last night at home, and you've got to make an early start tomorrow, *(He hesitates, then finishes earnestly)* 'n' your Ma'll be wantin' to see all she kin o' you the little time left.

ROBERT: I'm not forgetting, Pa. I'll be home right away.

MAYO: That's right. I'll tell your Maw you're acomin'. *(He chucks to the horses.)* Giddap, old bones! Don't you want no supper tonight?

(The horses walk off, and he follows them. There is a pause. ANDREW *and* ROBERT *sit silently, without looking at each other.)*

ANDREW: *(After a while)* Ma's going to miss you a lot, Rob.

ROBERT: Yes—and I'll miss her.

ANDREW: And Pa ain't feeling none too happy to have you go—though he's been trying not to show it.

ROBERT: I can see how he feels.

ANDREW: And you can bet that I'm not giving any cheers about it. *(He puts one hand on the fence near* ROBERT.*)*

ROBERT: *(Putting one hand on top of* ANDREW'S *with a gesture almost of shyness)* I know that too, Andy.

ANDREW: I'll miss you as much as anybody, I guess. I know how lonesome the old place was winter before last when you was away to college—and even then you used to come home once in a while; but this time— *(He stops suddenly.)*

ROBERT: Let's not think about it—'til afterward. We'll only spoil this last night if we do.

ANDREW: That's good advice. *(But after a pause, he returns to the subject again.)* You see, you and I ain't like most brothers—always fighting and separated a lot of the time, while we've always been together—just the two of us. It's different with us. That's why it hits so hard, I guess.

ROBERT: *(With feeling)* It's just as hard for me, Andy—believe that! I hate to leave you and the old folks—but—I feel I've got to. There's something calling me— *(He points to the horizon.)* calling to me from over there, beyond— and I feel as if— no matter what happens— Oh, I can't just explain it to you, Andy.

ANDREW: No need to, Rob. *(Angry at himself)* You needn't try to explain. It's all just as it ought to be. Hell! You want to go. You feel you ought to, and you got to!— that's all there is to it; and I wouldn't have you miss this chance for the world.

ROBERT: It's fine of you to feel that way, Andy.

ANDREW: Huh! I'd be a nice son-of-a-gun if I didn't, wouldn't I? When I know how you need this sea trip to make a new man of you—in the body, I mean—and give you your full health back.

ROBERT: *(A trifle impatiently)* All of you seem to keep harping on my health. You were so used to seeing me lying around the house in the old days that you never will get over the notion that I'm a chronic invalid, and have to be looked after like a baby all the time, or wheeled round in a chair like Misses Atkins. You don't realize how I've bucked up in the past few years. Why, I bet right now I'm just as healthy as you are—I mean just as sound in wind and limb; and if I was staying on at the farm, I'd prove it to you. You're suffering from a fixed idea about my delicateness—and so are Pa and Ma. Every time I've offered to help, Pa has stared at me as if he thought I was contemplating suicide.

ANDREW: *(Conciliatingly)* Nobody claimed the undertaker was taking your measurements. All I was saying was the sea trip would be bound to do anybody good.

ROBERT: If I had no other excuse for going on Uncle Dick's ship but just my health, I'd stay right here and start in plowing.

ANDREW: Can't be done. No use in your talking that way, Rob. Farming ain't your nature. There's all the difference shown in just the way us two feel about the farm. I like it, all of it, and you—well, you like the home part of it, I expect; but as a place to work and grow things, you hate it. Ain't that right?

ROBERT: Yes, I suppose it is. I've tried to take an interest but—well, you're the Mayo branch of the family, and I take after Ma and Uncle Dick. It's natural enough when you come to think of it. The Mayos have been farmers from way back, while the Scotts have been mostly sea-faring folks, with a school teacher thrown in now and then on the woman's side—just as Ma was before her marriage.

ANDREW: You do favor Ma. I remember she used always to have her nose in a book when I was a kid; but she seems to have given it up of late years.

ROBERT: *(With a trace of bitterness)* The farm has claimed her in spite of herself. That's what I'm afraid it might do to me in time; and that's why I feel I ought to get away. *(Fearing he has hurt ANDREW's feelings.)* You mustn't misunderstand me, Andy. For you it's a different thing. You're a Mayo through and through. You're wedded to the soil. You're as much a product of it as an ear of corn is, or a tree. Father is the same. This farm is his life-work, and he's happy in knowing that another Mayo, inspired by the same love, will take up the work where he leaves off. I can understand your attitude, and Pa's; and I think it's wonderful and sincere. But I—well, I'm not made that way.

ANDREW: No, you ain't; but when it comes to understanding, I guess I realize that you've got your own angle of looking at things.

ROBERT: *(Musingly)* I wonder if you do, really.

ANDREW: *(Confidently)* Sure I do. You've seen a bit of the world, enough to make the farm seem small, and you've got the itch to see it all.

ROBERT: It's more than that, Andy.

ANDREW: Oh, of course. I know you're going to learn navigation, and all about a ship, so's you can be an officer. That's natural, too. There's fair pay in it, I expect, when you consider that you've always got a home and grub thrown in; and if you're set on travelling, you can go anywhere you've a mind to, without paying fare.

ROBERT: *(With a smile that is half-sad)* It's more than that, Andy.

ANDREW: Sure it is. There's always a chance of a good thing coming your way in some of those foreign ports or other. I've heard there are great opportunities for a young fellow with his eyes open in some of those new countries that are just being opened up. And with your education you ought to pick up the language quick. *(Jovially)* I'll bet that's what you've been turning over in your mind under all your quietness! *(He slaps his brother on the back with a laugh.)* Well, if you get to be a millionaire all of a sudden, call 'round once in a while and I'll pass the plate to you. We could use a lot of money right here on the farm without hurting it any.

ROBERT: *(Forced to laugh)* I've never considered that practical side of it for a minute, Andy.

(As ANDREW *looks incredulous.)*

ROBERT: That's the truth.

ANDREW: Well, you ought to.

ROBERT: No, I oughtn't. You're trying to wish an eye-for-business on me I don't possess. *(Pointing to the horizon—dreamily)* Supposing I was to tell you that it's just Beauty that's calling me, the beauty of the far off and unknown, the mystery and spell of the East, which lures me in the books I've read, the need of the freedom of great wide spaces, the joy of wandering on and on—in quest of the secret which is hidden just over there, beyond the horizon? Suppose I told you that was the one and only reason for my going?

ANDREW: I should say you were nutty.

ROBERT: Then I must be—because it's so.

ANDREW: I don't believe it. You've got that idea out of your poetry books. A good dose of sea-sickness will get that out of your system.

ROBERT: *(Frowning)* Don't, Andy. I'm serious.

ANDREW: Then you might as well stay right here, because we've got all you're looking for right on this farm. There's wide space enough, Lord knows; and you can have all the sea you want by walking a mile down to the beach; and there's plenty of horizon to look at, and beauty enough for anyone, except in the winter. *(He grins.)* As for the mystery and spell, and other things you mentioned, I haven't met 'em yet, but they're probably lying around somewheres. I'll have you understand this is a first-class farm with all the fixings. *(He laughs.)*

ROBERT: *(Joining in the laughter in spite of himself)* It's no use talking to you, you chump!

ANDREW: Maybe; but you'll see I'm right before you've gone far. You're not as big a nut as you'd like to make out. You'd better not say anything to Uncle Dick about spells and things when you're on the ship. He'll likely chuck you overboard for a Jonah. *(He jumps down from the fence.)* I'd better run along. I've got to wash up some as long as Ruth's Ma is coming over for supper.

ROBERT: *(Pointedly—almost bitterly)* And Ruth.

ANDREW: *(Confused—looking everywhere except at ROBERT; trying to appear unconcerned)* Yes, Pa did say she was staying too. Well, I better hustle, I guess, and— *(He steps over the ditch to the road while he is talking.)*

ROBERT: *(Who appears to be fighting some strong inward emotion—impulsively)* Wait a minute, Andy! *(He jumps down from the fence.)* There is something I want to— *(He stops abruptly, biting his lips, his face coloring.)*

ANDREW: *(Facing him; half-defiantly)* Yes?

ROBERT: *(Confusedly)* No— never mind— it doesn't matter, it was nothing.

ANDREW: *(After a pause, during which he stares fixedly at ROBERT's averted face)* Maybe I can guess— what you were going to say—but I guess you're right not to talk about it.

(He pulls ROBERT's hand from his side and grips it tensely; the two brothers stand looking into each other's eyes for a minute.)

ANDREW: We can't help those things, Rob. *(He turns away, suddenly releasing ROBERT's hand.)* You'll be coming along shortly, won't you?

ROBERT: *(Dully)* Yes.

ANDREW: See you later, then.

(He walks off down the road to the left. ROBERT *stares after him for a moment; then climbs to the fence rail again, and looks out over the hills, an expression of deep grief on his face. After a moment or so,* RUTH *enters hurriedly from the left. She is a healthy, blonde, out-of-door girl of twenty, with a graceful, slender figure. Her face, though inclined to roundness, is undeniably pretty, its large eyes of a deep blue set off strikingly by the sun-bronzed complexion. Her small, regular features are marked by a certain strength—an underlying, stubborn fixity of purpose hidden in the frankly-appealing charm of her fresh youthfulness. She wears a simple white dress but no hat.)*

RUTH: *(Seeing him)* Hello, Rob!

ROBERT: *(Startled)* Hello, Ruth!

RUTH: *(Jumps the ditch and perches on the fence beside him)* I was looking for you.

ROBERT: *(Pointedly)* Andy just left here.

RUTH: I know. I met him on the road a second ago. He told me you were here. *(Tenderly playful)* I wasn't looking for Andy, Smarty, if that's what you mean. I was looking for you.

ROBERT: Because I'm going away tomorrow?

RUTH: Because your mother was anxious to have you come home and asked me to look for you. I just wheeled Ma over to your house.

ROBERT: *(Perfunctorily)* How is your mother?

RUTH: *(A shadow coming over her face)* She's about the same. She never seems to get any better or any worse. Oh, Rob, I do wish she'd pick up a little or—or try to make the best of things that can't be helped.

ROBERT: Has she been nagging at you again?

RUTH: *(Nods her head, and then breaks forth rebelliously)* She never stops nagging. No matter what I do for her she finds fault. She's growing more irritable every day. Oh, Rob, you've no idea how hard it is living there alone with her in that big lonely house. It's enough to drive anyone mad. If only Pa was still living— *(She stops as if ashamed of her outburst.)* I suppose I shouldn't complain this way. I wouldn't to anyone but you. *(She sighs.)* Poor Ma, Lord knows it's hard enough for her—having to be wheeled around in a chair ever since I was born. I suppose it's natural to be cross when you're not able ever to walk a step. But why should she be in a temper with me all the time? Oh, I'd like to be going away some place—like you!

ROBERT: It's hard to stay—and equally hard to go, sometimes.

RUTH: There! If I'm not the stupid body! I swore I wasn't going to speak about your trip—until after you'd gone; and there I go, first thing!

ROBERT: Why didn't you want to speak of it?

RUTH: Because I didn't want to spoil this last night you're here. Oh, Rob, I'm going to—we're all going to miss you so awfully. Your mother is going around looking as if she'd burst out crying any minute. You ought to know how I feel. Andy and you and I—why it seems as if we'd always been together.

ROBERT: *(With a wry attempt at a smile)* You and Andy will still have each other. It'll be harder for me without anyone.

RUTH: But you'll have new sights and new people to take your mind off; while we'll be here with the old, familiar place to remind us every minute of the day. It's a shame you're going—just at this time, in spring, when everything is getting so nice. *(With a sigh)* I oughtn't to talk that way when I know going's the best thing for you—on account of your health. The sea trip's bound to do you so much good, everyone says.

ROBERT: *(With a half-resentful grimace)* Don't tell me you think I'm a hopeless invalid, too! I've heard enough of that talk from the folks. Honestly, Ruth, I feel better than I ever did in my life. I'm disgustingly healthy. I wouldn't even consider my health an excuse for this trip.

RUTH: *(Vaguely)* Of course you're bound to find all sorts of opportunities to get on, your father says.

ROBERT: *(Heatedly)* I don't give a damn about that! I wouldn't take a voyage across the road for the best opportunity in the world of the kind Pa thinks of. I'd run away from it instead. *(He smiles at his own irritation.)* Excuse me, Ruth, for getting worked up over it; but Andy gave me an overdose of the practical considerations.

RUTH: *(Slowly puzzled)* Well, then, if it isn't any of those reasons— *(With sudden intensity)* Oh, Rob, why do you want to go?

ROBERT: *(Turning to her quickly, in surprise—slowly)* Why do you ask that, Ruth?

RUTH: *(Dropping her eyes before his searching glance)* Because— *(Lamely)* It seems such a shame.

ROBERT: *(Insistently)* Why?

RUTH: Oh, because—everything.

ROBERT: I could hardly back out now, even if I wanted to. And I'll be forgotten before you know it.

RUTH: *(Indignantly)* You won't! I'll never forget— *(She stops and turns away to hide her confusion.)*

ROBERT: *(Softly)* Will you promise me that?

RUTH: *(Evasively)* Of course. It's mean of you to think that any of us would forget so easily.

ROBERT: *(Disappointedly)* Oh!

RUTH: *(With an attempt at lightness)* But you haven't told me your reason for leaving yet? Aren't you going to?

ROBERT: *(Moodily)* I doubt if you'll understand. It's difficult to explain, even to myself. It's more an instinctive longing that won't stand dissection. Either you feel it, or you don't. The cause of it all is in the blood and the bone, I guess, not in the brain, although imagination plays a large part in it. I can remember being conscious of it first when I was only a kid—you haven't forgotten what a sickly specimen I was then, in those days, have you?

RUTH: *(With a shudder)* They're past. Let's not think about them.

ROBERT: You'll have to, to understand. Well, in those days, when Ma was fixing meals, she used to get me out of the way by pushing my chair to the west window and telling me to look out and be quiet. That wasn't hard. I guess I was always quiet.

RUTH: *(Compassionately)* Yes, you always were—and you suffering so much, too!

ROBERT: *(Musingly)* So I used to stare out over the fields to the hills, out there—*(He points to the horizon.)* and somehow after a time I'd forget any pain I was in, and start dreaming. I knew the sea was over beyond those hills,—the folks had told me—and I used to wonder what the sea was like, and try to form a picture of it in my mind. *(With a smile)* There was all the mystery in the world to me then about that—far-off sea—and there still is! It called to me then just as it does now. *(After a slight pause)* And other times my eyes would follow this road, winding off into the distance, toward the hills, as if it, too, was searching for the sea. And I'd promise myself that when I grew up and was strong, I'd follow that road, and it and I would find the sea together. *(With a smile)* You see, my making this trip is only keeping that promise of long ago.

RUTH: *(Charmed by his low, musical voice telling the dreams of his childhood)* Yes, I see.

ROBERT: Those were the only happy moments of my life then, dreaming there at the window. I liked to be all alone—those times. I got to know all the different kinds of sunsets by heart—the clear ones and the cloudy ones, and all the color schemes of their countless variations—although I could hardly name more than three or four colors correctly. And all those sunsets took place over there—*(He points.)* beyond the horizon. So gradually I came to believe that all the wonders of the world happened on the other side of those hills. There was the home of the good fairies who performed beautiful miracles. *(He smiles.)* I believed in fairies then, although I suppose I ought to have been ashamed of it from a boy's standpoint. But you know how contemptuous of all religion Pa's always been—even the mention of it in the house makes him angry.

RUTH: Yes. *(Wearily)* It's just the opposite to our house.

ROBERT: He'd bullied Ma into being ashamed of believing in anything and he'd forbidden her to teach Andy or me. There wasn't much about our home but the life on the farm. I didn't like that, so I had to believe in fairies. *(With a smile)* Perhaps I still do believe in them. Anyway, in those days they were real enough, and sometimes—I suppose the mental science folks would explain it by self-hypnosis—I could actually hear them calling to me in soft whispers to come out and play with them, dance with them down the road in the dusk in a game of hide-and-seek to find out where the sun was hiding himself. They sang their little songs to me, songs that told of all the wonderful things they had in their home on the other side of the hills; and they promised to show me all of them, if I'd only come, come! But I couldn't come then, and I used to cry sometimes and Ma would think I was in pain. *(He breaks off suddenly with a laugh.)* That's why I'm going now, I suppose. For I can still hear them calling, although I'm a man and have seen the other side of many hills. But the horizon is as far away and as luring as ever. *(He turns to her—softly.)* Do you understand now, Ruth?

RUTH: *(Spellbound, in a whisper)* Yes.

ROBERT: You feel it then?

RUTH: Yes, yes, I do!

(Unconsciously she snuggles close against his side. His arm steals about her as if he were not aware of the action.)

RUTH: Oh, Rob, how could I help feeling it? You tell things so beautifully!

ROBERT: *(Suddenly realizing that his arm is around her, and that her head is resting on his shoulder, gently takes his arm away. RUTH, brought back to herself, is overcome with confusion.)* So now you know why I'm going. It's for that reason—that and one other.

RUTH: You've another? Then you must tell me that, too.

ROBERT: *(Looking at her searchingly. She drops her eyes before his gaze.)* I wonder if I ought to. I wonder if you'd really care to hear it—if you knew. You'll promise not to be angry—whatever it is?

RUTH: *(Softly, her face still averted)* Yes, I promise.

ROBERT: *(Simply)* I love you. That's the other reason.

RUTH: *(Hiding her face in her hands)* Oh, Rob!

ROBERT: You must let me finish now I've begun. I wasn't going to tell you, but I feel I have to. It can't matter to you now that I'm going so far away, and for so long—perhaps forever. I've loved you all these years, but the realization of it never came to me 'til I agreed to go away with Uncle Dick. Then I thought of leaving you, and the pain of that thought revealed the truth to me in a flash—that I loved you, had loved you as long as I could remember. *(He gently pulls one of RUTH's hands away from her face.)* You mustn't mind my telling you this, Ruth. I realize how impossible it all is—and I understand; for the revelation of my own love seemed to open my eyes to the love of others. I saw Andy's love for you—and I knew that you must love him.

RUTH: *(Breaking out stormily)* I don't! I don't love Andy! I don't!

(ROBERT *stares at her in stupid astonishment.* RUTH *weeps hysterically.*)

RUTH: Whatever—put such a fool notion into—into your head? *(She suddenly throws her arms about his neck and hides her head on his shoulder.)* Oh, Rob! Don't go away! Please! You mustn't, now! You can't! I won't let you! It'd break my—my heart!

ROBERT: *(The expression of stupid bewilderment giving way to one of overwhelming joy. He presses her close to him—slowly and tenderly.)* Do you mean that—that you love me?

RUTH: *(Sobbing)* Yes, yes—of course I do—what d'you s'pose? *(She lifts up her head and looks into his eyes with a tremulous smile.)* You stupid thing!

(He kisses her.)

RUTH: I've loved you right along.

ROBERT: *(Mystified)* But you and Andy were always together!

RUTH: Because you never seemed to want to go any place with me. You were always reading an old book, and not paying any attention to me. I was too proud to let you see I cared because I thought the year you had away to college had made you stuck-up, and you thought yourself too educated to waste any time on me.

ROBERT: *(Kissing her)* And I was thinking— *(With a laugh)* What fools we've both been!

RUTH: *(Overcome by a sudden fear)* You won't go away on the trip, will you, Rob? You'll tell them you can't go on account of me, won't you? You can't go now! You can't!

ROBERT: *(Bewildered)* Perhaps—you can come too.

RUTH: Oh, Rob, don't be so foolish. You know I can't. Who'd take care of Ma? She has no one in the world but me. I can't leave her—the way she is. It'd be different if she was well and healthy like other people. Don't you see I couldn't go—on her account?

ROBERT: *(Vaguely)* I could go—and then send for you both—when I'd settled some place out there.

RUTH: Ma never could. She'd never leave the farm for anything; and she couldn't make a trip anywhere 'til she got better—if she ever does. And oh,

Rob, I wouldn't want to live in any of those outlandish places you were going to. I couldn't stand it there, I know I couldn't—not knowing anyone. It makes me afraid just to think of it. I've never been away from here, hardly and—I'm just a home body, I'm afraid. *(She clings to him imploringly.)* Please don't go—not now. Tell them you've decided not to. They won't mind. I know your mother and father'll be glad. They'll all be. They don't want you to go so far away from them. Please, Rob! We'll be so happy here together where it's natural and we know things. Please tell me you won't go!

ROBERT: *(Face to face with a definite, final decision, betrays the conflict going on within him)* But—Ruth—I—Uncle Dick—

RUTH: He won't mind when he knows it's for your happiness to stay. How could he? *(As ROBERT remains silent she bursts into sobs again.)* Oh, Rob! And you said—you loved me!

ROBERT: *(Conquered by this appeal—an irrevocable decision in his voice)* I won't go, Ruth. I promise you. There! Don't cry! *(He presses her to him, stroking her hair tenderly. After a pause he speaks with happy hopefulness.)* Perhaps after all Andy was right—righter than he knew—when he said I could find all the things I was seeking for here, at home on the farm. The mystery and the wonder—our love should bring them home to us. I think love must have been the secret—the secret that called to me from over the world's rim—the secret beyond every horizon; and when I did not come, it came to me. *(He clasps RUTH to him fiercely.)* Oh, Ruth, you are right! Our love is sweeter than any distant dream. It is the meaning of all life, the whole world. The kingdom of heaven is within—us!

(He kisses her passionately and steps to the ground, lifting RUTH in his arms and carrying her to the road where he puts her down.)

RUTH: *(With a happy laugh)* My, but you're strong!

ROBERT: Come! We'll go and tell them at once.

RUTH: *(Dismayed)* Oh, no, don't, Rob, not 'til after I've gone. Then you can tell your folks and I'll tell Ma when I get her home. There'd be bound to be such a scene with them all together.

ROBERT: *(Kissing her—gaily)* As you like—little Miss Common Sense!

RUTH: Let's go, then.

(She takes his hand, and they start to go off left. ROBERT suddenly stops and turns as though for a last look at the hills and the dying sunset flush.)

ROBERT: *(Looking upward and pointing)* See! The first star. *(He bends down and kisses her tenderly.)* Our star!

RUTH: *(In a soft murmur)* Yes. Our very own star.

(They stand for a moment looking up at it, their arms around each other. Then RUTH *takes his hand again and starts to lead him away.)*

RUTH: Come, Rob, let's go.

(His eyes are fixed again on the horizon as he half turns to follow her. RUTH *urges.)*

RUTH: We'll be late for supper, Rob.

ROBERT: *(Shakes his head impatiently, as though he were throwing off some disturbing thought—with a laugh.)* All right. We'll run then. Come on!

(They run off laughing as the curtain falls.)

Scene Two

(The sitting room of the Mayo farm house about nine o'clock the same night. On the left, two windows looking out on the fields. Against the wall between the windows, an old-fashioned walnut desk. In the left corner, rear, a sideboard with a mirror. In the rear wall to the right of the sideboard, a window looking out on the road. Next to the window a door leading out into the yard. Farther right, a black horsehair sofa, and another door opening on a bedroom. In the corner, a straight-backed chair. In the right wall, near the middle, an open doorway leading to the kitchen. Farther forward a double-heater stove with coal scuttle, etc. In the center of the newly carpeted floor, an oak dining-room table with a red cover. In the center of the table, a large oil reading lamp. Four chairs, three rockers with crocheted tidies on their backs, and one straight-backed, are placed about the table. The walls are papered a dark red with a scrolly-figured pattern.)

(Everything in the room is clean, well-kept, and in its exact place, yet there is no suggestion of primness about the whole. Rather the atmosphere is one of the orderly comfort of a simple, hard-earned prosperity, enjoyed and maintained by the family as a unit.)

*(*JAMES MAYO, *his wife, her brother,* CAPTAIN DICK SCOTT, *and* ANDREW *are discovered.* MRS MAYO *is a slight, round-faced, rather prim-looking woman of fifty-five who had once been a school teacher. The labors of a farmer's wife have bent but not broken her, and she retains a certain refinement of movement and expression foreign to the Mayo part of the family. Whatever of resemblance* ROBERT *has to his parents may be traced to her. Her brother, the* CAPTAIN, *is short and stocky, with a weather-beaten, jovial face and a white moustache—a typical old salt, loud of voice and given to gesture. He is fifty-eight years old.)*

*(*JAMES MAYO *sits in front of the table. He wears spectacles, and a farm journal which he has been reading lies in his lap. The* CAPTAIN *leans forward from a chair in the rear, his hands on the table in front of him.* ANDREW *is tilted back on the straight-backed chair to the left, his chin sunk forward on his chest, staring at the carpet, preoccupied and frowning.)*

(As the curtain rises the CAPTAIN *is just finishing the relation of some sea episode. The others are pretending an interest which is belied by the absent-minded expressions on their faces.)*

THE CAPTAIN: *(Chuckling)* And that mission woman, she hails me on the dock as I was acomin' ashore, and she says—with her silly face all screwed up serious as judgment—"Captain," she says, "would you be so kind as to tell me where the sea-gulls sleeps at nights?" Blow me if them warn't her exact words! *(He slaps the table with the palm of his hands and laughs loudly. The others force smiles.)* Ain't that just like a fool woman's question? And I looks at her serious as I could, "Ma'm," says I, "I couldn't rightly answer that question. I ain't never seed a sea-gull in his bunk yet. The next time I hears one snorin'," I says, "I'll make a note of where he's turned in, and write you a letter 'bout it." And then she calls me a fool real spiteful and tacks away from me quick. *(He laughs again uproariously.)* So I got rid of her that way.

(The others smile but immediately relapse into expressions of gloom again.)

MRS MAYO: *(Absent-mindedly—feeling that she has to say something)* But when it comes to that, where *do* sea-gulls sleep, Dick?

SCOTT: *(Slapping the table)* Ho! Ho! Listen to her, James. 'Nother one! Well, if that don't beat all hell—'scuse me for cussin', Kate.

MAYO: *(With a twinkle in his eyes)* They unhitch their wings, Katey, and spreads 'em out on a wave for a bed.

SCOTT: And then they tells the fish to whistle to 'em when it's time to turn out. Ho! Ho!

MRS MAYO: *(With a forced smile)* You men folks are too smart to live, aren't you?

(She resumes her knitting. MAYO *pretends to read his paper;* ANDREW *stares at the floor.)*

SCOTT: *(Looks from one to the other of them with a puzzled air. Finally he is unable to bear the thick silence a minute longer, and blurts out)* You folks look as if you was settin' up with a corpse. *(With exaggerated concern)* God A'mighty, there ain't anyone dead, be there?

MAYO: *(Sharply)* Don't play the dunce, Dick! You know as well as we do there ain't no great cause to be feelin' chipper.

SCOTT: *(Argumentatively)* And there ain't no cause to be wearin' mourning, either, I can make out.

MRS MAYO: *(Indignantly)* How can you talk that way, Dick Scott, when you're taking our Robbie away from us, in the middle of the night, you might say, just to get on that old boat of yours on time! I think you might wait until morning when he's had his breakfast.

SCOTT: *(Appealing to the others hopelessly)* Ain't that a woman's way o' seein' things for you? God A'mighty, Kate, I can't give orders to the tide that it's got to be high just when it suits me to have it. I ain't gettin' no fun out o' missin' sleep and leavin' here at six bells myself. *(Protestingly)* And the *Sunda* ain't an old ship—leastways, not very old—and she's good's she ever was. Your boy Robert'll be as safe on board o' her as he'd be home in bed here.

MRS MAYO: How can you say that, Dick, when we read in almost every paper about wrecks and storms, and ships being sunk.

SCOTT: You've got to take your chances with such things. They don't happen often—not nigh as often as accidents do ashore.

MRS MAYO: *(Her lips trembling)* I wish Robbie weren't going—not so far away and for so long.

MAYO: *(Looking at her over his glasses—consolingly)* There, Katey!

MRS MAYO: *(Rebelliously)* Well, I do wish he wasn't! It'd be different if he'd ever been away from home before for any length of time. If he was healthy and strong too, it'd be different. I'm so afraid he'll be taken down ill when you're miles from land, and there's no one to take care of him.

MAYO: That's the very reason you was willin' for him to go, Katey—'count o' your bein' 'fraid for his health.

MRS MAYO: *(Illogically)* But he seems to be all right now without Dick taking him away.

SCOTT: *(Protestingly)* You'd think to hear you, Kate, that I was kidnappin' Robert agin your will. Now I ain't asayin' I ain't tickled to death to have him along, because I be. It's a'mighty lonesome for a captain on a sailin' vessel at times, and Robert'll be company for me. But what I'm sayin' is, I didn't propose it. I never even suspicioned that he was hankerin' to ship out, or that you'd let him go 'til you and James speaks to me 'bout it. And now you blames me for it.

MAYO: That's so. Dick's speaking the truth, Katey.

SCOTT: You shouldn't be taking it so hard, 's far as I kin see. This vige'll make a man of him. I'll see to it he learns how to navigate, 'n' study for a mate's c'tificate right off—and it'll give him a trade for the rest of his life, if he wants to travel.

MRS MAYO: —But I don't want him to travel all his life. You've got to see he comes home when this trip is over. Then he'll be all well, and he'll want to—to marry—

(ANDREW *sits forward in his chair with an abrupt movement.*)

MRS MAYO: —and settle down right here.

SCOTT: Well, in any case it won't hurt him to learn things when he's travellin'. And then he'll get to see a lot of the world in the ports we put in at, 'n' that 'll help him afterwards, no matter what he takes up.

MRS MAYO: *(Staring down at the knitting in her lap—as if she hadn't heard him)* I never realized how hard it was going to be for me to have Robbie go—or I wouldn't have considered it a minute. *(On the verge of tears)* Oh, if only he wouldn't go!

SCOTT: It ain't no good goin' on that way, Kate, now it's all settled.

MRS MAYO: *(Half-sobbing)* It's all right for you to talk. You've never had any children of your own, and you don't know what it means to be parted from them—and Robbie my youngest, too.

(ANDREW *frowns and fidgets in his chair.*)

MAYO: *(A trace of command in his voice)* No use takin' on so, Katey! It's best for the boy. We've got to take that into consideration—no matter how much we hate to lose him. *(Firmly)* And like Dick says, it's all settled now.

ANDREW: *(Suddenly turning to them)* There's one thing none of you seem to take into consideration—that Rob wants to go. He's dead set on it. He's been dreaming over this trip ever since it was first talked about. It wouldn't be fair to him not to have him go. *(A sudden thought seems to strike him and he continues doubtfully.)* At least, not if he still feels the same way about it he did when he was talking to me this evening.

MAYO: *(With an air of decision)* Andy's right, Katey. Robert wants to go. That ends all argyment, you can see that.

MRS MAYO: *(Faintly, but resignedly)* Yes. I suppose it must be, then.

MAYO: *(Looking at his big silver watch)* It's past nine. Wonder what's happened to Robert. He's been gone long enough to wheel the widder to home, certain. He can't be out dreamin' at the stars his last night.

MRS MAYO: *(A bit reproachfully)* Why didn't you wheel Mrs. Atkins back tonight, Andy? You usually do when she and Ruth come over.

ANDREW: *(Avoiding her eyes)* I thought maybe Robert wanted to go tonight. He offered to go right away when they were leaving.

MRS MAYO: He only wanted to be polite.

ANDREW: *(Gets to his feet)* Well, he'll be right back, I guess. *(He turns to his father.)* Guess I'll go take a look at the black cow, Pa—see if she's ailing any.

MAYO: Yes—better had, son.

(ANDREW *goes into the kitchen on the right.*)

SCOTT: *(As he goes out—in a low tone)* There's the boy that would make a good, strong sea-farin' man—if he'd a mind to.

MAYO: *(Sharply)* Don't you put no such fool notions in Andy's head, Dick— or you 'n' me's goin' to fall out. *(Then he smiles.)* You couldn't tempt him, no ways. Andy's a Mayo bred in the bone, and he's a born farmer, and a damn good one, too. He'll live and die right here on this farm, like I expect to. *(With proud confidence)* And he'll make this one of the slickest, best-payin' farms in the state, too, afore he gits through!

SCOTT: Seems to me it's a pretty slick place right now.

MAYO: *(Shaking his head)* It's too small. We need more land to make it amount to much, and we ain't got the capital to buy it.

(ANDREW *enters from the kitchen. His hat is on, and he carries a lighted lantern in his hand. He goes to the door in the rear leading out.)*

ANDREW: *(Opens the door and pauses)* Anything else you can think of to be done, Pa?

MAYO: No, nothin' I know of.

(ANDREW *goes out, shutting the door.)*

MRS MAYO: *(After a pause)* What's come over Andy tonight, I wonder? He acts so strange.

MAYO: He does seem sort o' glum and out of sorts. It's 'count o' Robert leavin', I s'pose. *(To* SCOTT*)* Dick, you wouldn't believe how them boys o' mine sticks together. They ain't like most brothers. They've been thick as thieves all their lives, with nary a quarrel I kin remember.

SCOTT: No need to tell me that. I can see how they take to each other.

MRS MAYO: *(Pursuing her train of thought)* Did you notice, James, how queer everyone was at supper? Robert seemed stirred up about something; and Ruth was so flustered and giggly; and Andy sat there dumb, looking as if he'd lost his best friend; and all of them only nibbled at their food.

MAYO: Guess they was all thinkin' about tomorrow, same as us.

MRS MAYO: *(Shaking her head)* No. I'm afraid somethin's happened— somethin' else.

MAYO: You mean—'bout Ruth?

MRS MAYO: Yes.

MAYO: *(After a pause—frowning)* I hope her and Andy ain't had a serious fallin'-out. I always sorter hoped they'd hitch up together sooner or later. What d'you say, Dick? Don't you think them two'd pair up well?

SCOTT: *(Nodding his head approvingly)* A sweet, wholesome couple they'd make.

MAYO: It'd be a good thing for Andy in more ways than one. I ain't what you'd call calculatin' generally, and I b'lieve in lettin' young folks run their affairs to suit themselves; but there's advantages for both o' them in this match you can't overlook in reason. The Atkins farm is right next to ourn. Jined together they'd make a jim-dandy of a place, with plenty o' room to work in. And bein' a widder with only a daughter, and laid up all the time to boot, Mrs. Atkins can't do nothin' with the place as it ought to be done. Her hired help just goes along as they pleases, in spite o' her everlastin' complainin' at 'em. She needs a man, a first-class farmer, to take hold o' things; and Andy's just the one.

MRS MAYO: *(Abruptly)* I don't think Ruth loves Andy.

MAYO: You don't? Well, maybe a woman's eyes is sharper in such things, but—they're always together. And if she don't love him now, she'll likely come around to it in time.

MAYO: *(As MRS MAYO shakes her head)* You seem mighty fixed in your opinion, Katey. How d'you know?

MRS MAYO: It's just—what I feel.

MAYO: *(A light breaking over him)* You don't mean to say—

(MRS MAYO nods. MAYO chuckles scornfully.)

MAYO: Shucks! I'm losin' my respect for your eyesight, Katey. Why, Robert ain't got no time for Ruth, 'cept as a friend!

MRS MAYO: *(Warningly)* Sss-h-h!

(The door from the yard opens, and ROBERT enters. He is smiling happily, and humming a song to himself, but as he comes into the room an undercurrent of nervous uneasiness manifests itself in his bearing.)

MAYO: So here you be at last!

(ROBERT comes forward and sits on ANDY'S chair. MAYO smiles slyly at his wife.)

MAYO: What have you been doin' all this time—countin' the stars to see if they all come out right and proper?

ROBERT: There's only one I'll ever look for any more, Pa.

MAYO: *(Reproachfully)* You might've even not wasted time lookin' for that one—your last night.

MRS MAYO: *(As if she were speaking to a child)* You ought to have worn your coat a sharp night like this, Robbie.

ROBERT: I wasn't cold, Ma. It's beautiful and warm on the road.

SCOTT: *(Disgustedly)* God A'mighty, Kate, you treat Robert as if he was one year old!

ROBERT: *(With a smile)* I'm used to that, Uncle.

SCOTT: *(With joking severity)* You'll learn to forget all that baby coddlin' nights down off the Horn when you're haulin' hell-bent on the braces with a green sea up to your neck, and the old hooker doin' summersaults under you. That's the stuff 'll put iron in your blood, eh Kate?

MRS MAYO: *(Indignantly)* What are you trying to do, Dick Scott—frighten me out of my senses? If you can't say anything cheerful, you'd better keep still.

SCOTT: Don't take on, Kate. I was only joshin' him and you.

MRS MAYO: You have strange notions of what's a joke, I must say! *(She notices ROBERT's nervous uneasiness.)* You look all worked up over something, Robbie. What is it?

ROBERT: *(Swallowing hard, looks quickly from one to the other of them—then begins determinedly)* Yes, there is something—something I must tell you—all of you.

(As he begins to talk ANDREW enters quietly from the rear, closing the door behind him, and setting the lighted lantern on the floor. He remains standing by the door, his arms folded, listening to ROBERT with a repressed expression of pain on his face. ROBERT is so much taken up with what he is going to say that he does not notice ANDREW'S presence.)

ROBERT: Something I discovered only this evening—very beautiful and wonderful—something I did not take into consideration previously because I hadn't dared to hope that such happiness could ever come to me. *(Appealingly)* You must all remember that fact, won't you?

MAYO: *(Frowning)* Let's get to the point, son.

ROBERT: You were offended because you thought I'd been wasting my time star-gazing on my last night at home. *(With a trace of defiance)* Well, the point is this, Pa; it *isn't* my last night at home. I'm not going—I mean—I can't go tomorrow with Uncle Dick—or at any future time, either.

MRS MAYO: *(With a sharp sigh of joyful relief)* Oh, Robbie, I'm so glad!

MAYO: *(Astounded)* You ain't serious, be you, Robert?

ROBERT: Yes, I mean what I say.

MAYO: *(Severely)* Seems to me it's a pretty late hour in the day for you to be upsettin' all your plans so sudden!

ROBERT: I asked you to remember that until this evening I didn't know myself—the wonder which makes everything else in the world seem sordid and pitifully selfish by comparison. I had never dared to dream—

MAYO: *(Irritably)* Come to the point. What is this foolishness you're talkin' of?

ROBERT: *(Flushing)* Ruth told me this evening that—she loved me. It was after I'd confessed I loved her. I told her I hadn't been conscious of my love until after the trip had been arranged, and I realized it would mean—leaving her. That was the truth. I didn't know until then. *(As if justifying himself to the others)* I hadn't intended telling her anything but—suddenly—I felt I must. I didn't think it would matter, because I was going away, and before I came back I was sure she'd have forgotten. And I thought she loved—someone else. *(Slowly—his eyes shining)* And then she cried and said it was I she'd loved all the time, but I hadn't seen it. *(Simply)* So we're going to be married—very soon—and I'm happy—and that's all there is to say. *(Appealingly)* But you see, I couldn't go away now—even if I wanted to.

MRS MAYO: *(Getting up from her chair)* Of course not! *(Rushes over and throws her arms about him)* I knew it! I was just telling your father when you came in—and, oh, Robbie, I'm so happy you're not going!

ROBERT: *(Kissing her)* I knew you'd be glad, Ma.

MAYO: *(Bewilderedly)* Well, I'll be damned! You do beat all for gettin' folks' minds all tangled up, Robert. And Ruth too! Whatever got into her all of a sudden? Why, I was thinkin'—

MRS MAYO: *(Hurriedly—in a tone of warning)* Never mind what you were thinking, James. It wouldn't be any use telling us that now. *(Meaningly)* And what you were hoping for turns out just the same almost, doesn't it?

MAYO: *(Thoughtfully—beginning to see this side of the argument)* Yes; I suppose you're right, Katey. *(Scratching his head in puzzlement)* But how it ever come about! It do beat anything ever I heard. *(Finally he gets up with a sheepish grin and walks over to* ROBERT.*)* We're glad you ain't goin', your Ma and I, for we'd have missed you terrible, that's certain and sure; and we're glad you've found happiness. Ruth's a fine girl and'll make a good wife to you.

ROBERT: *(Much moved)* Thank you, Pa. *(He grips his father's hand in his.)*

ANDREW: *(His face tense and drawn comes forward and holds out his hand, forcing a smile)* I guess it's my turn to offer congratulations, isn't it?

ROBERT: *(With a startled cry when his brother appears before him so suddenly)* Andy! *(Confused)* Why—I—I didn't see you. Were you here when—

ANDREW: I heard everything you said; and here's wishing you every happiness, you and Ruth. You both deserve the best there is.

ROBERT: *(Taking his hand)* Thanks, Andy, it's fine of you to— *(His voice dies away as he sees the pain in* ANDREW's *eyes.)*

ANDREW: *(Giving his brother's hand a final grip)* Good luck to you both! *(He turns away and goes back to the rear where he bends over the lantern, fumbling with it to hide his emotion from the others.)*

MRS MAYO: *(To the* CAPTAIN, *who has been too flabbergasted by* ROBERT's *decision to say a word.)* What's the matter, Dick? Aren't you going to congratulate Robbie?

SCOTT: *(Embarrassed)* Of course I be! *(He gets to his feet and shakes* ROBERT's *hand, muttering a vague)* Luck to you, boy. *(He stands beside* ROBERT *as if he wanted to say something more but doesn't know how to go about it.)*

ROBERT: Thanks, Uncle Dick.

SCOTT: So you're not acomin' on the *Sunda* with me? *(His voice indicates disbelief.)*

ROBERT: I can't, Uncle—not now. I'm very grateful to you for having wanted to take me. I wouldn't miss it for anything else in the world under any other circumstances. *(He sighs unconsciously.)* But you see I've found—a bigger dream.

SCOTT: *(Gruffly)* Bring the girl along with you. I'll fix it so there's room.

MRS MAYO: *(Sharply)* How can you propose such a crazy idea, Dick—to take a young girl on a sail-boat all over the world and not a woman on the boat but herself. Have you lost your senses?

ROBERT: *(Regretfully)* It would be wonderful if we could both go with you, Uncle—but it's impossible. Ruth couldn't go on account of her mother, and besides, I'm afraid she doesn't like the idea of the sea.

SCOTT: *(Putting all his disapproval into an exclamation)* Humph! *(He goes back and sits down at the table.)*

ROBERT: *(In joyous high spirits)* I want you all to understand one thing—I'm not going to be a loafer on your hands any longer. This means the beginning of a new life for me in every way. I'm sick and disgusted at myself for sitting around and seeing everyone else hard at work, while all I've been doing is keep the accounts—a couple of hours work a week! I'm going to settle right down and take a real interest in the farm, and do my share. I'll prove to you, Pa, that I'm as good a Mayo as you are—or Andy, when I want to be.

MAYO: *(Kindly but skeptically)* That's the right spirit, Robert, but it ain't needful for you to—

MRS MAYO: *(Interrupting him)* No one said you weren't doing your part, Robbie. You've got to look out for—

ROBERT: I know what you're going to say, and that's another false idea you've got to get out of your heads. It's ridiculous for you to persist in looking on me as an invalid. I'm as well as anyone, and I'll prove it to you if you'll give me half a chance. Once I get the hang of it, I'll be able to do as hard a day's work as any one. You wait and see.

MAYO: Ain't none of us doubts your willin'ness, but you ain't never learned—

ROBERT: Then I'm going to start learning right away, and you'll teach me, won't you?

MAYO: *(Mollifyingly)* Of course I will, boy, and be glad to, only you'd best go easy at first.

ROBERT: With the two farms to look after, you'll need me; and when I marry Ruth I'll have to know how to take care of things for her and her mother.

MAYO: That's so, son.

SCOTT: *(Who has listened to this conversation in mingled consternation and amazement)* You don't mean to tell me you're goin' to let him stay, do you, James?

MAYO: Why, things bein' as they be, Robert's free to do as he's a mind to.

MRS MAYO: Let him! The very idea!

SCOTT: *(More and more ruffled)* Then all I got to say is, you're a soft, weak-willed critter to be permittin' a boy—and women, too—to be layin' your course for you wherever they damn pleases.

MAYO: *(Slyly amused)* It's just the same with me as 'twas with you, Dick. You can't order the tides on the seas to suit you, and I ain't pretendin' I can reg'late love for young folks.

SCOTT: *(Scornfully)* Love! They ain't old enough to know love when they sight it! Love! I'm ashamed of you, Robert, to go lettin' a little huggin' and kissin' in the dark spile your chances to make a man out o' yourself. It ain't common sense—no siree, it ain't—not by a hell of a sight! *(He pounds the table with his fists in exasperation.)*

ROBERT: *(Smiling)* I'm afraid I can't help it, Uncle.

SCOTT: Humph! You ain't got any sand, that's what! And you, James Mayo, lettin' boys and women run things to the devil and back—you've got less sense than he has!

MAYO: *(With a grin)* If Robert can't help it, I'm sure I ain't able, Dick.

MRS MAYO: *(Laughing provokingly at her brother)* A fine one you are to be talking about love, Dick—an old cranky bachelor like you. Goodness sakes!

SCOTT: *(Exasperated by their joking)* I've never been a damn fool like most, if that's what you're steerin' at.

MRS MAYO: *(Tauntingly)* Sour grapes, aren't they, Dick?

(She laughs. ROBERT and his father chuckle. SCOTT sputters with annoyance.)

MRS MAYO: Good gracious, Dick, you do act silly, flying into a temper over nothing.

SCOTT: *(Indignantly)* Nothin'! Is that what you call it—nothin'? You talk as if I wasn't concerned nohow in this here business. Seems to me I've got a right to have my say. Ain't I gone to all sorts o' trouble gettin' the sta'b'd cabin all cleaned out and painted and fixed up so's that Robert o' yours 'd be comfortable? Ain't I made all arrangements with the owners and stocked up with some special grub all on Robert's account?

ROBERT: You've been fine, Uncle Dick; and I appreciate it. Truly.

MAYO: 'Course; we all does, Dick.

MRS MAYO: And don't spoil it now by getting angry at us.

SCOTT: *(Unplacated)* It's all right for you to say don't this and don't that; but you ain't seen things from my side of it. I've been countin' sure on havin' Robert for company on this vige—to sorta talk to and show things to, and teach, kinda, and I got my mind so set on havin' him I'm goin' to be double lonesome this vige. *(He pounds on the table, attempting to cover up this confession of weakness.)* Darn all this silly lovin' business, anyway.

MRS MAYO: *(Touched)* It's too bad you have to be so lonesome, Dick. Why don't you give up the old boat? You've been on the sea long enough, heaven's knows. Why don't you make up your mind and settle down here with us?

SCOTT: *(Emphatically)* And go diggin' up the dirt and plantin' things? Not by a hell of a sight! You can have all the darned dirt in the earth for all o' me. I ain't sayin' it ain't all right—if you're made that way—but *I ain't*. No settlin' down for me. No sirree! *(Irritably)* But all this talk ain't tellin' me what I'm to do with that sta'b'd cabin I fixed up. It's all painted white, an a bran new mattress on the bunk, 'n' new sheets 'n' blankets 'n' things. And Chips built in a book-case so's Robert could take his books along—with a slidin' bar fixed across't it, mind, so's they couldn't fall out no matter how she rolled. *(With excited consternation)* What d'you suppose my officers is goin' to think when there's no one comes aboard to occupy that sta'b'd cabin? And the men what did the work on it—what'll they *think*? *(He shakes his finger indignantly.)* They're liable as not to suspicion it was a woman I'd planned to ship along, and that she gave me the go-by at the last moment! *(He wipes his perspiring brow in anguish at this thought.)* Gawd A'mighty! They're only lookin' to have the laugh on me for something like that. They're liable to b'lieve anything, those fellers is!

MAYO: *(With a wink)* Then there's nothing to it but for you to get right out and hunt up a wife somewheres for that spic 'n' span cabin. She'll have to be a pretty one, too, to match it. *(He looks at his watch with exaggerated concern.)* You ain't got much time to find her, Dick.

SCOTT: *(As the others smile—sulkily)* You kin go to thunder, Jim Mayo!

ANDREW: *(Comes forward from where he has been standing by the door, rear, brooding. His face is set in a look of grim determination.)* You needn't worry about that spare cabin, Uncle Dick, if you've a mind to take me in Robert's place.

ROBERT: *(Turning to him quickly)* Andy! *(He sees at once the fixed resolve in his brother's eyes, and realizes immediately the reason for it—in consternation.)* Andy, you mustn't!

ANDREW: You've made your decision, Rob, and now I've made mine. You're out of this, remember.

ROBERT: *(Hurt by his brother's tone)* But Andy—

ANDREW: Don't interfere, Rob—that's all I ask. *(Turning to his uncle)* You haven't answered my question, Uncle Dick.

SCOTT: *(Clearing his throat, with an uneasy side glance at* JAMES MAYO *who is staring at his elder son as if he thought he had suddenly gone mad)* O' course, I'd be glad to have you, Andy.

ANDREW: It's settled then. I can pack the little I want to take in a few minutes.

MRS MAYO: Don't be a fool, Dick. Andy's only joking you. He wouldn't go for anything.

SCOTT: *(Disgruntledly)* It's hard to tell who's jokin' and who's not in this house.

ANDREW: *(Firmly)* I'm not joking, Uncle Dick—and since I've got your permission, I'm going with you.

(As SCOTT *looks at him uncertainly)*

ANDREW: You needn't be afraid I'll go back on my word. When I say I'll go, I'll go.

ROBERT: *(Hurt by the insinuation he feels in* ANDREW's *tone)* Andy! That isn't fair!

MRS MAYO: *(Beginning to be disturbed)* But I know he must be fooling us. Aren't you, Andy?

ANDREW: No, Ma, I'm not.

MAYO: *(Frowning)* Seems to me this ain't no subject to joke over—not for Andy.

ANDREW: *(Facing his father)* I agree with you, Pa, and I tell you again, once and for all, that I've made up my mind to go.

MAYO: *(Dumbfounded—unable to doubt the determination in* ANDREW's *voice—helplessly)* But why, son? Why?

ANDREW: *(Evasively)* I've always wanted to go, even if I ain't said anything about it.

ROBERT: Andy!

ANDREW: *(Half-angrily)* You shut up, Rob! I told you to keep out of this. *(Turning to his father again)* I didn't ever mention it because as long as Rob was going I knew it was no use; but now Rob's staying on here, and Uncle Dick wants someone along with him, there isn't any reason for me not to go.

MAYO: *(Breathing hard)* No reason? Can you stand there and say that to me, Andrew?

MRS MAYO: *(Hastily—seeing the gathering storm)* He doesn't mean a word of it, James.

MAYO: *(Making a gesture to her to keep silence)* Let me talk, Katey. *(In a more kindly tone)* What's come over you so sudden, Andy? You know's well as I do that it wouldn't be fair o' you to run off at a moment's notice right now when we're up to our necks in hard work.

ANDREW: *(Avoiding his eyes)* Rob'll hold his end up as soon as he learns.

MAYO: You know that ain't so. Robert was never cut out for a farmer, and you was.

ANDREW: You can easily get a man to do my work.

MAYO: *(Restraining his anger with an effort)* It sounds strange to hear you, Andy, that I always thought had good sense, talkin' crazy like that. And you don't believe yourself one bit of what you've been sayin'—not 'less you've suddenly gone out of your mind. *(Scornfully)* Get a man to take your place! Where'd I get him, tell me, with the shortage of farm labor hereabouts? And if I could get one, what int'rest d'you suppose he'd take beyond doin' as little work as he could for the money I paid him? You ain't been workin' here for no hire, Andy, that you kin give me your notice to quit like you've done. The farm is your'n as well as mine. You've always worked on it with that understanding; and what you're sayin' you intend doin' is just skulkin' out o' your rightful responsibility.

ANDREW: *(Looking at the floor—simply)* I'm sorry, Pa. *(After a slight pause)* It's no use talking any more about it.

MRS MAYO: *(In relief)* There! I knew Andy'd come to his senses!

ANDREW: Don't get the wrong idea, Ma. I'm not backing out.

MAYO: You mean you're goin' in spite of—everythin'?

ANDREW: Yes. I'm going. I want to—and—I've got to. *(He looks at his father defiantly.)* I feel I oughtn't to miss this chance to go out into the world and see things, and—I want to go.

MAYO: *(With bitter scorn)* So—you want to go out into the world and see thin's! *(His voice raised and quivering with anger)* I never thought I'd live to see the day when a son o' mine 'd look me in the face and tell a bare-faced lie! *(Bursting out)* You're a liar, Andy Mayo, and a mean one to boot!

MRS MAYO: James!

ROBERT: Pa!

SCOTT: Steady there, Jim!

MAYO: *(Waving their protests aside)* He is and he knows it.

ANDREW: *(His face flushed)* I won't argue with you, Pa. You can think as badly of me as you like. I can't help that. Let's not talk about it any more. I've made up my mind, and nothing you can say will change it.

MAYO: *(Shaking his finger at* ANDREW, *in a cold rage)* You know I'm speakin' truth—that's why you're afraid to argy! You lie when you say you want to go 'way—and see things! You ain't got no likin' in the world to go. Your place is right here on this farm—the place you was born to by nature—and you can't tell me no different. I've watched you grow up, and I know your ways, and they're my ways. You're runnin' against your own nature, and you're goin' to be a'mighty sorry for it if you do. You're tryin' to pretend to me something that don't fit in with your make-up, and it's damn fool pretendin' if you think you're foolin' me. 'S if I didn't know your real reason for runnin' away! And runnin' away's the only words to fit it. You're runnin' away 'cause you're put out and riled 'cause your own brother's got Ruth 'stead o' you, and—

ANDREW: *(His face crimson—tensely)* Stop, Pa! I won't stand hearing that—not even from you!

MRS MAYO: *(Rushing to* ANDREW *and putting her arms about him protectingly.)* Don't mind him, Andy dear. He don't mean a word he's saying!

(ROBERT *stands rigidly, his hands clenched, his face contracted by pain.* SCOTT *sits dumbfounded and open-mouthed.* ANDREW *soothes his mother who is on the verge of tears.)*

MAYO: *(In angry triumph)* It's the truth, Andy Mayo! And you ought to be bowed in shame to think of it!

ROBERT: *(Protestingly.)* Pa! You've gone far enough. It's a shame for you to talk that way!

MRS MAYO: *(Coming from* ANDREW *to his father; puts her hands on his shoulders as though to try and push him back in the chair from which he has risen)* Won't you be still, James? Please won't you?

MAYO: *(Looking at* ANDREW *over his wife's shoulder—stubbornly)* The truth—God's truth!

MRS MAYO: Sh-h-h! *(She tries to put a finger across his lips, but he twists his head away.)*

ANDREW: *(Who has regained control over himself)* You're wrong, Pa, it isn't truth. *(With defiant assertiveness)* I don't love Ruth. I never loved her, and the thought of such a thing never entered my head.

MAYO: *(With an angry snort of disbelief)* Hump! You're pilin' lie on lie!

ANDREW: *(Losing his temper—bitterly)* I suppose it'd be hard for you to explain anyone's wanting to leave this blessed farm except for some outside reason like that. You think these few measly acres are heaven, and that none'd want to ever do nothing in all their lives but stay right here and work like a dog all the time. But I'm sick and tired of it—whether you want to believe me or not—and that's why I'm glad to get a chance to move on. I've been sick and tired of farm life for a long time, and if I hadn't said anything about it, it was only to save your feelings. Just because you love it here, you've got your mind set that I like it, too. You want me to stay on so's you can know that I'll be taking care of the rotten farm after you're gone. Well, Rob'll be here, and he's a Mayo, too. You can leave it in his hands.

ROBERT: Andy! Don't! You're only making it worse.

ANDREW: *(Sulkily)* I don't care. I've done my share of work here. I've earned my right to quit when I want to. *(Suddenly overcome with anger and grief; with rising intensity)* I'm sick and tired of the whole damn business. I hate the farm and every inch of ground in it. I'm sick of digging in the dirt and sweating in the sun like a slave without getting a word of thanks for it. *(Tears of rage starting to his eyes—hoarsely)* I'm through, through for good and all; and if Uncle Dick won't take me on his ship, I'll find another. I'll get away somewhere, somehow.

MRS MAYO: *(In a frightened voice)* Don't you answer him, James. He doesn't know what he's saying to you. Don't say a word to him 'til he's in his right senses again. Please James, don't—

MAYO: *(Pushes her away from him; his face is drawn and pale with the violence of his passion. He glares at ANDREW as if he hated him.)* You dare to—you dare to speak like that to me? You talk like that 'bout this farm—the Mayo farm—where you was born—you—you— *(He clenches his fist above his head and advances threateningly on ANDREW.)* You damned whelp!

MRS MAYO: *(With a shriek)* James! *(She covers her face with her hands and sinks weakly into MAYO's chair. ANDREW remains standing motionless, his face pale and set.)*

SCOTT: *(Starting to his feet and stretching his arms across the table toward MAYO)* Easy there, Jim!

ROBERT: *(Throwing himself between father and brother)* Stop! Are you mad?

MAYO: *(Grabs* ROBERT's *arm and pushes him aside—then stands for a moment gasping for breath before* ANDREW. *He points to the door with a shaking finger.)* Yes—go!—go!—You're no son o' mine—no son o' mine! You can go to hell if you want to! Don't let me find you here—in the mornin'—or—or—I'll *throw* you out!

ROBERT: Pa! For God's sake!

(MRS MAYO *bursts into noisy sobbing.)*

SCOTT: *(Placatingly)* Ain't you goin' too far, Jim?

MAYO: *(Turning on him furiously)* Shut up, you—you Dick! It's your fault—a lot o' this—you and your cussed ship! Don't you take him—if you do—don't you dare darken this door again. Let him go by himself and learn to starve—starve! *(He gulps convulsively and turns again to* ANDREW.) And you go—tomorrow mornin'—and by God—don't come back—don't dare come back—by God, not while I'm livin'—or I'll—I'll— *(He shakes over his muttered threat and strides toward the door rear, right.)*

MRS MAYO: *(Rising and throwing her arms around him—hysterically)* James! James! Where are you going?

MAYO: *(Incoherently)* I'm goin'—to bed, Katey. It's late, Katey—it's late. *(He goes out.)*

MRS MAYO: *(Following him, pleading hysterically)* James! Take back what you've said to Andy. James!

(*She follows him out.* ROBERT *and the* CAPTAIN *stare after them with horrified eyes.* ANDREW *stands rigidly looking straight in front of him, his fists clenched at his sides.)*

SCOTT: *(The first to find his voice—with an explosive sigh)* Well, if he ain't the devil himself when he's roused! You oughtn't to have talked to him that way, Andy 'bout the damn farm, knowin' how touchy he is about it. *(With another sigh)* Well, you won't mind what he's said in anger. He'll be sorry for it when he's calmed down a bit.

ANDREW: *(In a dead voice)* No, he won't. You don't know him. *(Defiantly)* What's said is said and can't be unsaid; and I've chosen.

SCOTT: *(Uncertainly)* You don't mean—you're still a mind to go—go with me, do you?

ANDREW: *(Stubbornly)* I haven't said I've changed my mind, have I? There's all the reason in the world for me to go—now. And I'm going if you're not afraid to take me after what he said.

ROBERT: *(With violent protest)* Andy! You can't! Don't be a fool! This is all so stupid—and terrible.

ANDREW: *(Coldly)* I'll talk to you in a minute, Rob, when we're alone. This is between Uncle and me.

(Crushed by his brother's cold indifference, ROBERT *sinks down into a chair, holding his head in his hands.* ANDREW *turns again to* SCOTT.*)*

ANDREW: If you don't want to take me, it's all right—there's no hard feelings. I can understand you don't like to fall out with Pa.

SCOTT: *(Indignantly)* Gawd A'mighty, Andy, I ain't scared o' your Pa, nor no man livin,' I want t'have you come along! Only I was thinkin' o' Kate. We don't want her to have to suffer from his contrariness. Let's see. *(He screws up his brows in thought.)* S'posing we both lie a little, eh? I'll tell 'em you're not comin' with me, and you tell 'em you're goin' to the port to get another ship. We can leave here in the team together. That's natural enough. They can't suspect nothin' from that. And then you can write home the first port we touch and explain things. *(He winks at* ANDREW *cunningly.)* Are you on to the course?

ANDREW: *(Frowning)* Yes—if you think it's best.

SCOTT: For your Ma's sake. I wouldn't ask it, else.

ANDREW: *(Shrugging his shoulders)* All right then.

SCOTT: *(With a great sigh of relief—comes and slaps* ANDREW *on the back—beaming)* I'm damned glad you're shippin' on, Andy. I like your spirit, and the way you spoke up to him. *(Lowering his voice to a cautious whisper)* You was right not to want to waste your life plowin' dirt and pattin' it down again. The sea's the place for a young feller like you that isn't half dead 'n' alive. *(He gives* ANDY *a final approving slap.)* You'n' me 'll get along like twins, see if we don't. I'm durned glad you're comin', boy.

ANDREW: *(Wearily)* Let's not talk about it any more, Uncle. I'm tired of talking.

SCOTT: Right! I'm goin' aloft to turn in, and leave you two alone. Don't forget to pack your dunnage. And git some sleep, if you kin. We'll want to sneak out extra early b'fore they're up. It'll do away with more argyments. Robert can drive us down to the town, and bring back the team. *(He goes to the door in the rear, left.)* Well, good night.

ANDREW: Good night.

*(*SCOTT *goes out. The two brothers remain silent for a moment. Then* ANDREW *comes over to his brother and puts a hand on his back. He speaks in a low voice, full of feeling.)*

ANDREW: Buck up, Rob. It ain't any use crying over spilt milk; and it'll all turn out for the best—let's hope. It couldn't be helped—what's happened.

ROBERT: *(Wildly)* But it's a lie, Andy, a lie!

ANDREW: Of course it's a lie. You know it and I know it—but that's all ought to know it.

ROBERT: Pa'll never forgive you. Oh, why did you want to anger him like that? You know how he feels about the farm. Oh, the whole affair is so senseless—and tragic. Why did you think you must go away?

ANDREW: You know better than to ask that. You know why. *(Fiercely)* I can wish you and Ruth all the good luck in the world, and I do, and I mean it; but you can't expect me to stay around here and watch you two together, day after day—and me alone. You couldn't expect that! I couldn't stand it—not after all the plans I'd made to happen on this place thinking— *(His voice breaks.)* Thinking she cared for me.

ROBERT: *(Putting a hand on his brother's arm)* God! It's horrible! I feel so guilty—to think that I should be the cause of your suffering, after we've been such pals all our lives. If I could have foreseen what'd happen, I swear to you I'd have never said a word to Ruth. I swear I wouldn't have, Andy.

ANDREW: I know you wouldn't; and that would've been worse, for Ruth would've suffered then. *(He pats his brother's shoulder.)* It's best as it is. It had to be, and I've got to stand the gaff, that's all. Pa'll see how I felt—after a time.

(As ROBERT *shakes his head)*

ANDREW: —and if he don't—well, it can't be helped.

ROBERT: But think of Ma! God, Andy, you can't go! You can't!

ANDREW: *(Fiercely)* I've got to go—to get away! I've got to, I tell you. I'd die here. I'd kill myself! Can't you understand what it'd mean to me, how I'd suffer? You don't know how I'd planned—for Ruth and me—the hopes I'd had about what the future'd be like. You can't blame me to go. You'd do the same yourself. I'd go crazy here, bein' reminded every second of the day how my life's been smashed, and what a fool I'd made of myself. I'd have nothing to hope or live for. I've got to get away and try and forget, if I can. I never could stay here—seeing her. And I'd hate the farm if I stayed, hate it for bringin' things back. I couldn't take interest in the work any more, work with no purpose in sight. Can't you see what a hell it'd be? You love her too, Rob. Put yourself in my place, and remember I haven't stopped loving her, and couldn't if I was to stay. Would that be fair to you or to her? Put yourself in my place. *(He shakes his brother fiercely by the shoulder.)* What'd you do then? Tell me the truth! You love her. What'd you do? In spite of all hell, what'd you do?

ROBERT: *(Chokingly)* I'd—I'd go, Andy! *(He buries his face in his hands with a shuddering sob.)* God!

ANDREW: *(Seeming to relax suddenly all over his body—in a low, steady voice)* Then you know why I got to go; and there's nothing more to be said.

ROBERT: *(In a frenzy of rebellion)* Why did this have to happen to us? It's damnable! *(He looks about him wildly, as if his vengeance were seeking the responsible fate.)*

ANDREW: *(Soothingly—again putting his hands on his brother's shoulder)* It's no use fussing any more, Rob. It's done. *(Affectionately)* You'll forget anything I said to hurt when I was mad, won't you? I wanted to keep you out of it.

ROBERT: Oh, Andy, it's me who ought to be asking your forgiveness for the suffering I've brought on you.

ANDREW: *(Forcing a smile)* I guess Ruth's got a right to have who she likes; you ain't to blame for that. She made a good choice—and God bless her for it!

ROBERT: Andy! Oh, I wish I could tell you half I feel of how fine you are!

ANDREW: *(Interrupting him quickly)* Shut up! Let's go to bed. We've talked long enough, and I've got to be up long before sun-up. You, too, if you're going to drive us down.

ROBERT: Yes. Yes.

ANDREW: *(Turning down the lamp)* And I've got to pack yet. *(He yawns with utter weariness.)* I'm as tired as if I'd been plowing twenty-four hours at a stretch. *(Dully)* I feel—dead.

(ROBERT *covers his face again with his hands.* ANDREW *shakes his head as if to get rid of his thoughts, and continues with a poor attempt at cheery briskness.)*

ANDREW: I'm going to douse the light. Come on.

(He slaps his brother on the back. ROBERT *does not move.* ANDREW *bends over and blows out the lamp. His voice comes from the darkness.)*

ANDREW: Don't sit there mourning, Rob. It'll all come out in the wash. Come on and get some sleep. Everything 'll turn out all right in the end.

(ROBERT *can be heard stumbling to his feet, and the dark figures of the two brothers can be seen groping their way toward the doorway in the rear as)*

(The curtain falls.)

END OF ACT ONE

ACT TWO

Scene One

(Same as ACT ONE, Scene Two. Sitting room of the farm house about half past twelve in the afternoon of a hot, sun-baked day in mid-summer, three years later. All the windows are open, but no breeze stirs the soiled white curtains. A patched screen door is in the rear. Through it the yard can be seen, its small stretch of lawn divided by the dirt path leading to the door from the gate in the white picket fence which borders the road.)

(The room has changed, not so much in its outward appearance as in its general atmosphere. Little significant details give evidence of carelessness, of inefficiency, of an industry gone to seed. The chairs appear shabby from lack of paint; the table cover is spotted and askew; holes show in the curtains; a child's doll, with one arm gone, lies under the table; a hoe stands in a corner; a man's coat is flung on the couch in the rear; the desk is cluttered up with odds and ends; a number of books are piled carelessly on the side-board. The noon enervation of the sultry, scorching day seems to have penetrated indoors, causing even inanimate objects to wear an aspect of despondent exhaustion.)

(A place is set at the end of the table, left, for someone's dinner. Through the open door to the kitchen comes the clatter of dishes being washed, interrupted at intervals by a woman's irritated voice and the peevish whining of a child.)

(At the rise of the curtain MRS MAYO *and* MRS ATKINS *are discovered sitting facing each other,* MRS MAYO *to the rear,* MRS ATKINS *to the right of the table.* MRS MAYO'S *face has lost all character, disintegrated, become a weak mask wearing a helpless, doleful expression of being constantly on the verge of comfortless tears. She speaks in an uncertain voice, without assertiveness, as if all power of willing had deserted her.* MRS ATKINS *is in her wheel chair. She is a thin, pale-faced, unintelligent looking woman of about forty-eight, with hard, bright eyes. A victim of partial paralysis for many years, condemned to be pushed from day to day of her life in a wheel chair, she has developed the selfish, irritable nature of the chronic invalid. Both women are dressed in black.* MRS ATKINS *knits nervously as she talks. A ball of unused yarn, with needles stuck through it, lies on the table before* MRS MAYO.*)*

MRS ATKINS: *(With a disapproving glance at the place set on the table)* Robert's late for his dinner again, as usual. I don't see why Ruth puts up with it, and I've told her so. Many's the time I've said to her "It's about time you put a stop to his nonsense. Does he suppose you're runnin' a hotel—with no one to help with things?" But she don't pay no attention. She's as bad as he is, a'most—thinks she knows better than an old, sick body like me.

MRS MAYO: *(Dully)* Robbie's always late for things. He can't help it, Sarah.

MRS ATKINS: *(With a snort)* Can't help it! How you do go on, Kate, findin' excuses for him! Anybody can help anything they've a mind to—as long as they've got health, and ain't rendered helpless like me, *(She adds as a pious afterthought.)*—through the will of God.

MRS MAYO: Robbie can't.

MRS ATKINS: Can't! It do make me mad, Kate Mayo, to see folks that God gave all the use of their limbs to potterin' round and wastin' time doin' every thing the wrong way—and me powerless to help and at their mercy, you might say. And it ain't that I haven't pointed the right way to 'em. I've talked to Robert thousands of times and told him how things ought to be done. You know that, Kate Mayo. But d'you s'pose he takes any notice of what I say? Or Ruth, either—my own daughter? No, they think I'm a crazy, cranky old woman, half dead a'ready, and the sooner I'm in the grave and out o' their way the better it'd suit them.

MRS MAYO: You mustn't talk that way, Sarah. They're not as wicked as that. And you've got years and years before you.

MRS ATKINS: You're like the rest, Kate. You don't know how near the end I am. Well, at least I can go to my eternal rest with a clear conscience. I've done all a body could do to avert ruin from this house. On their heads be it!

MRS MAYO: *(With hopeless indifference)* Things might be worse. Robert never had any experience in farming. You can't expect him to learn in a day.

MRS ATKINS: *(Snappily)* He's had three years to learn, and he's gettin' worse 'stead of better. He hasn't got it in him, that's what; and I do say it to you, Kate Mayo, even if he is your son. He doesn't want to learn. Everything I've told him he's that pig-headed he's gone and done the exact opposite. And now look where things are! They couldn't be worse, spite o' what you say. Not on'y your place but mine too is driftin' to rack and ruin, and I can't do nothin' to prevent, 'cause Ruth backs him up in his folly and shiftlessness.

MRS MAYO: *(With a spark of assertiveness)* You can't say but Robbie works hard, Sarah.

MRS ATKINS: What good's workin' hard if it don't accomplish anythin', I'd like to know?

MRS MAYO: Robbie's had bad luck against him.

MRS ATKINS: Say what you've a mind to, Kate, the proof of the puddin's in the eatin'; and you can't deny that things have been goin' from bad to worse ever since your husband died two years back.

MRS MAYO: *(Wiping tears from her eyes with her handkerchief)* It was God's will that he should be taken.

MRS ATKINS: *(Triumphantly)* It was God's punishment on James Mayo for the blasphemin' and denyin' of God he done all his sinful life!

(MRS MAYO *begins to weep softly.*)

MRS ATKINS: There, Kate, I shouldn't be remindin' you, I know. He's at peace, poor man, and forgiven, let's pray.

MRS MAYO: *(Wiping her eyes—simply)* James was a good man.

MRS ATKINS: *(Ignoring this remark)* What I was sayin' was that since Robert's been in charge things've been goin' down hill steady. You don't know how bad they are. Robert don't let on to you what's happinin'; and you'd never see it yourself if 'twas under your nose. But, thank God, Ruth still comes to me once in a while for advice when she's worried near out of her senses by his goin's-on. Do you know what she told me last night? But I forgot, she said not to tell you—still I think you've got a right to know, and it's my duty not to let such things go on behind your back.

MRS MAYO: *(Wearily)* You can tell me if you want to.

MRS ATKINS: *(Bending over toward her—in a low voice)* Ruth was almost crazy about it. Robert told her he'd have to mortgage the farm—said he didn't know how he'd pull through 'til harvest without it, and he can't get money any other way. *(She straightens up—indignantly.)* Now what do you think of your Robert?

MRS MAYO: *(Resignedly)* If it has to be—

MRS ATKINS: You don't mean to say you're goin' to sign away your farm, Kate Mayo—after me warnin' you?

MRS MAYO: I'll do what Robbie says is needful.

MRS ATKINS: *(Holding up her hands)* Well, of all the foolishness!—well, it's your farm, not mine, and I've nothin' more to say.

MRS MAYO: Maybe Robbie'll manage till Andy gets back and sees to things. It can't be long now.

MRS ATKINS: *(With keen interest)* Ruth says Andy ought to turn up any day. When does Robert figger he'll get here?

MRS MAYO: He says he can't calculate exactly on account o' the *Sunda* being a sail boat. Last letter he got was from England, the day they were sailing for home. That was over a month ago, and Robbie thinks they're overdue now.

MRS ATKINS: We can give praise to God then that he'll be back in the nick o' time. I've got confidence in Andy and always did have, when it comes to farmin'; and he ought to be tired of travellin' and anxious to get home and settle down to work again.

MRS MAYO: Andy *has* been working. He's head officer on Dick's boat, he wrote Robbie. You know that.

MRS ATKINS: That foolin' on ships is all right for a spell, but he must be right sick of it by this. Andy's got to the age where it's time he took hold of things serious and got this farm workin' as it ought to be again.

MRS MAYO: *(Musingly)* I wonder if he's changed much. He used to be so fine-looking and strong. *(With a sigh)* Three years! It seems more like three hundred. *(Her eyes filling—piteously)* Oh, if James could only have lived 'til he came back—and forgiven him!

MRS ATKINS: He never would have—not James Mayo! Didn't he keep his heart hardened against him till the last in spite of all you and Robert did to soften him?

MRS MAYO: *(With a feeble flash of anger)* Don't you dare say that! *(Brokenly)* Oh, I know deep down in his heart he forgave Andy, though he was too stubborn ever to own up to it. It was that brought on his death—breaking his heart just on account of his stubborn pride. *(She wipes her eyes with her handkerchief and sobs.)*

MRS ATKINS: *(Piously)* It was the will of God.

(The whining crying of the child sounds from the kitchen. MRS ATKINS frowns irritably.)

MRS ATKINS: Drat that young one! Seems as if she cries all the time on purpose to set a body's nerves on edge.

MRS MAYO: *(Wiping her eyes)* It's the heat upsets her. Mary doesn't feel any too well these days, poor little child!

MRS ATKINS: She gets it right from her Pa—bein' sickly all the time. You can't deny Robert was always ailin' as a child. *(She sighs heavily.)* It was a crazy mistake for them two to get married. I argyed against it at the time, but Ruth was so spelled with Robert's wild poetry notions she wouldn't listen to sense. Andy was the one would have been the match for her. I always thought so in those days, same as your James did; and I know she liked Andy. Then 'long comes Robert with his book-learnin' and high-fangled talk—and off she goes and marries him.

MRS MAYO: I've often thought since it might have been better the other way. But Ruth and Robbie seem happy enough together.

MRS ATKINS: At any rate it was God's work—and His will be done.

(The two women sit in silence for a moment. RUTH enters from the kitchen, carrying in her arms her two-year-old daughter, MARY, a pretty but sickly and

aenemic looking child with a tear-stained face. RUTH *has aged appreciably. Her face has lost its youth and freshness. There is a trace in her expression of something hard and spiteful. She sits in the rocker in front of the table and sighs wearily. She wears a gingham dress with a soiled apron tied around her waist.)*

RUTH: Land sakes, if this isn't a scorcher! That kitchen's like a furnace. Phew! *(She pushes the damp hair back from her forehead.)*

MRS MAYO: Why didn't you call me to help with the dishes?

RUTH: *(Shortly)* No. The heat in there'd kill you.

MARY: *(Sees the doll under the table and struggles on her mother's lap)* Mary wants Dolly, Mama! Give Mary Dolly!

RUTH: *(Pulling her back)* It's time for your nap. You can't play with Dolly now.

MARY: *(Commencing to cry whiningly)* Mary wants Dolly!

MRS ATKINS: *(Irritably)* Can't you keep that child still? Her racket's enough to split a body's ears. Put her down and let her play with the doll if it'll quiet her.

RUTH: *(Lifting* MARY *to the floor)* There! I hope you'll be satisfied and keep still. You're only to play for a minute, remember. Then you've got to take your nap.

(MARY *sits down on the floor before the table and plays with the doll in silence.* RUTH *glances at the place set on the table.)*

RUTH: It's a wonder Rob wouldn't try to get to meals on time once in a while. Does he think I've nothing to do on a hot day like this but stand in that kitchen washing dishes?

MRS MAYO: *(Dully)* Something must have gone wrong again.

RUTH: *(Wearily)* I s'pose so. Something's always going wrong these days, it looks like.

MRS ATKINS: *(Snappily)* It wouldn't if you possessed a bit of spunk. The idea of you permittin' him to come in to meals at all hours—and you doin' the work! You ought to force him to have more consideration. I never heard of such a thin'. You mind my words and let him go to the kitchen and get his own once in a while, and see if he don't toe the mark. You're too easy goin', that's the trouble.

RUTH: Do stop your nagging at me, Ma! I'm sick of hearing you. I'll do as I please about it; and thank you for not interfering. *(She wipes her moist forehead—wearily.)* Phew! It's too hot to argue. Let's talk of something pleasant. *(Curiously)* Didn't I hear you speaking about Andy a while ago?

MRS MAYO: We were wondering when he'd get home.

RUTH: *(Brightening)* Rob says any day now he's liable to drop in and surprise us—him and the Captain. I wonder if he's changed much—what he'll be like. It'll certainly look natural to see him around the farm again.

MRS ATKINS: Let's hope the farm'll look more natural, too, when he's had a hand at it. The way thin's are now!

RUTH: *(Irritably)* Will you stop harping on that, Ma? We all know things aren't as they might be. What's the good of your complaining all the time?

MRS ATKINS: There, Kate Mayo! Ain't that just what I told you? I can't say a word of advice to my own daughter even, she's that stubborn and self-willed.

RUTH: *(Putting her hands over her ears—in exasperation)* For goodness sakes, Ma!

MRS MAYO: *(Dully)* Never mind. Andy'll fix everything when he comes.

RUTH: *(Hopefully)* Oh, yes, I know he will. He always did know just the right thing ought to be done. *(With weary vexation)* It's a shame for him to come home and have to start in with things in such a topsy-turvy.

MRS MAYO: Andy'll manage.

RUTH: *(Sighing)* I s'pose it isn't Rob's fault things go wrong with him.

MRS ATKINS: *(Scornfully)* Hump! *(She fans herself nervously.)* Land o' Goshen, but it's bakin' in here! Let's go out in under the trees in back where there's a breath of fresh air. Come, Kate.

(MRS MAYO *gets up obediently and starts to wheel the invalid's chair toward the screen door.*)

MRS ATKINS: You better come too, Ruth. It'll do you good. Learn him a lesson and let him get his own dinner. Don't be such a fool.

RUTH: *(Going and holding the screen door open for them—listlessly)* He wouldn't mind. He tells me never to wait—but he wouldn't know where to find anything.

MRS ATKINS: Let him go hungry then—and serve him right.

RUTH: He wouldn't mind that, either. He doesn't eat much. But I can't go anyway. I've got to put baby to bed.

MRS ATKINS: Let's go, Kate. I'm boilin' in here.

(MRS MAYO *wheels her out and off left.* RUTH *comes back and sits down in her chair.*)

RUTH: *(Mechanically)* Come and let me take off your shoes and stockings, Mary, that's a good girl. You've got to take your nap now.

(The child continues to play as if she hadn't heard, absorbed in her doll. An eager expression comes over RUTH's *tired face. She glances toward the door furtively—then gets up and goes to the desk. Her movements indicate a guilty fear of discovery. She takes a letter from a pigeon hole and retreats swiftly to her chair with it. She opens the envelope and reads the letter with great interest, a flush of excitement coming to her cheeks.* ROBERT *walks up the path and opens the screen door quietly and comes into the room. He, too, has aged. His shoulders are stooped as if under too great a burden. His eyes are dull and lifeless, his face burned by the sun and unshaven for days. Streaks of sweat have smudged the layer of dust on his cheeks. His lips, drawn down at the corners, give him a hopeless, resigned expression. The three years have accentuated the weakness of his mouth and chin. He is dressed in overalls, laced boots, and a flannel shirt open at the neck.)*

ROBERT: *(Throwing his hat over on the sofa—with a great sigh of exhaustion)* Phew! The sun's hot today!

*(*RUTH *is startled. At first she makes an instinctive motion as if to hide the letter in her bosom. She immediately thinks better of this and sits with the letter in her hands looking at him with defiant eyes. He bends down and kisses her.)*

RUTH: *(Feeling of her cheek—irritably)* Why don't you shave? You look awful.

ROBERT: *(Indifferently)* I forgot—and it's too much trouble this weather.

MARY: *(Throwing aside her doll, runs to him with a happy cry)* Dada! Dada!

ROBERT: *(Swinging her up above his head—lovingly)* And how's this little girl of mine this hot day, eh?

MARY: *(Screeching happily)* Dada! Dada!

RUTH: *(In annoyance)* Don't do that to her! You know it's time for her nap and you'll get her all waked up; then I'll be the one that'll have to sit beside her till she falls asleep.

ROBERT: *(Sitting down in the chair on the left of table and cuddling* MARY *on his lap)* You needn't bother. I'll put her to bed.

RUTH: *(Shortly)* You've got to get back to your work, I s'pose.

ROBERT: *(With a sigh)* Yes, I was forgetting. *(He glances at the open letter on* RUTH's *lap.)* Reading Andy's letter again? I should think you'd know it by heart by this time.

RUTH: *(Coloring as if she'd been accused of something—defiantly)* I've got a right to read it, haven't I? He says it's meant for all of us.

ROBERT: *(With a trace of irritation)* Right? Don't be so silly. There's no question of right. I was only saying that you must know all that's in it after so many readings.

RUTH: Well, I don't. *(She puts the letter on the table and gets wearily to her feet.)* I s'pose you'll be wanting your dinner now.

ROBERT: *(Listlessly)* I don't care. I'm not hungry. It's almost too hot to eat.

RUTH: And here I been keeping it hot for you!

ROBERT: *(Irritably)* Oh, all right then. Bring it in and I'll try to eat.

RUTH: I've got to get her to bed first. *(She goes to lift MARY off his lap.)* Come, dear. It's after time and you can hardly keep your eyes open now.

MARY: *(Crying)* No, no, I don't wanter sleep! *(Appealing to her father)* Dada! No!

RUTH: *(Accusingly to ROBERT)* There! Now see what you've done! I told you not to—

ROBERT: *(Shortly)* Let her alone, then. She's all right where she is. She'll fall asleep on my lap in a minute if you'll stop bothering her.

RUTH: *(Hotly)* She'll not do any such thing! She's got to learn to mind me, that she has! *(Shaking her finger at MARY)* You naughty child! Will you come with Mama when she tells you for your own good?

MARY: *(Clinging to her father)* No, Dada!

RUTH: *(Losing her temper)* A good spanking's what you need, my young lady—and you'll get one from me if you don't mind better, d'you hear?

(MARY starts to whimper frightenedly.)

ROBERT: *(With sudden anger)* Leave her alone! How often have I told you not to threaten her with whipping? It's barbarous, and I won't have it. That's got to be understood. *(Soothing the wailing MARY)* There! There, little girl! Baby mustn't cry. Dada won't like you if you do. Dada'll hold you and you must promise to go to sleep like a good little girl. Will you when Dada asks you?

MARY: *(Cuddling up to him)* Yes, Dada.

RUTH: *(Looking at them, her pale face set and drawn)* I won't be ordered by you! She's my child as much as yours. A fine one you are to be telling folks how to do things, you—

(She bites her lips. Husband and wife look into each other's eyes with something akin to hatred in their expressions; then RUTH turns away with a shrug of affected indifference.)

RUTH: All right, take care of her then, if you think it's so easy. You'll be whipping her yourself inside of a week. *(She walks away into the kitchen.)*

ROBERT: *(Smoothing MARY's hair—tenderly)* We'll show Mama you're a good little girl, won't we?

MARY: *(Crooning drowsily)* Dada, Dada.

ROBERT: Let's see: Does your mother take off your shoes and stockings before your nap?

MARY: *(Nodding with half-shut eyes)* Yes, Dada.

ROBERT: *(Taking off her shoes and stockings)* We'll show Mama we know how to do those things, won't we? There's one old shoe off—and there's the other old shoe—and here's one old stocking—and there's the other old stocking. There we are, all nice and cool and comfy. *(He bends down and kisses her.)* And now will you promise to go right to sleep if Dada takes you to bed?

(MARY nods sleepily.)

ROBERT: That's the good little girl.

(He gathers her up in his arms carefully and carries her into the bedroom. His voice can be heard faintly as he lulls the child to sleep. RUTH comes out of the kitchen and gets the plate from the table. She hears the voice from the room and tiptoes to the door to look in. Then she starts for the kitchen but stands for a moment thinking, a look of ill-concealed jealousy on her face. At a noise from inside she hurriedly disappears into the kitchen. A moment later ROBERT reenters. He comes forward and picks up the shoes and stockings which he shoves carelessly under the table. Then, seeing no one about, he goes to the sideboard and selects a book. Coming back to his chair, he sits down and immediately becomes absorbed in reading. RUTH returns from the kitchen bringing his plate heaped with food, and a cup of tea. She sets those before him and sits down in her former place. ROBERT continues to read, oblivious to the food on the table.)

RUTH: *(After watching him irritably for a moment)* For heaven's sakes, put down that old book! Don't you see your dinner's getting cold?

ROBERT: *(Closing his book)* Excuse me, Ruth. I didn't notice. *(He picks up his knife and fork and begins to eat gingerly, without appetite.)*

RUTH: I should think you might have some feeling for me, Rob, and not always be late for meals. If you think it's fun sweltering in that oven of a kitchen to keep things warm for you, you're mistaken.

ROBERT: I'm sorry, Ruth, really I am.

RUTH: That's what you always say; but you keep coming late just the same.

ROBERT: I know; and I can't seem to help it. Something crops up every day to delay me. I mean to be here on time.

RUTH: *(With a sigh)* Mean-tos don't count.

ROBERT: *(With a conciliating smile)* Then punish me, Ruth. Let the food get cold and don't bother about me. Just set it to one side. I won't mind.

RUTH: I'd have to wait just the same to wash up after you.

ROBERT: But I can wash up.

RUTH: A nice mess there'd be then!

ROBERT: *(With an attempt at lightness)* The food is lucky to be able to get cold this weather.

(As RUTH *doesn't answer or smile he opens his book and resumes his reading, forcing himself to take a mouthful of food every now and then.* RUTH *stares at him in annoyance.*)

RUTH: And besides, you've got your own work that's got to be done.

ROBERT: *(Absent-mindedly, without taking his eyes from the book)* Yes, of course.

RUTH: *(Spitefully)* Work you'll never get done by reading books all the time.

ROBERT: *(Shutting the book with a snap)* Why do you persist in nagging at me for getting pleasure out of reading? Is it because— *(He checks himself abruptly.)*

RUTH: *(Coloring)* Because I'm too stupid to understand them, I s'pose you were going to say.

ROBERT: *(Shame-facedly)* No—no. *(In exasperation)* Oh, Ruth, why do you want to pick quarrels like this? Why do you goad me into saying things I don't mean? Haven't I got my share of troubles trying to work this cursed farm without your adding to them? You know how hard I've tried to keep things going in spite of bad luck—

RUTH: *(Scornfully)* Bad luck!

ROBERT: And my own very apparent unfitness for the job, I was going to add; but you can't deny there's been bad luck to it, too. You know how unsuited I am to the work and how I hate it; and I've managed to fight along somehow. Why don't you take things into consideration? Why can't we pull together? We used to. I know it's hard on you also. Then why can't we help each other instead of hindering? That's the only way we can make life bearable for each other.

RUTH: *(Sullenly)* I do the best I know how.

ROBERT: *(Gets up and puts his hand on her shoulder)* I know you do. But let's both of us try to do better. We can both improve. Say a word of encouragement once in a while when things go wrong, even if it is my fault. You know the odds I've been up against since Pa died. I'm not a farmer. I've never claimed to be one. But there's nothing else I can do under the circumstances, and I've got to pull things through somehow. With your help, I can do it. With you against me— *(He shrugs his shoulders. There is a pause. Then he bends down and kisses her hair—with an attempt at cheerfulness.)* So you promise that; and I'll promise to be here when the clock strikes—and anything else you tell me to. Is it a bargain?

RUTH: *(Dully)* I s'pose so.

ROBERT: The reason I was late today—it's more bad news, so be prepared.

RUTH: *(As if this was only what she expected)* Oh!

(They are interrupted by the sound of a loud knock at the kitchen door.)

RUTH: There's someone at the kitchen door. *(She hurries out. A moment later she reappears.)* It's Ben. He says he wants to see you.

ROBERT: *(Frowning)* What's the trouble now, I wonder? *(In a loud voice)* Come on in here, Ben.

(BEN slouches in from the kitchen. He is a hulking, awkward young fellow with a heavy, stupid face and shifty, cunning eyes. He is dressed in overalls, boots, etc., and wears a broad-brimmed hat of coarse straw pushed back on his head.)

ROBERT: Well, Ben, what's the matter?

BEN: *(Drawlingly)* The mowin' machine's bust.

ROBERT: Why, that can't be. The man fixed it only last week.

BEN: It's bust just the same.

ROBERT: And can't you fix it?

BEN: No. Don't know what's the matter with the goll-darned thing. 'Twon't work, anyhow.

ROBERT: *(Getting up and going for his hat)* Wait a minute and I'll go look it over. There can't be much the matter with it.

BEN: *(Impudently)* Don't make no diff'rence t'me whether there be or not. I'm quittin'.

ROBERT: *(Anxiously)* You're quitting? You don't mean you're throwing up your job here?

BEN: That's what! My month's up today and I want what's owin' t'me.

ROBERT: But why are you quitting now, Ben, when you know I've so much work on hand? I'll have a hard time getting another man at such short notice.

BEN: That's for you to figger. I'm quittin'.

ROBERT: But what's your reason? You haven't any complaint to make about the way you've been treated, have you?

BEN: No. 'Tain't that. *(Shaking his finger)* Look-a-here. I'm sick o' bein' made fun at, that's what; an' I got a job up to Timms' place; an' I'm quittin' here.

ROBERT: Being made fun of? I don't understand you. Who's making fun of you?

BEN: They all do. When I drive down with the milk in the mornin' they all laughs and jokes at me—that boy up to Harris' and the new feller up to Slocum's, and Bill Evans down to Meade's, and all the rest on 'em.

ROBERT: That's a queer reason for leaving me flat. Won't they laugh at you just the same when you're working for Timms?

BEN: They wouldn't dare to. Timms is the best farm hereabouts. They was laughin' at me for workin' for you, that's what! "How're things up to the Mayo place?" they hollers every mornin'. "What's Robert doin' now—pasturin' the cattle in the corn-lot? Is he seasonin' his hay with rain this year, same as last?" they shouts. "Or is he inventin' some 'lectrical milkin' engine to fool them dry cows o' his into givin' hard cider?" *(Very much ruffled)* That's like they talks; and I ain't goin' to put up with it no longer. Everyone's always knowd me as a first-class hand hereabouts, and I ain't wantin' 'em to get no different notion. So I'm quittin' you. And I wants what's comin' to me.

ROBERT: *(Coldly)* Oh, if that's the case, you can go to the devil.

BEN: This farm'd take me there quick 'nuff if I was fool 'nuff to stay.

ROBERT: *(Angrily)* None of your damned cheek! You'll get your money tomorrow when I get back from town—not before!

BEN: *(Turning to doorway to kitchen)* That suits me. *(As he goes out he speaks back over his shoulder)* And see that I do get it, or there'll be trouble. *(He disappears and the slamming of the kitchen door is heard.)*

ROBERT: *(As RUTH comes from where she has been standing by the doorway and sits down dejectedly in her old place)* The stupid damn fool! And now what about the haying? That's an example of what I'm up against. No one can say I'm responsible for that.

RUTH: Yes you are! He wouldn't dare act that way with anyone else. They do like they please with you, because you don't know how to treat 'em. They think you're easy—and you are!

ROBERT: *(Indignantly)* I suppose I ought to be a slave driver like the rest of the farmers—stand right beside them all day watching every move they make, and work them to their last ounce of strength? Well, I can't do it, and I won't do it!

RUTH: It's better to do that than have to ask your Ma to sign a mortgage on the place.

ROBERT: *(Distractedly)* Oh, damn the place! *(He walks to the window on left and stands looking out.)*

RUTH: *(After a pause, with a glance at ANDREW's letter on the table)* It's lucky Andy's coming back.

ROBERT: *(Coming back and sitting down)* Yes, Andy'll see the right thing to do in a jiffy. He has the knack of it; and he ought to be home any time now. The *Sunda*'s overdue. Must have met with head winds all the way across.

RUTH: *(Anxiously)* You don't think—anything's happened to the boat?

ROBERT: Trust Uncle Dick to bring her through all right! He's too good a sailor to be caught napping. Besides we'll never know the ship's here till Andy steps in the door. He'll want to surprise us. *(With an affectionate smile)* I wonder if the old chump's changed much? He doesn't seem to from his letters, does he? Still the same practical hard-head. *(Shaking his head)* But just the same I doubt if he'll want to settle down to a hum-drum farm life, after all he's been through.

RUTH: *(Resentfully)* Andy's not like you. He likes the farm.

ROBERT: *(Immersed in his own thoughts—enthusiastically)* Gad, the things he's seen and experienced! Think of the places he's been! Hong-Kong, Yokohoma, Batavia, Singapore, Bangkok, Rangoon, Bombay—all the marvelous East! And Honolulu, Sydney, Buenos Aires! All the wonderful far places I used to dream about! God, how I envy him! What a trip! *(He springs to his feet and instinctively goes to the window and stares out at the horizon.)*

RUTH: *(Bitterly)* I s'pose you're sorry now you didn't go?

ROBERT: *(Too occupied with his own thoughts to hear her—vindictively)* Oh, those cursed hills out there that I used to think promised me so much! How I've grown to hate the sight of them! They're like the walls of a narrow prison yard shutting me in from all the freedom and wonder of life! *(He turns back to the room with a gesture of loathing.)* Sometimes I think if it wasn't for you, Ruth, and—*(His voice softening)*—little Mary, I'd chuck everything up and walk down the road with just one desire in my heart—to put the whole rim of the world between me and those hills, and be able to breathe freely once more! *(He sinks down into his chair and smiles with bitter self-scorn.)* There I go dreaming again—my old fool dreams.

RUTH: *(In a low, repressed voice—her eyes smoldering)* You're not the only one!

ROBERT: *(Buried in his own thoughts—bitterly)* And Andy, who's had the chance—what has he got out of it? His letters read like the diary of a—of a farmer! "We're in Singapore now. It's a dirty hole of a place and hotter than hell. Two of the crew are down with fever and we're short-handed on the work. I'll be damn glad when we sail again, although tacking back and forth in these blistering seas is a rotten job too!" *(Scornfully)* That's about the way he summed up his impressions of the East. Every port they touched at he found the same silly fault with. God! The only place he appeared to like was Buenos Aires—and that only because he saw the business opportunities in a booming country like Argentine.

RUTH: *(Her repressed voice trembling)* You needn't make fun of Andy.

ROBERT: Perhaps I am too hard on him; but when I think—but what's the use? You know I wasn't making fun of Andy personally. No one loves him better than I do, the old chump! But his attitude toward things is—is rank, in my estimation.

RUTH: *(Her eyes flashing—bursting into uncontrollable rage)* You was too making fun of him! And I ain't going to stand for it! You ought to be ashamed of yourself! A fine one you be!

(ROBERT *stares at her in amazement. She continues furiously.*)

RUTH: A fine one to talk about anyone else—after the way you've ruined everything with your lazy loafing!—and the stupid way you do things!

ROBERT: *(Angrily)* Stop that kind of talk, do you hear?

RUTH: You findin' fault—with your own brother who's ten times the man you ever was or ever will be—a thing like you to be talking. You're jealous, that's what! Jealous because he's made a man of himself, while you're nothing but a—but a— *(She stutters incoherently, overcome by rage.)*

ROBERT: Ruth! Ruth! Don't you dare—! You'll be sorry for talking like that.

RUTH: I won't! I won't never be sorry! I'm only saying what I've been thinking for years.

ROBERT: *(Aghast)* Ruth! You can't mean that!

RUTH: What do you think—living with a man like you—having to suffer all the time because you've never been man enough to work and do things like other people. But no! You never own up to that. You think you're so much better than other folks, with your college education, where you never learned a thing, and always reading your stupid books instead of working. I s'pose you think I ought to be proud to be your wife—a poor, ignorant thing like me! *(Fiercely)* But I'm not. I hate it! I hate the sight of you! Oh, if I'd only known! If I hadn't been such a fool to listen to your cheap, silly, poetry talk that you learned out of books! If I could have seen how you were in your true self—like you are now—I'd have killed myself before I'd have married you! I was sorry for it before we'd been together a month. I knew what you were really like—when it was too late.

ROBERT: *(His voice raised loudly)* And now—I'm finding out what you're really like—what a—a creature I've been living with. *(With a harsh laugh)* God! It wasn't that I haven't guessed how mean and small you are—but I've kept on telling myself that I must be wrong—like a fool!—like a damned fool!

RUTH: You were saying you'd go out on the road if it wasn't for me. Well, you can go, and the sooner the better! I don't care! I'll be glad to get rid of you! The farm'll be better off too. There's been a curse on it ever since you took hold. So go! Go and be a tramp like you've always wanted. It's all you're good for. I can get along without you, don't you worry. I'll get some peace. *(Exulting fiercely)* And Andy's coming back, don't forget that! He'll attend to things like they should be. He'll show what a man can do! I don't need you. Andy's coming!

ROBERT: *(They are both standing. ROBERT grabs her by the shoulders and glares into her eyes.)* What do you mean? *(He shakes her violently.)* What are you thinking of? What's in your evil mind, you—you— *(His voice is a harsh shout.)*

RUTH: *(In a defiant scream)* Yes I do mean it! I'd say it if you was to kill me! I do love Andy. I do! I do! I always loved him. *(Exultantly)* And he loves me! He loves me! I know he does. He always did! And you know he did, too! So go! Go if you want to!

ROBERT: *(Throwing her away from him. She staggers back against the table—thickly.)* You—you slut!

(He stands glaring at her as she leans back, supporting herself by the table, gasping for breath. A loud frightened whimper sounds from the awakened child in the bedroom. It continues. The man and woman stand looking at one another in horror, the extent of their terrible quarrel suddenly brought home to them. A pause. The noise of a horse and carriage comes from the road before the house. The two, suddenly struck by the same premonition, listen to it breathlessly, as to a sound heard in a dream. It stops. They hear ANDY's voice from the road shouting a long hail—"Ahoy there!")

RUTH: *(With a strangled cry of joy)* Andy! Andy! *(She rushes and grabs the knob of the screen door, about to fling it open.)*

ROBERT: *(In a voice of command that forces obedience)* Stop!

(He goes to the door and gently pushes the trembling RUTH away from it. The child's crying rises to a louder pitch.)

ROBERT: I'll meet Andy. You better go in to Mary, Ruth.

(She looks at him defiantly for a moment, but there is something in his eyes that makes her turn and walk slowly into the bedroom.)

ANDY'S VOICE: *(In a louder shout)* Ahoy there, Rob!

ROBERT: *(In an answering shout of forced cheeriness)* Hello, Andy!

(He opens the door and walks out as the curtain falls.)

Scene Two

(The top of a hill on the farm. It is about eleven o'clock the next morning. The day is hot and cloudless. In the distance the sea can be seen.)

(The top of the hill slopes downward slightly toward the left. A big boulder stands in the center toward the rear. Further right, a large oak tree. The faint trace of a path leading upward to it from the left foreground can be detected through the bleached, sun-scorched grass.)

(ROBERT is discovered sitting on the boulder, his chin resting on his hands, staring out toward the horizon seaward. His face is pale and haggard, his expression one of utter despondency. MARY is sitting on the grass near him in the shade, playing with her doll, singing happily to herself. Presently she casts a curious glance at her father, and, propping her doll up against the tree, comes over and clambers to his side.)

MARY: *(Pulling at his hand—solicitously)* Is Dada sick?

ROBERT: *(Looking at her with a forced smile)* No, dear. Why?

MARY: Then why don't he play with Mary?

ROBERT: *(Gently)* No, dear, not today. Dada doesn't feel like playing today.

MARY: *(Protestingly)* Yes, please, Dada!

ROBERT: No, dear. Dada does feel sick—a little. He's got a bad headache.

MARY: Let Mary see.

(He bends his head. She pats his hair.)

MARY: Bad head.

ROBERT: *(Kissing her—with a smile)* There! It's better now, dear, thank you.

(She cuddles up close against him. There is a pause during which each of them looks out seaward.)

MARY: *(Pointing toward the sea)* Is that all wa-wa, Dada?

ROBERT: Yes, dear.

MARY: *(Amazed by the magnitude of this conception)* Oh-oh! *(She points to the horizon.)* And it all stops there, over farver?

ROBERT: No, it doesn't stop. That line you see is called the horizon. It's where the sea and sky meet. Just beyond that is where the good fairies live. *(Checking himself—with a harsh laugh)* But you mustn't ever believe in fairies. It's bad luck. And besides, there aren't any good fairies.

(MARY looks up into his face with a puzzled expression.)

MARY: Then if fairies don't live there, what lives there?

ROBERT: *(Bitterly)* God knows! Mocking devils, I've found them.

(MARY frowns in puzzlement, turning this over in her mind. There is a pause. Finally ROBERT turns to her tenderly.)

ROBERT: Would you miss Dada very much if he went away?

MARY: Far—far away?

ROBERT: Yes. Far, far away.

MARY: And Mary wouldn't see him, never?

ROBERT: No; but Mary'd forget him very soon, I'm sure.

MARY: *(Tearfully)* No! No! Dada mustn't go 'way. No, Dada, no!

ROBERT: Don't you like Uncle Andy—the man that came yesterday—not the old man with the white moustache—the other?

MARY: But Dada mustn't go 'way. Mary loves Dada.

ROBERT: *(With fierce determination)* He won't go away, baby. He was only joking. He couldn't leave his little Mary. *(He presses the child in his arms.)*

MARY: *(With an exclamation of pain)* Oh! Dada hurts!

ROBERT: I'm sorry, little girl. *(He lifts her down to the grass.)* Go play with Dolly, that's a good girl; and be careful to keep in the shade.

(She reluctantly leaves him and takes up her doll again. A moment later she points down the hill to the left.)

MARY: Here comes mans, Dada.

ROBERT: *(Looking that way)* It's your Uncle Andy.

MARY: Will he play wiv me, Dada?

ROBERT: Not now, dear. You mustn't bother him. After a while he will, maybe.

(A moment later ANDREW comes up from the left, whistling cheerfully. He has changed but little in appearance, except for the fact that his face has been deeply bronzed by his years in the tropics; but there is a decided change in his manner. The old easy-going good-nature seems to have been partly lost in a breezy, business-like briskness of voice and gesture. There is an authoritative note in his speech as though he were accustomed to give orders and have them obeyed as a matter of course. He is dressed in the simple blue uniform and cap of a merchant ship's officer.)

ANDREW: Here you are, eh?

ROBERT: Hello, Andy.

ANDREW: *(Going over to MARY)* And who's this young lady I find you all alone with, eh? Who's this pretty young lady?

(He tickles the laughing, squirming MARY, then lifts her up at arm's length over his head.)

ANDREW: Upsy—daisy! *(He sets her down on the ground again.)* And there you are!

(He walks over and sits down on the boulder beside ROBERT *who moves to one side to make room for him.)*

ANDREW: Ruth told me I'd probably find you up top-side here; but I'd have guessed it, anyway. *(He digs his brother in the ribs affectionately.)* Still up to your old tricks, you old beggar! I can remember how you used to come up here to mope and dream in the old days.

ROBERT: *(With a smile)* I come up here now because it's the coolest place on the farm. I've given up dreaming.

ANDREW: *(Grinning)* I don't believe it. You can't have changed that much.

ROBERT: *(Wearily)* One gets tired of dreaming—when they never come true.

ANDREW: *(Scrutinizing his brother's face)* You've changed in looks all right. You look all done up, as if you'd been working too hard. Better let up on yourself for a while.

ROBERT: Oh, I'm all right!

ANDREW: Take a fool's advice and go it easy. You remember—your old trouble. You wouldn't want that coming back on you, eh? It pays to keep top-notch in your case.

ROBERT: *(Betraying annoyance)* Oh, that's all a thing of the past, Andy. Forget it!

ANDREW: Well—a word to the wise does no harm? Don't be touchy about it. *(Slapping his brother on the back)* You know I mean well, old man, even if I do put my foot in it.

ROBERT: Of course, Andy. I'm not touchy about it. I don't want you to worry about dead things, that's all. I've a headache today, and I expect I do look done up.

ANDREW: Mum's the word, then! *(After a pause—with boyish enthusiasm)* Say, it sure brings back old times to be up here with you having a chin all by our lonesomes again. I feel great being back home.

ROBERT: It's great for us to have you back.

ANDREW: *(After a pause—meaningly)* I've been looking over the old place with Ruth. Things don't seem to be—

ROBERT: *(His face flushing—interrupts his brother shortly)* Never mind the damn farm! There's nothing about it we don't both know by heart. Let's talk about something interesting. This is the first chance I've had to have a word with you alone. To the devil with the farm for the present. They think of nothing else at home. Tell me about your trip. That's what I've been anxious to hear about.

ANDREW: *(With a quick glance of concern at* ROBERT*)* I suppose you do get an overdose of the farm at home. *(Indignantly)* Say, I never realized that Ruth's mother was such an old rip 'till she talked to me this morning. *(With a grin)* Phew! I pity you, Rob, when she gets on her ear!

ROBERT: She is—difficult sometimes; but one must make allowances. *(Again changing the subject abruptly)* But this isn't telling me about the trip.

ANDREW: Why, I thought I told you everything in my letters.

ROBERT: *(Smiling)* Your letters were—sketchy, to say the least.

ANDREW: Oh, I know I'm no author. You needn't be afraid of hurting my feelings. I'd rather go through a typhoon again than write a letter.

ROBERT: *(With eager interest)* Then you were through a typhoon?

ANDREW: Yes—in the China sea. Had to run before it under bare poles for two days. I thought we were bound down for Davy Jones, sure. Never dreamed waves could get so big or the wind blow so hard. If it hadn't been for Uncle Dick being such a good skipper we'd have gone to the sharks, all of us. As it was we came out minus a main top-mast and had to beat back to Hong-Kong for repairs. But I must have written you all this.

ROBERT: You never mentioned it.

ANDREW: Well, there was so much dirty work getting things ship-shape again I must have forgotten about it.

ROBERT: *(Looking at* ANDREW: *marvelling)* Forget a typhoon? *(With a trace of scorn)* You're a strange combination, Andy. And is what you've told me all you remember about it?

ANDREW: Oh, I could give you your bellyful of details if I wanted to turn loose on you; but they're not the kind of things to fit in with your pretty notions of life on the ocean wave, I'll give you that straight.

ROBERT: *(Earnestly)* Tell me. I'd like to hear them—honestly!

ANDREW: What's the use? They'd make a man want to live in the middle of America without even a river in a hundred miles of him so he'd feel safe. It was rotten, that's what it was! Talk about work! I was wishin' the ship'd sink and give me a rest, I was so dog tired toward the finish. We didn't get a warm thing to eat for nearly two weeks. There was enough China Sea in the galley to float the stove, and the fo' c's'tle was flooded, too. And you couldn't sleep a wink. No place on the darned old tub stayed still long enough for you to lie on it. And every one was soaked to the skin all the time, with green seas boiling over the deck keeping you busy jumping for the rat-lines to keep from being washed over. Oh, it was all-wool-and-a-yard-wide-Hell, I'll tell you. You ought to have been there. I remember thinking about you at the worst of it when you couldn't force a breath out against the wind, and saying to myself: 'This'd cure Rob of them ideas of his about the beautiful sea, if he could see it.' And it would have too, you bet! *(He nods emphatically.)*

ROBERT: And you don't see any romance in that?

ANDREW: Romance be blowed! It was hell! *(As an afterthought)* Oh, I was forgetting! One of the men *was* washed overboard—a Norwegian—Ollie we called him. *(With a grin of sarcasm)* I suppose that's romance, eh? Well, it might be for a fish, but not for me, old man!

ROBERT: *(Dryly)* The sea doesn't seem to have impressed you very favorably.

ANDREW: I should say it didn't! It's a dog's life. You work like the devil and put up with all kinds of hardships—for what? For a rotten wage you'd be ashamed to take on shore.

ROBERT: Then you're not going to—follow it up?

ANDREW: Not me! I'm through! I'll never set foot on a ship again if I can help it—except to carry me some place I can't get to by train. No. I've had enough. Dry land is the only place for me.

ROBERT: But you studied to become an officer!

ANDREW: Had to do something or I'd gone mad. The days were like years. Nothing to look at but sea and sky. No place to go. A regular prison. *(He laughs.)* And as for the East you used to rave about—well, you ought to see it, and smell it! And the Chinks and Japs and Hindus and the rest of them—you can have them! One walk down one of their filthy narrow streets with the tropic sun beating on it would sicken you for life with the "wonder and mystery" you used to dream of. I can say one thing for it though—it certainly has the stink market cornered.

ROBERT: *(Shrinking from his brother with a glance of aversion)* So all you found in the East was a stench?

ANDREW: A stench! Ten thousand of them! That and the damned fever! You can have the tropics, old man. I never want to see them again. At that, there's lots of money to be made down there—for a white man. The natives are too lazy to work, that's the only trouble.

ROBERT: But you did like some of the places, judging from your letters—Sydney, Buenos Aires—

ANDREW: Yes, Sydney's a good town. *(Enthusiastically)* But Buenos Aires—there's the place for you. Argentine's a country where a fellow has a chance to make good. You're right I liked it. And I'll tell you, Rob, that's right where I'm going just as soon as I've seen you folks a while and can get a ship. I don't intend to pay for my passage now I can get a berth as second officer, and I'll jump the ship when I get there. I'll need every cent of the wages Uncle's paid me to get a start at something in B A.

ROBERT: *(Staring at his brother—slowly)* So you're not going to stay on the farm?

ANDREW: Why sure not! Did you think I was? There wouldn't be any sense. One of us is enough to run this little place.

ROBERT: I suppose it does seem small to you now.

ANDREW: *(Not noticing the sarcasm in* ROBERT's *tone)* You've no idea, Rob, what a splendid place Argentine is. I went around Buenos Aires quite a lot and got to know people—English speaking people, of course. The town is full of them. It's foreign capital that's developed the country, you know. I had a letter from a marine insurance chap that I'd made friends with in Hong-Kong to his brother, who's in the grain business in Buenos Aires. He took quite a fancy to me, and what's more important, he offered me a job if I'd come back there. I'd have taken it on the spot, only I couldn't leave Uncle Dick in the lurch, and I'd promised you folks to come home. But I'm going back there very soon, you bet, and then you watch me get on! *(He slaps* ROBERT *on the back.)* But don't you think it's a big chance, Rob?

ROBERT: It's fine—for you, Andy.

ANDREW: We call this a farm—but you ought to hear about the farms down there—ten square miles where we've got an acre. It's a new country where big things are opening up—and I want to get in on something big before I die. That job I'm offered'll furnish the wedge. I'm no fool when it comes to farming, and I know something about grain. I've been reading up a lot on it, too, lately. *(He notices* ROBERT's *absent-minded expression and laughs.)* Wake up, you old poetry book worm, you! I know my talking about business makes you want to choke me, doesn't it?

ROBERT: *(With an embarrassed smile)* No, Andy, I—I just happened to think of something else. *(Frowning)* There've been lots of times lately that I've wished I had some of your faculty for business.

ANDREW: *(Soberly)* There's something I want to talk about, Rob,—the farm. You don't mind, do you?

ROBERT: No.

ANDREW: I walked over it this morning with Ruth—and she told me about things— *(Evasively)*—the hard luck you'd had and how things stood at present—and about your thinking of raising a mortgage.

ROBERT: *(Bitterly)* It's all true I guess, and probably worse than she told you.

ANDREW: I could see the place had run down; but you mustn't blame yourself. When luck's against anyone—

ROBERT: Don't, Andy! It is my fault—my inability. You know it as well as I do. The best I've ever done was to make ends meet, and this year I can't do that without the mortgage.

ANDREW: *(After a pause)* You mustn't raise the mortgage, Rob. I've got over a thousand saved, and you can have that.

ROBERT: *(Firmly)* No. You need that for your start in Buenos Aires.

ANDREW: I don't. I can—

ROBERT: *(Determinedly)* No, Andy! Once and for all, no! I won't hear of it!

ANDREW: *(Protestingly)* You obstinate old son of a gun! *(There is a pause.)* Well, I'll do the best I can while I'm here. I'll get a real man to superintend things for you—if he can be got. That'll relieve you some. If he gets results, you can afford to pay him.

ROBERT: Oh, everything'll be on a sound footing after harvest. Don't worry about it.

ANDREW: *(Doubtfully)* Maybe. The prospects don't look so bad.

ROBERT: And then I can pay the mortgage off again. It's just to tide over.

ANDREW: *(After a pause)* I wish you'd let me help, Rob.

ROBERT: *(With a tone of finality)* No. Please don't suggest it any more. My mind's made up on that point.

ANDREW: *(Slapping his brother on the back—with forced joviality)* Well, anyway, you've got to promise to let me step in when I've made my pile; and I'll make it down there, I'm certain; and it won't take me long, either.

ROBERT: I've no doubt you will with your determination.

ANDREW: I'll be able to pay off all the mortgages you can raise! Still, a mortgage isn't such a bad thing at that—it makes a place heaps easier to sell—and you may want to cut loose from this farm some day—come down and join me in Buenos Aires, that's the ticket.

ROBERT: If I had only myself to consider—

ANDREW: Yes, I suppose they wouldn't want to come. *(After a pause)* It's too bad Pa couldn't have lived to see things through. *(With feeling)* It cut me up a lot—hearing he was dead. Tell me about it. You didn't say much in your letter.

ROBERT: *(Evasively)* He's at peace, Andy. It'll only make you feel bad to talk of it.

ANDREW: He never—softened up, did he—about me, I mean?

ROBERT: He never understood, that's a kinder way of putting it. He does now.

ANDREW: *(After a pause)* You've forgotten all about what—caused me to go, haven't you Rob?

(ROBERT *nods but keeps his face averted.*)

ANDREW: I was a slushier damn fool in those days than you were. But it was an act of Providence I did go. It opened my eyes to how I'd been fooling myself. Why, I'd forgotten all about—that—before I'd been at sea six months.

ROBERT: *(Turns and looks into* ANDREW's *eyes searchingly)* You're speaking of—Ruth?

ANDREW: *(Confused)* Yes. I didn't want you to get false notions in your head, or I wouldn't say anything. *(Looking* ROBERT *squarely in the eyes)* I'm telling you the truth when I say I'd forgotten long ago. It don't sound well for me, getting over things so easy, but I guess it never really amounted to more than a kid idea I was letting rule me. I'm certain now I never was in love—I was getting fun out of thinking I was—and being a hero to myself. *(He heaves a great sigh of relief.)* There! Gosh, I'm glad that's off my chest. I've been feeling sort of awkward ever since I've been home, thinking of what you two might think. *(A trace of appeal in his voice)* You've got it all straight now, haven't you, Rob?

ROBERT: *(In a low voice)* Yes, Andy.

ANDREW: And I'll tell Ruth, too, if I can get up the nerve. She must feel kind of funny having me round—after what used to be—and not knowing how I feel about it.

ROBERT: *(Slowly)* Perhaps—for her sake—you'd better not tell her.

ANDREW: For her sake? Oh, you mean she wouldn't want to be reminded of my foolishness? Still, I think it'd be worse if—

ROBERT: *(Breaking out—in an agonized voice)* Do as you please, Andy; but for God's sake, let's not talk about it!

(There is a pause. ANDREW *stares at* ROBERT *in hurt stupefaction.* ROBERT *continues after a moment in a voice which he vainly attempts to keep calm.)*

ROBERT: Excuse me, Andy. This rotten headache has my nerves shot to pieces.

ANDREW: *(Mumbling)* It's all right, Rob—long as you're not sore at me.

ROBERT: Where did Uncle Dick disappear to this morning?

ANDREW: He went down to the port to see to things on the *Sunda*. He said he didn't know exactly when he'd be back. I'll have to go down and tend to the ship when he comes. That's why I dressed up in these togs.

MARY: *(Pointing down the hill to the left)* See Dada! Mama! Mama! *(She jumps to her feet and starts to run down the path.)*

ANDREW: *(Standing and looking down)* Yes, here comes Ruth. Must be looking for you, I guess. *(Jumping forward and stopping* MARY*)* Hey up! You mustn't run down hill like that, little girl. You'll take a bad fall, don't you know it?

ROBERT: Stay here and wait for your mother, Mary.

MARY: *(Struggling to her feet)* No! No! Mama! Dada!

ANDREW: Here she is!

(RUTH *appears at left. She is dressed in white, shows she has been fixing up. She looks pretty, flushed and full of life.*)

MARY: *(Running to her mother)* Mama!

RUTH: *(Kissing her)* Hello, dear! *(She walks toward the rock and addresses* ROBERT *coldly.)* Jake wants to see you about something. He finished working where he was. He's waiting for you at the road.

ROBERT: *(Getting up—wearily)* I'll go down right away. *(As he looks at* RUTH, *noting her changed appearance, his face darkens with pain.)*

RUTH: And take Mary with you, please. *(To* MARY) Go with Dada, that's a good girl. Grandma has your dinner most ready for you.

ROBERT: *(Shortly)* Come, Mary!

MARY: *(Taking his hand and dancing happily beside him)* Dada! Dada!

(*They go down the hill to the left.* RUTH *looks after them for a moment, frowning—then turns to* ANDY *with a smile.*)

RUTH: I'm going to sit down. Come on, Andy. It'll be like old times. *(She jumps lightly to the top of the rock and sits down.)* It's so fine and cool up here after the house.

ANDREW: *(Half-sitting on the side of the boulder)* Yes. It's great.

RUTH: I've taken a holiday in honor of your arrival—from work in the kitchen. *(Laughing excitedly)* I feel so free I'd like to have wings and fly over the sea. You're a man. You can't know how awful and stupid it is—cooking and washing dishes all the time.

ANDREW: *(Making a wry face)* I can guess.

RUTH: Besides, your mother just insisted on getting your first dinner to home, she's that happy at having you back. You'd think I was planning to poison you the flurried way she shooed me out of the kitchen.

ANDREW: That's just like Ma, bless her!

RUTH: She's missed you terrible. We all have. And you can't deny the farm has, after what I showed you and told you when we was looking over the place this morning.

ANDREW: *(With a frown)* Things are run down, that's a fact! It's too darn hard on poor old Rob.

RUTH: *(Scornfully)* It's his own fault. He never takes any interest in things.

ANDREW: *(Reprovingly)* You can't blame him. He wasn't born for it; but I know he's done his best for your sake and the old folks and the little girl.

RUTH: *(Indifferently)* Yes, I suppose he has. *(Gaily)* But thank the Lord, all those days are over now. The "hard luck" Rob's always blaming won't last long when you take hold, Andy. All the farm's ever needed was someone with the knack of looking ahead and preparing for what's going to happen.

ANDREW: Yes, Rob hasn't got that. He's frank to own up to that himself. I'm going to try and hire a good man for him—an experienced farmer—to work the place on a salary and percentage. That'll take it off of Rob's hands, and he needn't be worrying himself to death any more. He looks all worn out, Ruth. He ought to be careful.

RUTH: *(Absent-mindedly)* Yes, I s'pose. *(Her mind is filled with premonitions by the first part of his statement.)*

ANDREW: It would be a good idea if Rob could pull out of here—get a job in town on a newspaper, or something connected with writing—and this plan of mine'd give him a chance.

RUTH: *(Vaguely)* He's always wanted to get away. *(Suspiciously)* Why do you want to hire a man to oversee things? Seems as if now that you're back it wouldn't be needful.

ANDREW: Oh, of course I'll attend to everything while I'm here. I mean after I'm gone.

RUTH: *(As if she couldn't believe her ears)* Gone!

ANDREW: Yes. When I leave for the Argentine again.

RUTH: *(Aghast)* You're going away to sea again!

ANDREW: Not to sea, no; I'm through with the sea for good as a job. I'm going down to Buenos Aires to get in the grain business.

RUTH: But—that's way far off—isn't it?

ANDREW: *(Easily)* Six thousand miles more or less. It's quite a trip. *(With enthusiasm)* I've got a peach of a chance down there, Ruth. Ask Rob if I haven't. I've just been telling him all about it. I won't bother you by repeating. Rob can tell you.

RUTH: *(A flush of anger coming over her face)* And didn't he try to stop you from going?

ANDREW: *(In surprise)* No, of course not. Why?

RUTH: *(Slowly and vindictively)* That's just like him—not to.

ANDREW: *(Resentfully)* Rob's too good a chum to try and stop me when he knows I'm set on a thing. And he could see just as soon's I told him what a good chance it was. You ask him about it.

RUTH: *(Dazedly)* And you're bound on going?

ANDREW: Sure thing. Oh, I don't mean right off. I'll have to wait for a ship sailing there for quite a while, likely. Anyway, I want to stay to home and visit with you folks a spell before I go.

RUTH: *(Dumbly)* I s'pose. *(With sudden anguish)* Oh, Andy, you can't go! You can't. Why we've all thought—we've all been hoping and praying you was coming home to stay, to settle down on the farm and see to things. You mustn't go! Think of how your Ma'll take on if you go—and how the farm'll be ruined if you leave it to Rob to look after. You can see that.

ANDREW: *(Frowning)* Rob hasn't done so bad. When I get a man to direct things the farm'll be safe enough.

RUTH: *(Insistently)* But your Ma—think of her.

ANDREW: She's used to me being away. She won't object when she knows it's best for her and all of us for me to go. You ask Rob. In a couple of years down there I'll make my pile, see if I don't; and then I'll come back and settle down and turn this farm to the crackiest place in the whole state. In the meantime, I can help you both from down there. *(Earnestly)* I tell you, Ruth, I'm going to make good right from the minute I land, if working hard and a determination to get on can do it; and I know they can! I'll have money and lots of it before long, and none of you'll have to worry about this pesky little farm any more. *(Excitedly—in a rather boastful tone)* I tell you, I feel ripe for bigger things than settling down here. The trip did that for me, anyway. It showed me the world in a larger proposition than ever I thought it was in the old days. I couldn't be content any more stuck here like a fly in molasses. There ain't enough to do. It all seems trifling, somehow. You ought to be able to understand what I feel.

RUTH: *(Dully)* Yes—I s'pose I ought.

ANDREW: I felt sure you'd see; and wait till Rob tells you about—

RUTH: *(A dim suspicion forming in her mind—interrupting him)* What did he tell you—about me?

ANDREW: Tell? About you? Why, nothing.

RUTH: *(Staring at him intensely)* Are you telling me the truth, Andy Mayo? Didn't he say—I—*(She stops confusedly.)*

ANDREW: *(Surprised)* No, he didn't mention you, I can remember. Why? What made you think he did?

RUTH: *(Wringing her hands)* Oh, I wish I could tell if you're lying or not!

ANDREW: *(Indignantly)* What're you talking about? I didn't used to lie to you, did I? And what in the name of God is there to lie for?

RUTH: *(Still unconvinced)* Are you sure—will you swear—it isn't the reason— *(She lowers her eyes and half turns away from him.)* The same reason

that made you go last time that's driving you away again? 'Cause if it is—
I was going to say—you mustn't go—on that account. *(Her voice sinks to a tremulous, tender whisper as she finishes.)*

ANDREW: *(Confused—forces a laugh)* Oh, is that what you're driving at? Well, you needn't worry about that no more— *(Soberly)* I don't blame you, Ruth, feeling embarrassed having me around again, after the way I played the dumb fool about going away last time. You'll have to put it down to me just being young and foolish and not responsible for my actions—and forgive me and forget it. Will you?

RUTH: *(In anguish buries her face in her hands)* Oh, Andy!

ANDREW: *(Misunderstanding)* I know I oughtn't to talk about such foolishness to you. Still I figure it's better to get it out of my system so's we three can be together same's years ago, and not be worried thinking one of us might have the wrong notion. No, don't you fret about me having any such reason for going this time. I'm not a calf any more. Why honest, Ruth, before the ship got to Hong Kong I'd near forgot all that part of it. All I remembered was the awful scrap I'd had with Pa—and I was darned cut up about that.

RUTH: Andy! Please! Don't!

ANDREW: Let me finish now that I've started. It'll help clear things up. I don't want you to think once a fool always a fool, and be upset all the time I'm here on my fool account. I want you to believe I put all that silly nonsense back of me a long time ago—and now—it seems—well—as if you'd always been my sister, that's what, Ruth.

RUTH: *(At the end of her endurance—laughing hysterically)* For God's sake, Andy—won't you please stop talking! *(She again hides her face in her hands, her bowed shoulders trembling.)*

ANDREW: *(Ruefully)* Seem's if I put my foot in it whenever I open my mouth today. Rob shut me up with almost them same words when I tried speaking to him about it.

RUTH: *(Fiercely)* You told him—what you've told me?

ANDREW: *(Astounded)* Why sure! Why not?

RUTH: *(Shuddering)* Oh, my God!

ANDREW: *(Alarmed)* Why? Shouldn't I have?

RUTH: *(Hysterically)* Oh, I don't care what you do! I don't care! Leave me alone!

(ANDREW gets up and walks down the hill to the left, embarrassed, hurt, and greatly puzzled by her behavior.)

ANDREW: *(After a pause—pointing down the hill)* Hello! Here they come back—and the Captain's with them. How'd he come to get back so soon, I wonder? That means I've got to hustle down to the port and get on board. Rob's got the baby with him.

(He comes back to the boulder. RUTH keeps her face averted from him.)

ANDREW: Gosh, I never saw a father so tied up in a kid as Rob is! He just watches every move she makes. And I don't blame him. You both got a right to feel proud of her. She's surely a little winner. *(He glances at RUTH to see if this very obvious attempt to get back in her good graces is having any effect.)* I can see the likeness to Rob standing out all over her, can't you? But there's no denying she's your young one, either. There's something about her eyes—

RUTH: *(Piteously)* Oh, Andy, I've a headache! I don't want to talk! Leave me alone, won't you please?

ANDREW: *(Stands staring at her for a moment—then walks away saying in a hurt tone)* Everybody hereabouts seems to be on edge today. I begin to feel as if I'm not wanted around.

(He stands near the path, left, kicking at the grass with the toe of his shoe. A moment later CAPTAIN DICK SCOTT enters, followed by ROBERT carrying MARY. The CAPTAIN seems scarcely to have changed at all from the jovial, booming person he was three years before. He wears a uniform similar to ANDREW's. He is puffing and breathless from his climb and mops wildly at his perspiring countenance. ROBERT casts a quick glance at ANDREW, noticing the latter's discomfited look, and then turns his eyes on RUTH who, at their approach, has moved so her back is toward them, her chin resting on her hands as she stares out seaward.)

MARY: Mama! Mama!

(ROBERT puts her down and she runs to her mother. RUTH turns and grabs her up in her arms with a sudden fierce tenderness, quickly turning away again from the others. During the following scene she keeps MARY in her arms.)

SCOTT: *(Wheezily)* Phew! I got great news for you, Andy. Let me get my wind first. Phew! God A'mighty, mountin' this damned hill is worser'n goin' aloft to the skys'l yard in a blow. I got to lay to a while. *(He sits down on the grass, mopping his face.)*

ANDREW: I didn't look for you this soon, Uncle.

SCOTT: I didn't figger it, neither; but I run across a bit o' news down to the Seamen's Home made me 'bout ship and set all sail back here to find you.

ANDREW: *(Eagerly)* What is it, Uncle?

SCOTT: Passin' by the Home I thought I'd drop in an' let 'em know I'd be lackin' a mate next trip count o' your leavin'. Their man in charge o' the shippin' asked after you 'special curious. 'Do you think he'd consider a berth as Second on a steamer, Captain?' he asks. I was goin' to say no when I thinks o' you wantin' to get back down south to the Plate agen; so I asks him: 'What is she and where's she bound?' 'She's the El Paso, a brand new tramp,' he says, 'and she's bound for Buenos Aires.'

ANDREW: *(His eyes lighting up—excitedly)* Gosh, that is luck! When does she sail?

SCOTT: Tomorrow mornin'. I didn't know if you'd want to ship away agen so quick an' I told him so. 'Tell him I'll hold the berth open for him until late this afternoon,' he says. So I said I'd tell you an' I catches the first car back to town. So there you be, an' you can make your own choice.

ANDREW: I'd like to take it. There may not be another ship for Buenos Aires with a vacancy in months. *(His eyes roving from* ROBERT *to* RUTH *and back again—uncertainly)* Still—damn it all—tomorrow morning is soon. I wish she wasn't leaving for a week or so. That'd give me a chance—it seems hard to go right away again when I've just got home. And yet it's a chance in a thousand— *(Appealing to* ROBERT*)* What do you think, Rob? What would you do?

ROBERT: *(Forcing a smile)* He who hesitates, you know. *(Frowning)* It's a piece of good luck thrown in your way—and—from what you've told me of your plans—I think you owe it to yourself to jump at it. But don't ask me to decide for you.

RUTH: *(Turning to look at* ANDREW; *in a tone of fierce resentment)* Yes go, Andy! *(She turns quickly away again. There is a moment of embarrassed silence.)*

ANDREW: *(Thoughtfully)* Yes, I guess I will. It'll be the best thing for all of us in the end, don't you think so, Rob?

(ROBERT *nods but remains silent.*)

SCOTT: *(Getting to his feet)* Then, that's settled.

ANDREW: *(Now that he has definitely made a decision his voice rings with hopeful strength and energy.)* Yes, I'll take the berth. The sooner I go the sooner I'll be back, that's a certainty; and I won't come back with empty hands next time. You bet I won't!

SCOTT: You ain't got so much time, Andy. To make sure you'd best leave here soon's you kin. You can't put too much trust in them fellers. I got to get right back aboard. You'd best come with me.

ANDREW: I'll go to the house and repack my bag right away.

ROBERT: *(Quietly)* You'll both be here for dinner, won't you?

ANDREW: *(Worriedly)* I don't know. Will there be time? What time is it now, I wonder?

ROBERT: *(Reproachfully)* Ma's been getting dinner especially for you, Andy.

ANDREW: *(Flushing—shamefacedly)* Hell! And I was forgetting! I'm a damn fool. Of course I'll stay for dinner if I missed every damned ship in the world. *(He turns to the* CAPTAIN—*briskly.)* Come on, Uncle. Walk down with me to the house and you can tell me more about this berth on the way. I've got to pack before dinner.

(He and the CAPTAIN *start down to the left.* ANDREW *calls back over his shoulder.)*

ANDREW: You're coming soon, aren't you, Rob?

ROBERT: Yes. I'll be right down.

*(*ANDREW *and the* CAPTAIN *leave.* RUTH *puts* MARY *on the ground and hides her face in her hands. Her shoulders shake as if she were sobbing.* ROBERT *stares at her with a grim, somber expression.* MARY *walks backward toward* ROBERT, *her wondering eyes fixed on her mother.)*

MARY: *(Her voice vaguely frightened, taking her father's hand)* Dada, Mama's cryin', Dada.

ROBERT: *(Bending down and stroking her hair—in a voice he endeavors to keep from being harsh)* No, she isn't, little girl. The sun hurts her eyes, that's all. Aren't you beginning to feel hungry, Mary?

MARY: *(Decidedly)* Yes, Dada.

ROBERT: *(Meaningly)* It must be your dinner time now.

RUTH: *(In a muffled voice)* I'm coming, Mary. *(She wipes her eyes quickly and, without looking at* ROBERT, *comes and takes* MARY's *hand—in a dead voice.)* Come on and I'll get your dinner for you. *(She walks out left, her eyes fixed on the ground, the skipping* MARY *tugging at her hand.* ROBERT *waits a moment for them to get ahead and then slowly follows as the curtain falls.)*

END OF ACT TWO

ACT THREE

Scene One

(Same as ACT TWO, Scene One—The sitting room of the farm house about six o'clock in the morning of a day toward the end of October five years later. It is not yet dawn, but as the action progresses the darkness outside the windows gradually fades to grey.)

(The room, seen by the light of the shadeless oil lamp with a smoky chimney which stands on the table, presents an appearance of decay, of dissolution. The curtains at the windows are torn and dirty and one of them is missing. The closed desk is grey with accumulated dust as if it had not been used in years. Blotches of dampness disfigure the wall paper. Threadbare trails, leading to the kitchen and outer doors, show in the faded carpet. The top of the coverless table is stained with the imprints of hot dishes and spilt food. The rung of one rocker has been clumsily mended with a piece of plain board. A brown coating of rust covers the unblacked stove. A pile of wood is stacked up carelessly against the wall by the stove.)

(The whole atmosphere of the room, contrasted with that of former years, is one of an habitual poverty too hopelessly resigned to be any longer ashamed or even conscious of itself.)

(At the rise of the curtain RUTH is discovered sitting by the stove, with hands outstretched to the warmth as if the air in the room were damp and cold. A heavy shawl is wrapped about her shoulders, half-concealing her dress of deep mourning. She has aged horribly. Her pale, deeply lined face has the stony lack of expression of one to whom nothing more can ever happen, whose capacity for emotion has been exhausted. When she speaks her voice is without timbre, low and monotonous. The negligent disorder of her dress, the slovenly arrangement of her hair, now streaked with grey, her muddied shoes run down at the heel, give full evidence of the apathy in which she lives.)

(Her mother is asleep in her wheel chair beside the stove toward the rear, wrapped up in a blanket.)

(There is a sound from the open bedroom door in the rear as if someone were getting out of bed. RUTH turns in that direction with a look of dull annoyance. A moment later ROBERT appears in the doorway, leaning weakly against it for support. His hair is long and unkempt, his face and body emaciated. There are bright patches of crimson over his cheek bones and his eyes are burning with fever. He is dressed in corduroy pants, a flannel shirt, and wears worn carpet slippers on his bare feet.)

RUTH: *(Dully)* S-s-s-h-h! Ma's asleep.

ROBERT: *(Speaking with an effort)* I won't wake her. *(He walks weakly to a rocker by the side of the table and sinks down in it exhausted.)*

RUTH: *(Staring at the stove)* You better come near the fire where it's warm.

ROBERT: No. I'm burning up now.

RUTH: That's the fever. You know the doctor told you not to get up and move round.

ROBERT: *(Irritably)* That old fossil! He doesn't know anything. Go to bed and stay there—that's his only prescription.

RUTH: *(Indifferently)* How are you feeling now?

ROBERT: *(Buoyantly)* Better! Much better than I've felt in ages. Really I'm quite healthy now—only very weak. It's the turning point, I guess. From now on I'll pick up so quick I'll surprise you—and no thanks to that old fool of a country quack, either.

RUTH: He's always tended to us.

ROBERT: Always helped us to die, you mean! He "tended" to Pa and Ma and—*(His voice breaks.)*—and to—Mary.

RUTH: *(Dully)* He did the best he knew, I s'pose. *(After a pause)* Well, Andy's bringing a specialist with him when he comes. That ought to suit you.

ROBERT: *(Bitterly)* Is that why you're waiting up all night?

RUTH: Yes.

ROBERT: For Andy?

RUTH: *(Without a trace of feeling)* Somebody had got to, when he's bringing that doctor with him. You can't tell when he might get here if he's coming from the port in an auto like he telegraphed us. And besides it's only right for someone to meet him after he's been gone five years.

ROBERT: *(With bitter mockery)* Five years! It's a long time.

RUTH: Yes.

ROBERT: *(Meaningly)* To wait!

RUTH: *(Indifferently)* It's past now.

ROBERT: Yes, it's past. *(After a pause)* Have you got his two telegrams with you?

*(*RUTH *nods.)*

ROBERT: Let me see them, will you? My head was so full of fever when they came I couldn't make head or tail to them. *(Hastily)* But I'm feeling fine now. Let me read them again.

(RUTH *takes them from the bosom of her dress and hands them to him.*)

RUTH: Here. The first one's on top.

ROBERT: (*Opening it*) New York. "Just landed from steamer. Have important business to wind up here. Will be home as soon as deal is completed." (*He smiles bitterly.*) Business first was always Andy's motto. (*He reads.*) "Hope you are all well. Andy." (*He repeats ironically.*) "Hope you are all well!"

RUTH: (*Dully*) He couldn't know you'd been took sick till I answered that and told him.

ROBERT: (*Contritely*) Of course he couldn't. You're right. I'm a fool. I'm touchy about nothing lately. Just what did you say in your reply? I forget.

RUTH: (*Inconsequentially*) I had to send it collect.

(ROBERT *frowns.*)

RUTH: I wrote you were pretty low and for him to hurry up here.

ROBERT: (*Irritably*) He'll think I'm dying or some such foolishness. What an idiotic exaggeration! What did you say was the matter with me? Did you mention that?

RUTH: I wrote you had lung trouble—just those two words. (*Dully*) The boy said it wouldn't cost any more for two words.

ROBERT: (*Flying into a petty temper*) You are a fool! How often have I explained to you that it's *pleurisy* is the matter with me. You can't seem to get it in your head that the pleura is outside the lungs, not in them!

RUTH: (*Callously*) I only wrote what Doctor Smith told me.

ROBERT: (*Angrily*) He's a damned ignoramus!

RUTH: (*Dully*) Makes no difference. I had to tell Andy something, didn't I?

ROBERT: (*After a pause, opening the other telegram*) He sent this last evening. Let's see. (*He reads.*) "Leave for home on midnight train. Just received your wire. Am bringing specialist to see Rob. Will motor to farm from Port." (*He calculates.*) The midnight gets in the Port about four-thirty, I think, or five. It should take a car an hour or more to get here. What time is it now?

RUTH: Round six, must be.

ROBERT: He ought to be here soon. I'm glad he's bringing a doctor who knows something. I'm tired of being at the mercy of that cheap old quack. A specialist will tell you in a second that there's nothing the matter with my lungs.

RUTH: (*Stolidly*) You've been coughing an awful lot lately.

ROBERT: *(Irritably)* What nonsense! For God's sake, haven't you ever had a bad cold yourself?

(RUTH *stares at the stove in silence.* ROBERT *fidgets in his chair. There is a pause. Finally* ROBERT's *eyes are fixed on the sleeping* MRS ATKINS.)

ROBERT: Your mother is lucky to be able to sleep so soundly.

RUTH: Ma's tired. She's been sitting up with me most of the night.

ROBERT: *(Mockingly)* Is she waiting for Andy, too? *(There is a pause. He sighs.)* I couldn't get to sleep to save my soul. I counted ten million sheep if I counted one. No use! My brain kept pounding out thoughts as if its life depended on it. I gave up trying finally and just laid there in the dark thinking. *(He pauses, then continues in a tone of tender sympathy.)* I was thinking about you, Ruth—of how hard these last years must have been for you. *(Appealingly)* I'm sorry, Ruth.

RUTH: *(In a dead voice)* I don't know. They're past now. They were hard on all of us.

ROBERT: Yes; on all of us but Andy. *(With a flash of sick jealousy)* Andy's made a big success of himself—the kind he wanted. He's got lots of money and, I suppose, a reputation for being a sharp business man. *(Mockingly)* What else is there in life to wish for, eh, Ruth? And now he's coming home to let us admire his greatness. *(Frowning—irritably)* What does it matter? What am I talking about? My brain must be sick, too. *(After a pause)* Yes, these years have been terrible for both of us. *(His voice is lowered to a trembling whisper.)* Especially the last eight months since Mary—died. *(He forces back a sob with a convulsive shudder—then breaks out in a passionate agony.)* Our last hope of happiness! I could curse God from the bottom of my soul—if there was a God! *(He is racked by a violent fit of coughing and hurriedly puts his handkerchief to his lips.)*

RUTH: *(Without looking at him)* Mary's better off—being dead.

ROBERT: *(Gloomily)* We'd all be better off for that matter. *(With sudden exasperation)* You tell that mother of yours she's got to stop saying that Mary's death was due to a weak constitution inherited from me. *(On the verge of tears of weakness)* It's got to stop, I tell you!

RUTH: *(Sullenly)* She's only saying what Doctor Smith said.

ROBERT: *(Fiercely)* He's an old ass, and I'll tell him if—

RUTH: *(Sharply)* S-h-h! You'll wake her; and then she'll nag at me—not you.

ROBERT: *(Coughs and lies back in his chair weakly—a pause)* It's all because your mother's down on me for not begging Andy for help when things got worse here.

RUTH: *(Resentfully)* You might have. He's got plenty, if what he says is true.

ROBERT: How can you of all people think of taking money from him?

RUTH: *(Dully)* I don't see the harm. He's your own brother.

ROBERT: *(Shrugging his shoulders)* What's the use of talking to you? Well, I couldn't. *(Proudly)* And I've managed to keep things going, thank God. You can't deny that without help I've succeeded in— *(He breaks off with a bitter laugh.)* My God, what am I boasting of? Debts to this one and that, taxes, interest unpaid! I'm a fool! *(He lies back in his chair closing his eyes for a moment, then speaks in a low voice.)* I'll be frank, Ruth. I've been an utter failure, and I've dragged you with me. I couldn't blame you in all justice—for hating me.

RUTH: *(Without feeling)* I don't hate you. It's been my fault too, I s'pose.

ROBERT: No. You couldn't help loving—Andy.

RUTH: *(Dully)* I don't love anyone.

ROBERT: *(Waving her remark aside)* You needn't deny it. It doesn't matter. *(After a pause—with a tender smile)* Do you know Ruth, what I've been dreaming back there in the dark? *(With a short laugh)* It may sound silly of me but—I was planning our future when I get well.

(He looks at her with appealing eyes as if afraid she will sneer at him. Her expression does not change. She stares at the stove. His voice takes on a note of eagerness.)

ROBERT: After all, why shouldn't we have a future? We're young yet. If we can only shake off the curse of this farm! It's the farm that's ruined our lives, damn it! And now that Andy's coming back—I'm going to sink my foolish pride, Ruth! I'll borrow the money from him to give us a good start in the city. We'll go where people live instead of stagnating, and start all over again. *(Confidently)* I won't be the failure there that I've been here, Ruth. You won't need to be ashamed of me there. I'll prove to you the reading I've done can be put to some use. *(Vaguely)* I'll write, or something of that sort. I've always wanted to write. *(Pleadingly)* You'll want to do that, won't you, Ruth?

RUTH: *(Dully)* There's Ma.

ROBERT: She can come with us.

RUTH: She wouldn't.

ROBERT: *(Angrily)* So that's your answer!

(He trembles with violent passion. His voice is so strange that RUTH *turns to look at him in alarm.)*

ROBERT: You're lying, Ruth! Your mother's just an excuse. You want to stay here. You think that because Andy's coming back that— *(He chokes and has an attack of coughing.)*

RUTH: *(Getting up—in a frightened voice)* What's the matter? *(She goes to him.)* I'll go with you, Rob. I don't care for Andy like you think. Stop that coughing for goodness sake! It's awful bad for you. *(She soothes him in dull tones.)* I'll go with you to the city—soon's you're well again. Honest I will, Rob, I promise!

(ROBERT *lies back and closes his eyes. She stands looking down at him anxiously.*)

RUTH: Do you feel better now?

ROBERT: Yes.

(RUTH *goes back to her chair. After a pause he opens his eyes and sits up in his chair. His face is flushed and happy.*)

ROBERT: Then you will go, Ruth?

RUTH: Yes.

ROBERT: *(Excitedly)* We'll make a new start, Ruth—just you and I. Life owes us some happiness after what we've been through. *(Vehemently)* It must! Otherwise our suffering would be meaningless—and that is unthinkable.

RUTH: *(Worried by his excitement)* Yes, yes, of course, Rob, but you mustn't—

ROBERT: Oh, don't be afraid. I feel completely well, really I do—now that I can hope again. Oh if you knew how glorious it feels to have something to look forward to—not just a dream, but something tangible, something already within our grasp! Can't you feel the thrill of it, too—the vision of a new life opening up after all the horrible years?

RUTH: Yes, yes, but do be—

ROBERT: Nonsense! I won't be careful. I'm getting back all my strength. *(He gets lightly to his feet.)* See! I feel light as a feather. *(He walks to her chair and bends down to kiss her smilingly.)* One kiss—the first in years, isn't it?—to greet the dawn of a new life together.

RUTH: *(Submitting to his kiss—worriedly)* Sit down, Rob, for goodness' sake!

ROBERT: *(With tender obstinacy—stroking her hair)* I won't sit down. You're silly to worry. *(He rests one hand on the back of her chair.)* Listen. All our suffering has been a test through which we had to pass to prove ourselves worthy of a finer realization. *(Exultingly)* And we did pass through it! It hasn't broken us! And now the dream is to come true! Don't you see?

RUTH: *(Looking at him with frightened eyes as if she thought he had gone mad)* Yes, Rob, I see; but won't you go back to bed now and rest?

ROBERT: No. I'm going to see the sun rise. It's an augury of good fortune.

(*He goes quickly to the window in the rear, left, and pushing the curtains aside, stands looking out.* RUTH *springs to her feet and comes quickly to the table, left, where she remains watching* ROBERT *in a tense, expectant attitude. As he peers out his body seems gradually to sag, to grow limp and tired. His voice is mournful as he speaks.)*

ROBERT: No sun yet. It isn't time. All I can see is the black rim of the damned hills outlined against a creeping greyness. *(He turns around, letting the curtains fall back, stretching a hand out to the wall to support himself. His false strength of a moment has evaporated leaving his face drawn and hollow eyed. He makes a pitiful attempt to smile.)* That's not a very happy augury, is it? But the sun'll come—soon. *(He sways weakly.)*

RUTH: *(Hurrying to his side and supporting him)* Please go to bed, won't you, Rob? You don't want to be all wore out when the specialist comes, do you?

ROBERT: *(Quickly)* No. That's right. He mustn't think I'm sicker than I am. And I feel as if I could sleep now—*(Cheerfully)*—a good, sound, restful sleep.

RUTH: *(Helping him to the bedroom door)* That's what you need most.

(They go inside. A moment later she reappears calling back.)

RUTH: I'll shut this door so's you'll be quiet. *(She closes the door and goes quickly to her mother and shakes her by the shoulder.)* Ma! Ma! Wake up!

MRS ATKINS: *(Coming out of her sleep with a start)* Glory be! What's the matter with you?

RUTH: It was Rob. He's just been talking to me out here. I put him back to bed. *(Now that she is sure her mother is awake her fear passes and she relapses into dull indifference. She sits down in her chair and stares at the stove—dully.)* He acted—funny; and his eyes looked so—so wild like.

MRS ATKINS: *(With asperity)* And is that all you woke me out of a sound sleep for, and scared me near out of my wits?

RUTH: I was afraid. He talked so crazy—staring out of the window as if he saw—something—and speaking about the hills, and wanting to see the sun rise—and all such notions. I couldn't quiet him. It was like he used to talk—only mad, kind of. I didn't want to be alone with him that way. Lord knows what he might do.

MRS ATKINS: *(Scornfully)* Humph! A poor help I'd be to you and me not able to move a step! Why didn't you run and get Jake?

RUTH: *(Dully)* Jake isn't here. I thought I'd told you. He quit last night. He hasn't been paid in three months. You can't blame him.

MRS ATKINS: *(Indignantly)* No, I can't blame him when I come to think of it. What decent person'd want to work on a place like this? *(With sudden exasperation)* Oh, I wish you'd never married that man!

RUTH: *(Wearily)* You oughtn't to talk about him now when he's sick in his bed.

MRS ATKINS: *(Working herself into a fit of rage)* It's lucky for me and you, too, I took my part of the place out of his hands years ago. You know very well, Ruth Mayo, if it wasn't for me helpin' you on the sly out of my savin's, you'd both been in the poor house—and all 'count of his pig-headed pride in not lettin' Andy know the state thin's were in. A nice thing for me to have to support him out of what I'd saved for my last days—and me an invalid with no one to look to!

RUTH: Andy'll pay you back, Ma. I can tell him so's Rob'll never know.

MRS ATKINS: *(With a snort)* What'd Rob think you and him was livin' on, I'd like to know?

RUTH: *(Dully)* He didn't think about it, I s'pose. *(After a slight pause)* He said he'd made up his mind to ask Andy for help when he comes.

(As a clock in the kitchen strikes six.)

RUTH: Six o'clock. Andy ought to get here directly.

MRS ATKINS: D'you think this special doctor'll do Rob any good?

RUTH: *(Hopelessly)* I don't know.

(The two women remain silent for a time staring dejectedly at the stove.)

MRS ATKINS: *(Shivering irritably)* For goodness' sake put some wood on that fire. I'm most freezin'!

RUTH: *(Pointing to the door in the rear)* Don't talk so loud. Let him sleep if he can. *(She gets wearily from the chair and puts a few pieces of wood in the stove. Then she tiptoes to the bedroom door and listens.)*

MRS ATKINS: *(In a sharp whisper)* Is he sleepin'?

RUTH: *(Coming back)* I couldn't hear him move. I s'pose he is. *(She puts another stick in the stove.)* This is the last of the wood in the pile. I don't know who'll cut more now that Jake's left. *(She sighs and walks to the window in the rear, left, pulls the curtains aside, and looks out.)* It's getting grey out. It'll be light soon and we can put out that lamp. *(She comes back to the stove.)* Looks like it'd be a nice day. *(She stretches out her hands to warm them.)* Must've been a heavy frost last night. We're paying for the spell of warm weather we've been having.

(The throbbing whine of a motor sounds from the distance outside.)

MRS ATKINS: *(Sharply)* S-h-h! Listen! Ain't that an auto I hear?

RUTH: *(Without interest)* Yes. It's Andy, I s'pose.

MRS ATKINS: *(With nervous irritation)* Don't sit there like a silly goose. Look at the state of this room! What'll this strange doctor think of us? Look at that lamp chimney all smoke! Gracious sakes, Ruth—

RUTH: *(Indifferently)* I've got a lamp all cleaned up in the kitchen.

MRS ATKINS: *(Peremptorily)* Wheel me in there this minute. I don't want him to see me looking a sight. I'll lay down in the room the other side. You don't need me now and I'm dead for sleep. I'll have plenty of time to see Andy.

(RUTH *wheels her mother off right. The noise of the motor grows louder and finally ceases as the car stops on the road before the farmhouse.* RUTH *returns from the kitchen with a lighted lamp in her hand which she sets on the table beside the other. The sound of footsteps on the path is heard—then a sharp rap on the door.* RUTH *goes and opens it.* ANDREW *enters, followed by* DOCTOR FAWCETT *carrying a small black bag.* ANDREW *has changed greatly. His face seems to have grown high-strung, hardened by the look of decisiveness which comes from being constantly under a strain where judgments on the spur of the moment are compelled to be accurate. His eyes are keener and more alert. There is even a suggestion of ruthless cunning about them. At present, however, his expression is one of tense anxiety.* DOCTOR FAWCETT *is a short, dark, middle-aged man with a Vandyke beard. He wears glasses.*)

RUTH: Hello, Andy! I've been waiting—

ANDREW: *(Kissing her hastily)* I know. I got here as soon as I could. (*He throws off his cap and heavy overcoat on the table, introducing* RUTH *and the* DOCTOR *as he does so. He is dressed in an expensive business suit and appears stouter.*) My sister-in-law, Mrs. Mayo—Doctor Fawcett.

(*They bow to each other silently.* ANDREW *casts a quick glance about the room.*)

ANDREW: Where's Rob?

RUTH: *(Pointing)* In there.

ANDREW: I'll take your coat and hat, Doctor. (*As he helps the* DOCTOR *with his things*) Is he very bad, Ruth?

RUTH: *(Dully)* He's been getting weaker.

ANDREW: Damn! This way, Doctor. Bring the lamp, Ruth.

(*He goes into the bedroom, followed by the* DOCTOR *and* RUTH *carrying the clean lamp.* RUTH *reappears almost immediately closing the door behind her, and goes slowly to the outside door, which she opens, and stands in the doorway looking out. The sound of* ANDREW's *and* ROBERT's *voices comes from the bedroom. A moment later* ANDREW *re-enters, closing the door softly. He comes forward and sinks down on the rocker on the right of table, leaning his head on his hand. His face is drawn in a shocked expression of great grief. He sighs heavily, staring mournfully in front of him.* RUTH *turns and stands watching him. Then she shuts the door and returns to her chair by the stove, turning it so she can face him.*)

ANDREW: *(Glancing up quickly—in a harsh voice)* How long has this been going on?

RUTH: You mean—how long has he been sick?

ANDREW: *(Shortly)* Of course! What else?

RUTH: It was last summer he had a bad spell first, but he's been ailin' ever since Mary died—eight months ago.

ANDREW: *(Harshly)* Why didn't you let me know—cable me? Do you want him to die, all of you? I'm damned if it doesn't look that way! *(His voice breaking)* Poor old chap! To be sick in this out-of-the-way hole without anyone to attend to him but a country quack! It's a damned shame!

RUTH: *(Dully)* I wanted to send you word once, but he only got mad when I told him. He was too proud to ask anything, he said.

ANDREW: Proud? To ask me? *(He jumps to his feet and paces nervously back and forth.)* I can't understand the way you've acted. Didn't you see how sick he was getting? Couldn't you realize—why, I nearly dropped in my tracks when I saw him! He looks—*(He shudders.)*—terrible! *(With fierce scorn)* I suppose you're so used to the idea of his being delicate that you took his sickness as a matter of course. God, if I'd only known!

RUTH: *(Without emotion)* A letter takes so long to get where you were—and we couldn't afford to telegraph. We owed everyone already, and I couldn't ask Ma. She'd been giving me money out of her savings for the last two years till she hadn't much left. Don't say anything to Rob about it. I never told him. He'd only be mad at me if he knew. But I had to, because—God knows how we'd have got on if I hadn't.

ANDREW: You mean to say— *(His eyes seem to take in the poverty-stricken appearance of the room for the first time.)* You sent that telegram to me collect. Was it because—

(RUTH nods silently. ANDREW pounds on the table with his fist.)

Good God! And all this time I've been—why I've had everything! *(He sits down in his chair and pulls it close to RUTH's—impulsively.)* But—I can't get it through my head. Why? Why? What has happened? How did it ever come about? Tell me!

RUTH: *(Dully)* There's nothing much to tell. Things kept getting worse, that's all—and Rob didn't seem to care.

ANDREW: But hasn't he been working the farm?

RUTH: He never took any interest since way back when your Ma died. After that he got men to take charge, and they nearly all cheated him—he couldn't tell—and left one after another. And then there'd be times when there was no one to see to it, when he'd be looking to hire someone new. And the hands wouldn't stay. It was hard to get them. They didn't want to work here, and as soon as they'd get a chance to work some other place they'd leave. Then after Mary died he didn't pay no heed to anything any more—

just stayed indoors and took to reading books again. So I had to ask Ma if she wouldn't help us some.

ANDREW: *(Surprised and horrified)* Why, damn it, this is frightful! Rob must be mad not to have let me know. Too proud to ask help of me! It's an insane idea! It's crazy! And for Rob, of all people, to feel that way! What's the matter with him in God's name? He didn't appear to have changed when I was talking to him a second ago. He seemed same old Rob—only very sick physically. *(A sudden, horrible suspicion, entering his mind)* Ruth! Tell me the truth. His mind hasn't gone back on him, has it?

RUTH: *(Dully)* I don't know. Mary's dying broke him up terrible—but he's used to her being gone by this, I s'pose.

ANDREW: *(Looking at her queerly)* Do you mean to say *you're* used to it?

RUTH: *(In a dead tone)* There's a time comes—when you don't mind any more—anything.

ANDREW: *(Looks at her fixedly for a moment—with great pity)* I'm sorry I talked the way I did just now, Ruth—if I seemed to blame you. I didn't realize— The sight of Rob lying in bed there, so gone to pieces—it made me furious at everyone. Forgive me, Ruth.

RUTH: There's nothing to forgive. It doesn't matter.

ANDREW: *(Springing to his feet again and pacing up and down)* Thank God I came back before it was too late. This doctor will know exactly what to do to bring him back to health. That's the first thing to think of. When Rob's on his feet again we can get the farm working on a sound basis once more. I'll see to it so that you'll never have any more trouble—before I leave.

RUTH: You're going away again?

ANDREW: Yes. Back to Argentine. I've got to.

RUTH: You wrote Rob you was coming back to stay this time.

ANDREW: I expected to—until I got to New York. Then I learned certain facts that make it necessary. *(With a short laugh)* To be candid, Ruth, I'm not the rich man you've probably been led to believe by my letters—not now. I was when I wrote them. I made money hand over fist as long as I stuck to legitimate trading; but I wasn't content with that. I wanted it to come easier, so like all the rest of the idiots, I tried speculation. It was funny, too. I'd always been dead set against that form of gambling before. I guess there's still enough of the farmer in me to make me feel squeamish about Wheat Pits. But I got into it just the same, and it seemed as if I never had a chance to get out. Oh, I won all right! Several times I've been almost a millionaire— on paper—and then come down to earth again with a bump. Finally the strain was too much. I got disgusted with myself and made up my mind to get out and come home and forget it and really live again. I got out—

with just a quarter of a million dollars more than I'd had when I landed there five years before. *(He gives a harsh laugh.)* And now comes the funny part. The day before the steamer sailed I saw what I thought was a chance to become a millionaire again. *(He snaps his fingers.)* That easy! I plunged. Then, before things broke, I left—I was so confident I couldn't be wrong— and I left explicit orders to friends. *(Bitterly)* Friends! Well, maybe it wasn't their fault. A fool deserves what he gets. Anyway, when I landed in New York—I wired you I had business to wind up, didn't I? Well, it was the business that wound me up! *(He smiles grimly, pacing up and down, his hands in his pockets.)*

RUTH: *(Dully)* You found—you'd lost everything?

ANDREW: *(Sitting down again)* Practically. *(He takes a cigar from his pocket, bites the end off, and lights it.)* Oh, I don't mean I'm dead broke. I've saved ten thousand from the wreckage, maybe twenty. But that's a poor showing for five years' hard work. That's why I'll have to go back. *(Confidently)* I can make it up in a year or so down there—and I don't need but a shoestring to start with. *(A weary expression comes over his face and he sighs heavily.)* I wish I didn't have to. I'm sick of it all. And I'd made so many plans about converting this place into a real home for all of us, and a working proposition that'd pay big at the same time. *(With another sigh)* It'll have to wait.

RUTH: It's too bad—things seem to go wrong so.

ANDREW: *(Shaking of his depression—briskly)* They might be much worse. There's enough left to fix the farm O K before I go. I won't leave 'til Rob's on his feet again. In the meantime I'll make things fly around here. *(With satisfaction)* I need a rest, and the kind of rest I need is hard work in the open—just like I used to do in the old days. I'll organize things on a working basis and get a real man to carry out my plans while I'm away— what I intended to do the last time. *(Stopping abruptly and lowering his voice cautiously)* Not a word to Rob about my losing money! Remember that, Ruth! You can see why. If he's grown so touchy he'd never accept a cent if he thought I was hard up; see?

RUTH: Yes, Andy.

(After a pause, during which ANDREW *puffs at his cigar abstractedly, his mind evidently busy with plans for the future, the bedroom door is opened and* DOCTOR FAWCETT *enters, carrying a bag. He closes the door quietly behind him and comes forward, a grave expression on his face.* ANDREW *springs out of his chair.)*

ANDREW: Ah, Doctor! *(He pushes a chair between his own and* RUTH's.) Won't you have a chair?

FAWCETT: *(Glancing at his watch)* I must catch the nine o'clock back to the city. It's imperative. I have only a moment. *(Sitting down and clearing his throat—in a perfunctory, impersonal voice.)* The case of your brother, Mr.

Mayo, is— *(He stops and glances at* RUTH *and says meaningly to* ANDREW.*)* Perhaps it would be better if you and I—

RUTH: *(With dogged resentment)* I know what you mean, Doctor; but I'm not going. I'm his wife, and I've got a right to hear what you're going to say. *(Dully)* Don't be afraid I can't stand it. I'm used to bearing trouble by this; and I can guess what you've found out. Don't you s'pose I could see it staring out of his eyes at me these last days? *(She hesitates for a moment—then continues in a monotonous voice.)* Rob's going to die.

ANDREW: *(Angrily)* Ruth!

FAWCETT: *(Raising his hand as if to command silence)* In view of what you have said, Misses Mayo, I see no reason to withhold the facts from you. *(He turns to* ANDREW.*)* I am afraid my diagnosis of your brother's condition forces me to the same conclusion as Misses Mayo's.

ANDREW: *(Groaning)* But Doctor, surely—

FAWCETT: *(Calmly)* I am concerned only with facts, my dear sir, and this is one of them. Your brother has not long to live—perhaps a few days, perhaps only a few hours. I would not dare to venture a prediction on that score. It is a marvel that he is alive at this moment. My examination revealed that both of his lungs are terribly affected. A hemorrhage, resulting from any exertion or merely through the unaided progress of the disease itself, will undoubtedly prove fatal.

ANDREW: *(Brokenly)* Good God!

*(*RUTH *keeps her eyes fixed on her lap in a trance-like stare.)*

FAWCETT: I am sorry I have to tell you this, sorry my trip should prove to be of such little avail. If there was anything that could be done—

ANDREW: There isn't anything?

FAWCETT: *(Shaking his head)* I am afraid not. It is too late. Six months ago there might have—

ANDREW: *(In anguish)* But if we were to take him to the mountains—or to Arizona—or—

FAWCETT: That might have prolonged his life six months ago.

*(*ANDREW *groans.)*

FAWCETT: But now— *(He shrugs his shoulders significantly.)* I would only be raising a hope in you foredoomed to disappointment if I encouraged any belief that a change of air could accomplish the impossible. He could not make a journey. The excitement, the effort required, would inevitably bring on the end.

ANDREW: *(Appalled by a sudden thought)* Good heavens, you haven't told him this, have you, Doctor?

FAWCETT: No. I lied to him. I said a change of climate to the mountains, the desert would bring about a cure. *(Perplexedly)* He laughed at that. He seemed to find it amusing for some reason or other. I am sure he knew I was lying. A clear foresight seems to come to people as near death as he is. *(He sighs.)* One feels foolish lying to them; and yet one feels one ought to do it, I don't know why. *(He looks at his watch again nervously.)* I must take my leave of you. It is really imperative that I take no risk of missing— *(He gets up.)*

ANDREW: *(Getting to his feet—insistently)* But there must still be a chance for him, isn't there, Doctor?

FAWCETT: *(As if he were reassuring a child)* There is always that last chance—the miracle. We doctors see it happen too often to disbelieve in it. *(He puts on his hat and coat—bowing to* RUTH.*)* Goodby, Misses Mayo.

RUTH: *(Without raising her eyes—dully)* Goodby.

ANDREW: *(Mechanically)* I'll walk to the car with you, Doctor.

(They go out the door. RUTH *sits motionlessly. The motor is heard starting and the noise gradually recedes into the distance.* ANDREW *re-enters and sits down in his chair, holding his head in his hands.)*

ANDREW: Ruth!

(She lifts her eyes to his.)

ANDREW: Hadn't we better go in and see him? God! I'm afraid to! I know he'll read it in my face.

(The bedroom door is noiselessly opened and ROBERT *appears in the doorway. His cheeks are flushed with fever, and his eyes appear unusually large and brilliant.* ANDREW *continues with a groan.)*

ANDREW: It can't be, Ruth. It can't be as hopeless as he said. There's always a fighting chance. We'll take Rob to Arizona. He's got to get well. There must be a chance!

ROBERT: *(In a gentle tone)* Why must there, Andy?

*(*RUTH *turns and stares at him with terrified eyes.)*

ANDREW: *(Whirling around)* Rob! *(Scoldingly)* What are you doing out of bed? *(He gets up and goes to him.)* Get right back now and obey the Doc, or you're going to get a licking from me!

ROBERT: *(Ignoring these remarks)* Help me over to the chair, please, Andy.

ANDREW: Like hell I will! You're going right back to bed, that's where you're going, and stay there! *(He takes hold of* ROBERT's *arm.)*

ROBERT: *(Mockingly)* Stay there 'til I die, eh, Andy? *(Coldly)* Don't behave like a child. I'm sick of lying down. I'll be more rested sitting up.

(As ANDREW *hesitates—violently)* I swear I'll get out of bed every time you put me there. You'll have to sit on my chest, and that wouldn't help my health any. Come on, Andy. Don't play the fool. I want to talk to you, and I'm going to. *(With a grim smile)*

ROBERT: A dying man has some rights, hasn't he?

ANDREW: *(With a shudder)* Don't talk that way, for God's sake! Remember.

(He helps ROBERT *to the chair between his own and* RUTH*'s.)*

ANDREW: Easy now! There you are! Wait, and I'll get a pillow for you.

(He goes into the bedroom. ROBERT *looks at* RUTH *who shrinks away from him in terror.* ROBERT *smiles bitterly.* ANDREW *comes back with the pillow which he places behind* ROBERT*'s back.)*

ANDREW: How's that?

ROBERT: *(With an affectionate smile)* Fine! Thank you!

(As ANDREW *sits down)*

ROBERT: Listen, Andy. You've asked me not to talk—and I won't after I've made my position clear. *(Slowly)* In the first place I know I'm dying.

(RUTH *bows her head and covers her face with her hands. She remains like this all during the scene between the two brothers.)*

ANDREW: Rob! That isn't so!

ROBERT: *(Wearily)* It is so! Don't lie to me. It's useless and it irritates me. After Ruth put me to bed before you came, I saw it clearly for the first time. *(Bitterly)* I'd been making plans for our future—Ruth's and mine—so it came hard at first—the realization. Then when the doctor examined me, I knew—although he tried to lie about it. And then to make sure I listened at the door to what he told you. So, for my sake, don't mock me with fairy tales about Arizona, or any such rot as that. Because I'm dying is no reason you should treat me as an imbecile or a coward. Now that I'm sure what's happening I can say Kismet to it with all my heart. It was only the silly uncertainty that hurt.

(There is a pause. ANDREW *looks around in impotent anguish, not knowing what to say.* ROBERT *regards him with an affectionate smile.)*

ANDREW: *(Finally blurts out)* It isn't foolish. You have got a chance. If you heard all the Doctor said that ought to prove it to you.

ROBERT: Oh, you mean when he spoke of the possibility of a miracle? *(Dryly)* The Doctor and I disagree on that point. I don't believe in miracles—in my case. Beside I know more than any doctor in earth could know—because I feel what's coming. *(Dismissing the subject)* But we've agreed not to talk of it. Tell me about yourself, Andy, and what you've done all these years. That's what I'm interested in. Your letters were too brief and far apart to be illuminating.

ANDREW: I meant to write oftener.

ROBERT: *(With a faint trace of irony)* I judge from them you've accomplished all you set out to do five years ago?

ANDREW: That isn't much to boast of.

ROBERT: *(Surprised)* Have you really, honestly reached that conclusion?

ANDREW: Well, it doesn't seem to amount to much now.

ROBERT: But you're rich, aren't you?

ANDREW: *(With a quick glance at* RUTH*)* Yes I s'pose so.

ROBERT: I'm glad. You can do to the farm all I've undone. *(With a smile)* Do you know I was too proud to ask you for money when things went bad here? You'll have to forgive me for that, Andy.

ANDREW: I knew it wasn't like you to feel that way.

ROBERT: But what did you do down there? Tell me. You went in the grain business with that friend of yours?

ANDREW: Yes. After two years I had a share in it. I sold out last year. *(He is answering* ROB's *questions with great reluctance.)*

ROBERT: And then?

ANDREW: I went in on my own.

ROBERT: Your own business?

ANDREW: I s'pose you'd call it that.

ROBERT: Still in grain?

ANDREW: Yes.

ROBERT: What's the matter? What's there to be ashamed of? You look as if I was accusing you of crimes.

ANDREW: I'm proud enough of the first four years. It's after that I'm not boasting of. You see, I couldn't make money easy enough that way, so I took to speculating.

ROBERT: In wheat?

ANDREW: Yes.

ROBERT: And you made money—gambling?

ANDREW: Yes.

ROBERT: I can't imagine you as the easy-come, easy-go kind.

ANDREW: I'm not. I'm sick of it.

ROBERT: *(Thoughtfully)* I've been wondering what the great change was in you. I can see now. It's your eyes. There's an expression about them as if you were constantly waiting to hear a cannon go off, and wincing at the bang beforehand.

ANDREW: *(Grimly)* I've felt just that way all the past year.

ROBERT: *(After a pause during which his eyes search* ANDREW's *face)* Why haven't you ever married?

ANDREW: Never wanted to. Didn't have time to think of it, I guess.

ROBERT: *(After a pause)* You—a farmer—to gamble in a wheat pit with scraps of paper. There's a spiritual significance in that picture, Andy. *(He smiles bitterly.)* I'm a failure, and Ruth's another—but we can both justly lay some of the blame for our stumbling on God. But you're the deepest-dyed failure of the three, Andy. You've spent eight years running away from yourself. Do you see what I mean? You used to be a creator when you loved the farm. You and life were in harmonious partnership. And now— *(He stops as if seeking vainly for words.)* My brain is muddled. But part of what I mean is that your gambling with the thing you used to love to create proves how far astray you've gotten from the truth. So you'll be punished. You'll have to suffer to win back— *(His voice grows weaker and he sighs wearily.)* It's no use. I can't say it. *(He lies back and closes his eyes, breathing pantingly.)*

ANDREW: *(Slowly)* I think I know what you're driving at, Rob—and it's true, I guess.

(ROBERT *smiles gratefully and stretches out his hand, which* ANDREW *takes in his.*)

ROBERT: I want you to promise me to do one thing, Andy, after—

ANDREW: I'll promise anything, as God is my Judge!

ROBERT: Remember, Andy, Ruth has suffered double her share, and you haven't suffered at all. *(His voice faltering with weakness.)* Only through contact with suffering, Andy, will you—awaken. Listen. You must marry Ruth—afterwards.

RUTH: *(With a cry)* Rob!

(ROBERT *lies back, his eyes closed, gasping heavily for breath.*)

ANDREW: *(Making signs to her to humor him—gently.)* You're tired out, Rob. You shouldn't have talked so much. You better lie down and rest a while, don't you think? We can talk later on.

ROBERT: *(With a mocking smile)* Later on! You always were an optimist, Andy! *(He sighs with exhaustion.)* Yes, I'll go and rest a while.

(As ANDREW *comes to help him*)

ROBERT: It must be near sunrise, isn't it? It's getting grey out.

ANDREW: Yes—pretty near. It's after six.

ROBERT: *(As* ANDREW *helps him to the bedroom)* Pull the bed around so it'll face the window, will you, Andy? I can't sleep, but I'll rest and forget if I can watch the rim of the hills and dream of what is waiting beyond.

(They go into the bedroom.)

ROBERT: And shut the door, Andy. I want to be alone.

(ANDREW *reappears and shuts the door softly. He comes and sits down on his chair again, supporting his head on his hands. His face is drawn with the intensity of his dry-eyed anguish.)*

RUTH: *(Glancing at him—fearfully)* He's out of his mind now, isn't he?

ANDREW: He may be a little delirious. The fever would do that. *(With impotent rage)* God, what a shame! And there's nothing we can do but sit and—wait! *(He springs from his chair and walks to the stove.)*

RUTH: *(Dully)* He was talking—wild—like he used to—only this time it sounded—unnatural, don't you think?

ANDREW: I don't know. The things he said to me had truth in them—even if he did talk them way up in the air, like he always sees things. Still— *(He glances down at* RUTH *keenly.)* Why do you suppose he wanted us to promise we'd— *(Confusedly)* You know what he said.

RUTH: *(Dully)* His mind was wandering, I s'pose.

ANDREW: *(With conviction)* No—there was something back of it.

RUTH: He wanted to make sure I'd be all right—after he'd gone, I expect.

ANDREW: No, it wasn't that. He knows very well I'd naturally look after you without—anything like that.

RUTH: He might be thinking of—something happened five years back, the time you came home from the trip.

ANDREW: What happened? What do you mean?

RUTH: *(Dully)* It was the day you came. We had a fight.

ANDREW: A fight? What has that to do with me?

RUTH: It was about you—in a way.

ANDREW: *(Amazed)* About *me*?

RUTH: Yes, mostly. You see I'd found out I'd made a mistake about Rob soon after we were married—when it was too late.

ANDREW: Mistake? *(Slowly)* You mean—you found out you didn't love Rob?

RUTH: Yes.

ANDREW: Good God!

RUTH: And then I thought that when Mary came it'd be different, and I'd love him; but it didn't happen that way. And I couldn't bear with his blundering and book-reading—and I grew to hate him, almost.

ANDREW: Ruth!

RUTH: I couldn't help it. No woman could. It had to be because I loved someone else, I'd found out. *(She sighs wearily.)* It can't do no harm to tell you now—when it's all past and gone—and dead. You were the one I really loved—only I didn't come to the knowledge of it 'til too late.

ANDREW: *(Stunned)* Ruth! Do you know what you're saying?

RUTH: It was true—then. *(With sudden fierceness)* How could I help it? No woman could.

ANDREW: Then—you loved me—that time I came home?

RUTH: Yes.

ANDREW: But—couldn't you see—I didn't love you—that way?

RUTH: *(Doggedly)* Yes—I saw then; but I'd known your real reason for leaving home the first time—everybody knew it—and for three years I'd been thinking—

ANDREW: That I loved you?

RUTH: Yes. Then that day on the hill you laughed about what a fool you'd been for loving me once—and I knew it was all over.

ANDREW: Good God, but I never thought— *(He stops, shuddering at his remembrance.)* And did Rob—

RUTH: That was what I'd started to tell. We'd had a fight just before you came and I got crazy mad—and I told him all I've told you.

ANDREW: *(Gaping at her speechlessly for a moment)* You told Rob—you loved me?

RUTH: Yes.

ANDREW: *(Shrinking away from her in horror)* You—you—you mad fool, you! How could you do such a thing?

RUTH: I couldn't help it. I'd got to the end of bearing things—without talking.

ANDREW: And the thought of the child—his child and yours—couldn't keep your mouth shut?

RUTH: I was crazy mad at him—when I told.

ANDREW: Then Rob must have known every moment I stayed here! And yet he never said or showed—God, how he must have suffered! Didn't you know how much he loved you?

RUTH: *(Dully)* Yes. I knew he liked me.

ANDREW: Liked you! How can you talk in that cold tone—now—when he's dying! What kind of a woman are you? I'd never believe it was in you to be so— Couldn't you have kept silent—no matter what you felt or thought? Did you have to torture him? No wonder he's dying. I don't see how he's lived through it as long as he has. I couldn't. No. I'd have killed myself—or killed you.

RUTH: *(Dully)* I wish he had—killed me.

ANDREW: And you've lived together for five years with this horrible secret between you?

RUTH: We've lived in the same house—not as man and wife.

ANDREW: But what does he feel about it now? Tell me! Does he still think—

RUTH: I don't know. We've never spoke a word about it since that day. Maybe, from the way he went on, he s'poses I care for you yet. Maybe that's one reason he said what he did.

ANDREW: But you don't. You can't. It's outrageous. It's stupid! You don't love me!

RUTH: *(Slowly)* I wouldn't know how to feel love, even if I tried, any more.

ANDREW: *(Brutally)* And I don't love you, that's sure! *(He sinks into his chair, his head between his hands.)* It's damnable such a thing should be between Rob and me—we that have been pals ever since we were born, almost. Why, I love Rob better'n anybody in the world and always did. There isn't a thing on God's green earth I wouldn't have done to keep trouble away from him. And now I have to be the very one—it's damnable! How am I going to face him again? What can I say to him now? *(He groans with anguished rage. After a pause)* He asked me to promise—what am I going to do?

RUTH: You can promise—so's it'll ease his mind—and not mean anything.

ANDREW: What? Lie to him now—when he's dying? Can you believe I'd descend as low as that? And there's no sense in my lying. He knows I don't love you. *(Determinedly)* No! It's you who'll have to do the lying, since it must be done. You're the cause of all this. You've got to! You've got a chance now to undo some of all the suffering you've brought on Rob. Go in to him! Tell him you never loved me—it was all a mistake. Tell him you only said so because you were mad and didn't know what you were saying, and you've been ashamed to own up to the truth before this. Tell him something, anything, that'll bring him peace and make him believe you've loved him all the time.

RUTH: *(Dully)* It's no good. He wouldn't believe me.

ANDREW: *(Furiously)* You've got to make him believe you, do you hear? You've got to—now—hurry—you never know when it may be too late.

(As she hesitates—imploringly)

ANDREW: For God's sake, Ruth! Don't you see you owe it to him? You'll never forgive yourself if you don't.

RUTH: *(Dully)* I'll go. *(She gets wearily to her feet and walks slowly toward the bedroom.)* But it won't do any good.

(ANDREW's eyes are fixed on her anxiously. She opens the door and steps inside the room. She remains standing there for a minute. Then she calls in a frightened voice.)

RUTH: Rob! Where are you? *(Then she hurries back, trembling with fright.)* Andy! Andy! He's gone!

ANDREW: *(Misunderstanding her—his face pale with dread)* He's not—

RUTH: *(Interrupting him—hysterically)* He's gone! He isn't in there. The bed's empty. The window's wide open. He must have crawled out into the yard!

ANDREW: *(Springing to his feet. He rushes into the bedroom and returns immediately with an expression of alarmed amazement on his face.)* Come! He can't have gone far! We've got to find him! *(Grabbing his hat he takes RUTH's arm and shoves her toward the door.)* Come on! *(Opening the door)* Let's hope to God— *(The door closes behind them, cutting off his words as the curtain falls.)*

Scene Two

(Same as ACT ONE, Scene One—A section of country highway. The sky to the east is already alight with bright color and a thin, quivering line of flame is spreading slowly along the horizon rim of the dark hills. The roadside, however, is still steeped in the greyness of the dawn, shadowy and vague. The field in the foreground has a wild uncultivated appearance as if it had been allowed to remain fallow the preceding summer. Parts of the snake-fence in the rear have been broken down. The apple tree is leafless and seems dead.)

(ROBERT staggers weakly in from the left. He stumbles into the ditch and lies there for a moment; then crawls with a great effort to the top of the bank where he can see the sun rise, and collapses weakly. RUTH and ANDREW come hurriedly along the road from the left.)

ANDREW: *(Stopping and looking about him)* There he is! I knew it! I knew we'd find him here.

ROBERT: *(Trying to raise himself to a sitting position as they hasten to his side—with a wan smile)* I thought I'd given you the slip.

ANDREW: *(With kindly bullying)* Well you didn't, you old scoundrel, and we're going to take you right back where you belong—in bed. *(He makes a motion to lift* ROBERT.*)* What d'you mean by running away like this, eh?

ROBERT: Don't, Andy. Don't, I tell you! I can't bear it!

ANDREW: You're in pain?

ROBERT: *(Simply)* No. I'm dying.

(He falls back weakly. RUTH *sinks down beside him with a sob and pillows his head on her lap.)*

ROBERT: Don't try to move me, Andy. It would mean—. I had a bad hemorrhage—trying to get here. I knew then— it was only—a few minutes more.

*(*ANDREW *stands looking down at him helplessly.* ROBERT *moves his head restlessly on* RUTH's *lap.)*

ROBERT: There! Just so I can see—the sun. I couldn't stand it back there in the room. It seemed as if all my life—I'd been cooped in a room. So I thought I'd try to end as I might have—if I'd had the courage to live my dream. Alone—in a ditch by the open road—watching the sun rise.

ANDREW: Rob! Don't talk. You're wasting your strength. Rest a while and then we'll carry you—

ROBERT: Still hoping, Andy? Don't. I know. *(There is a pause during which he breathes heavily, straining his eyes toward the horizon.)* The sun comes so slowly. I haven't long—to wait. *(With an ironical smile)* The doctor told me to go to the far-off places—and I'd be cured. He was right. That was always the cure for me. It's too late—for this world—but in the next I'll not miss—the secret. *(He has a fit of coughing which racks his body.)*

ANDREW: *(With a hoarse sob)* Rob! *(He clenches his fists in an impotent rage against fate.)* God! God!

*(*RUTH *sobs brokenly and wipes* ROBERT's *lips with her handkerchief.)*

ROBERT: *(In a voice which is suddenly ringing with the happiness of hope)* You mustn't feel sorry for me. It's ridiculous! Don't you see I'm happy at last—because I'm making a start to the far-off places—free—free!—freed from the farm—free to wander on and on—eternally! Even the hills are powerless to shut me in now. *(He raises himself on his elbow, his face radiant, and points to the horizon.)* Look! Isn't it beautiful beyond the hills? I can hear the old voices calling me to come— *(Exultantly)* And this time I'm going— I'm free! It isn't the end. It's a free beginning—the start of my voyage! Don't you see? I've won to my trip—the right of release—beyond the horizon! Oh, you ought to be glad—glad—for my sake! *(He collapses weakly.)* Andy!

(ANDREW *bends down to him.*)

ROBERT: Remember Ruth—

ANDREW: I'll take care of her, I swear to you, Rob!

ROBERT: Ruth has suffered—and for your own sake and hers—remember, Andy—only through sacrifice—the secret beyond there— (*He suddenly raises himself with his last remaining strength and points to the horizon where the edge of the sun's disc is rising from the rim of the hills.*) The sun! (*He remains with his eyes fixed on it for a moment. A rattling noise throbs from his throat. He mumbles:*) Remember!

(*And falls back and is still.* RUTH *gives a cry of horror and springs to her feet, shuddering, her hands over her eyes.* ANDREW *bends on one knee beside the body, placing a hand over* ROBERT's *heart, then he kisses his brother reverentially on the forehead and stands up.*)

ANDREW: (*Facing* RUTH, *the body between them—in a dead voice*) He's dead. (*With a sudden burst of fury*) God damn you, you never told him!

RUTH: (*Piteously*) He was so happy without my lying to him.

ANDREW: (*Pointing to the body—trembling with the violence of his rage*) This is your doing, you damn woman, you coward, you murderess! He's dead because you've killed him, do you hear?

RUTH: (*Sobbing*) Don't, Andy! Stop! I couldn't help it—and he knew how I'd suffered, too. He told you—to remember.

ANDREW: (*Stares at her for a moment, his rage ebbing away, an expression of deep pity gradually coming over his face. Then he glances down at his brother and speaks brokenly in a compassionate voice.*) Forgive me, Ruth—for his sake. I know he was right—and I'll remember what he said.

(RUTH *lets her hands fall from her face and looks at him uncomprehendingly. He lifts his eyes to hers and forces out falteringly:*)

ANDREW: I—you—we've both made such a mess of things! We must try to help each other—and—in time—we'll come to know what's right to do— (*Desperately*) And perhaps we—

(*But* RUTH, *if she is aware of his words, gives no sign. She remains silent, gazing at him dully with the sad humility of exhaustion, her mind already sinking back into that spent calm beyond the further troubling of any hope.*)

(*The curtain falls.*)

END OF PLAY

THE EMPEROR JONES

ORIGINAL PRODUCTION

THE EMPEROR JONES was first produced by The Provincetown Players at The Playwrights' Theatre, 133 MacDougal St. THE EMPEROR JONES was the second of a double bill that started out with MATINATA by Lawrence Langer, opening on 1 November 1920. The cast and creative contributors were:

BRUTUS JONES	Charles S Gilpin
HENRY SMITHERS	Jasper Deeter
AN OLD NATIVE WOMAN	Christine Ell
LEM	Charles Ellis
SOLDIERS	S I Thompson, Lawrence Vail, Leo Richman, James Martin & Owen White

THE LITTLE FORMLESS FEARS

JEFF	S I Thompson
THE NEGRO CONVICTS	Leo Richman, Lawrence Vail, S I Thompson & Owen White
THE PRISON GUARD	James Martin
THE PLANTERS	Frank Schwartz, C I Martin & W D Slager
THE SPECTATORS	Jeannie Begg, Charlotte Grauert
THE AUCTIONEER	Frederick Ward Roege
THE SLAVES	James Martin, S I Thompson, Leo Richman, Owen White & Lawrence Vail
THE CONGO WITCH DOCTOR	S I Thompson

Director	George Cram Cook
Sets	Cleon Throckmorton

THE EMPEROR JONES moved to the Selwyn Theatre on Broadway on 27 December 1920, playing special matinees. The production then moved to the Princess Theatre, opening on 29 January 1921 and played 204 performances.

THE EMPEROR JONES was revived by The Provincetown Players at The Playwrights' Theatre opening on 5 May 1924. The cast and creative contributors were:

AN OLD NATIVE WOMAN	Kirah Markham
HENRY SMITHERS	Charles Ellis
BRUTUS JONES	Paul Robeson
THE LITTLE FORMLESS FEARS	
JEFF	Clement O'Loghlen
THE NEGRO CONVICTS	John Brewster, James Meighan, William Stahl, John Taylor & Clement Wilenchick
THE SPECTATORS	Jeannie Begg & Kirah Markham
THE AUCTIONEER	Clement O'Loghlen
THE SLAVES	John Brewster, Mr Forsyth, James Meighan, William Stahl & Clement Wilenchick
THE CONGO WITCH-DOCTOR	John Taylor
LEM	William Stahl
SOLDIERS	John Brewster, Mr Forsyth, Mr Martin, James Meighan, William Stahl & Clement Wilenchick
Director	James Light
Sets	Cleon Throckmorton

CHARACTERS & SETTING

Brutus Jones, *Emperor*
Henry Smithers, *a Cockney Trader*
An Old Native Woman
Lem, *a Native Chief*
Soldiers, *adherents of* Lem

The Little Formless Fears
Jeff
The Negro Convicts
The Prison Guard
The Planters
The Auctioneer
The Slaves
The Congo Witch-Doctor
The Crocodile God

The action of the play takes place on an island in the West Indies as yet not self-determined by White Marines. The form of native government is, for the time being, an Empire.

Scene One

(*The audience chamber in the palace of the Emperor—a spacious, high-ceilinged room with bare, whitewashed walls. The floor is of white tiles. In the rear, to the left of center, a wide archway giving out on a portico with white pillars. The palace is evidently situated on high ground for beyond the portico nothing can be seen but a vista of distant hills, their summits crowned with thick groves of palm trees. In the right wall, center, a smaller arched doorway leading to the living quarters of the palace. The room is bare of furniture with the exception of one huge chair made of uncut wood which stands at center, its back to rear. This is very apparently the Emperor's throne. It is painted a dazzling, eye-smiting scarlet. There is a brilliant orange cushion on the seat and another smaller one is placed on the floor to serve as a footstool. Strips of matting, dyed scarlet, lead from the foot of the throne to the two entrances. It is late afternoon but the sunlight still blazes yellowly beyond the portico and there is an oppressive burden of exhausting heat in the air.*)

(*As the curtain rises, a native negro* WOMAN *sneaks in cautiously from the entrance on the right. She is very old, dressed in cheap calico, bare-footed, a red bandana handkerchief covering all but a few stray wisps of white hair. A bundle bound in colored cloth is carried over her shoulder on a stick. She hesitates beside the doorway, peering back as if in extreme dread of being discovered. Then she begins to glide noiselessly, a step at a time, toward the doorway in the rear. At this moment,* SMITHERS *appears beneath the portico.* SMITHERS *is a tall, stoop-shouldered man about forty. His bald head, perched on a long neck with an enormous Adam's apple, looks like an egg. The tropics have tanned his naturally pasty face with its small, sharp features to a sickly yellow, and native rum has painted his pointed nose to a startling red. His little, washy-blue eyes are red-rimmed and dart about him like a ferret's. His expression is one of unscrupulous meanness, cowardly and dangerous. He is dressed in a worn riding suit of dirty white drill, puttees, spurs, and wears a white cork helmet. A cartridge belt with an automatic revolver is around his waist. He carries a riding whip in his hand. He sees the* WOMAN *and stops to watch her suspiciously. Then, making up his mind, he steps quickly on tiptoe into the room. The* WOMAN, *looking back over her shoulder continually, does not see him until it is too late. When she does* SMITHERS *springs forward and grabs her firmly by the shoulder. She struggles to get away, fiercely but silently.*)

SMITHERS: (*Tightening his grasp—roughly*) Easy! None o' that, me birdie. You can't wriggle out now I got me 'ooks on yer.

WOMAN: *(Seeing the uselessness of struggling, gives way to frantic terror, and sinks to the ground, embracing his knees supplicatingly)* No tell him! No tell him, Mister!

SMITHERS: *(With great curiosity)* Tell 'im? *(Then scornfully)* Oh, you mean 'is bloomin' Majesty. What's the gaime, any 'ow? What you sneakin' away for? Been stealin' a bit, I s'pose. *(He taps her bundle with his riding whip significantly.)*

WOMAN: *(Shaking her head vehemently)* No, me no steal.

SMITHERS: Bloody liar! But tell me what's up. There's somethin' funny goin' on. I smelled it in the air first thing I got up this mornin'. You blacks are up to some devilment. This palace of 'is is like a bleedin' tomb. Where's all the 'ands?

(The WOMAN keeps sullenly silent. SMITHERS raises his whip threateningly.)

SMITHERS: Ow, yer won't, won't yer? I'll show yer what's what.

WOMAN: *(Coweringly)* I tell, Mister. You no hit. They go—all go. *(She makes a sweeping gesture toward the hills in the distance.)*

SMITHERS: Run away— to the 'ills?

WOMAN: Yes, Mister. Him Emperor—great Father. *(She touches her forehead to the floor with a quick mechanical jerk.)* Him sleep after eat. Then they go— all go. Me old woman. Me left only. Now me go too.

SMITHERS: *(His astonishment giving way to an immense, mean satisfaction)* Ow! So that's the ticket! Well, I know bloody well wot's in the air—when they runs orf to the 'ills. The tom-tom'll be thumping out there bloomin' soon. *(With extreme vindictiveness)* And I'm bloody glad of it, for one! Serve 'im right! Puttin' on airs, the stinkin' nigger! 'Is Majesty! Gawd blimey! I only 'opes I'm there when they takes 'im out to shoot 'im. *(Suddenly)* 'E's still 'ere all right, ain't 'e?

WOMAN: Yes. Him sleep.

SMITHERS: 'E's bound to find out soon as wakes up. 'E's cunnin' enough to know when 'is time's come.

(He goes to the doorway on right and whistles shrilly with his fingers in his mouth. The old WOMAN springs to her feet and runs out of the doorway, rear. SMITHERS goes after her, reaching for his revolver.)

SMITHERS: Stop or I'll shoot! *(Then stopping—indifferently)* Pop orf then, if yer like, yer black cow. *(He stands in the doorway, looking after her.)*

(JONES enters from the right. He is a tall, powerfully-built, full-blooded negro of middle age. His features are typically negroid, yet there is something decidedly distinctive about his face—an underlying strength of will, a hardy, self-reliant confidence in himself that inspires respect. His eyes are alive with a keen, cunning

intelligence. In manner he is shrewd, suspicious, evasive. He wears a light blue uniform coat, sprayed with brass buttons, heavy gold chevrons on his shoulders, gold braid on the collar, cuffs, etc. His pants are bright red with a light blue stripe down the side. Patent leather laced boots with brass spurs, and a belt with a long-barreled, pearl-handled revolver in a holster complete his makeup. Yet there is something not altogether ridiculous about his grandeur. He has a way of carrying it off.)

JONES: *(Not seeing anyone—greatly irritated and blinking sleepily—shouts)* Who dare whistle dat way in my palace? Who dare wake up de Emperor? I'll git de hide frayed off some o' you niggers sho'!

SMITHERS: *(Showing himself—in a manner half-afraid and half-defiant)* It was me whistled to yer.

(As JONES frowns angrily)

SMITHERS: I got news for yer.

JONES: *(Putting on his suavest manner, which fails to cover up his contempt for the white man)* Oh, it's you, Mister Smithers. *(He sits down on his throne with easy dignity.)* What news you got to tell me?

SMITHERS: *(Coming close to enjoy his discomfiture)* Don't yer notice nothin' funny today?

JONES: *(Coldly)* Funny? No. I ain't perceived nothin' of de kind!

SMITHERS: Then yer ain't so foxy as I thought yer was. Where's all your court? *(Sarcastically)* The Generals and the Cabinet Ministers and all?

JONES: *(Imperturbably)* where dey mostly runs to minute I closes my eyes—drinkin' rum and talkin' big down in de town. *(Sarcastically)* How come you don't know dat? Ain't you sousin' with 'em most everyday?

SMITHERS: *(Stung but pretending indifference—with a wink)* That's part of the day's work. I got ter—ain't I—in my business?

JONES: *(Contemptuously)* Yo' business!

SMITHERS: *(Imprudently enraged)* Gawd blimey, you was glad enough for me ter take yer in on it when you landed here first. You didn' 'ave no 'igh and mighty airs in them days!

JONES: *(His hand going to his revolver like a flash—menacingly)* Talk polite, white man! Talk polite, you heah me! I'm boss heah now, is you fergettin'?

(The Cockney seems about to challenge this last statement with the facts but something in the other's eyes holds and cowes him.)

SMITHERS: *(In a cowardly whine)* No 'arm meant, old top.

JONES: *(Condescendingly)* I accepts yo' apology. *(Lets his hand fall from his revolver)* No use'n you rakin' up ole times. What I was den is one thing.

What I is now 's another. You didn't let me in on yo' crooked work out o' no kind feelin's dat time. I done de dirty work fo' you—and most o' de brain work, too, fo' dat matter—and I was wu'th money to you, dat's de reason.

SMITHERS: Well, blimey, I give yer a start, didn't I—when no one else would. I wasn't afraid to 'ire yer like the rest was—'count of the story about your breakin' jail back in the States.

JONES: No, you didn't have no s'cuse to look down on me fo' dat. You been in jail you'self more'n once.

SMITHERS: *(Furiously)* It's a lie! *(Then trying to pass it off by an attempt at scorn)* Garn! Who told yer that fairy tale?

JONES: Dey's some tings I ain't got to be tole. I kin see 'em in folk's eyes. *(Then after a pause—meditatively)* Yes, you sho' give me a start. And it didn't take long from dat time to git dese fool, woods' niggers right where I wanted dem. *(With pride)* From stowaway to Emperor in two years! Dat's goin' some!

SMITHERS: *(With curiosity)* And I bet you got yer pile o' money 'id safe some place.

JONES: *(With satisfaction)* I sho' has! And it's in a foreign bank where no pusson don't ever git it out but me no matter what come. You didn't s'pose I was holdin' down dis Emperor job for de glory in it, did you? Sho'! De fuss and glory part of it, dat's only to turn de heads o' de low-flung, bush niggers dat's here. Dey wants de big circus show for deir money. I gives it to 'em an' I gits de money. *(With a grin)* De long green, dat's me every time! *(Then rebukingly)* But you ain't got no kick agin me, Smithers. I'se paid you back all you done for me many times. Ain't I pertected you and winked at all de crooked tradin' you been doin' right out in de broad day. Sho'. I has—and me makin' laws to stop it at de same time! *(He chuckles.)*

SMITHERS: *(Grinning)* But, meanin' no 'arm, you been grabbin' right and left yourself, ain't yer? Look at the taxes you've put on 'em! Blimey! You've squeezed 'em dry!

JONES: *(Chuckling)* No, dey ain't all dry yet. I'se still heah, ain't I?

SMITHERS: *(Smiling at his secret thought)* They're dry right now, you'll find out. *(Changing the subject abruptly)* And as for me breakin' laws, you've broke 'em all yerself just as fast as yer made 'em.

JONES: Ain't r de Emperor? De laws don't go for him. *(Judicially)* You heah what I tells you, Smithers. Dere's little stealin' like you does, and dere's big stealin' like I does. For de little stealin' dey gits you in jail soon or late. For de big stealin' dey makes you Emperor and puts you in de Hall o' Fame when you croaks. *(Reminiscently)* If dey's one thing I learns in ten years on de Pullman ca's listenin' to de white quality talk, it's dat same fact. And when I gits a chance to use it I winds up Emperor in two years.

SMITHERS: *(Unable to repress the genuine admiration of the small fry for the large)* Yes, yer turned the bleedin' trick, all fight. Blimey, I never seen a bloke 'as 'ad the bloomin' luck you 'as.

JONES: *(Severely)* Luck? What you mean—luck?

SMITHERS: I suppose you'll say as that swank about the silver bullet ain't luck—and that was what first got the fool blacks on yer side the time of the revolution, wasn't it?

JONES: *(With a laugh)* Oh, dat silver bullet! Sho' was luck! But I makes dat luck, you heah? I loads de dice! Yessuh! When dat murderin' nigger ole Lem hired to kill me takes aim ten feet away and his gun misses fire and I shoots him dead, what you heah me say?

SMITHERS: You said yer'd got a charm so's no lead bullet'd kill yer. You was so strong only a silver bullet could kill yer, you told 'em. Blimey, wasn't that swank for yer—and plain, fat-'eaded luck?

JONES: *(Proudly)* I got brains and I uses 'em quick. Dat ain't luck.

SMITHERS: Yer know they wasn't 'ardly likely to get no silver bullets. And it was luck 'e didn't 'it you that time.

JONES: *(Laughing)* And dere all dem fool, bush niggers was kneelin' down and bumpin' deir heads on de ground like I was a miracle out o' de Bible Oh Lawd, from dat time on I has dem all eatin' out of my hand. I cracks de whip and dey jumps through.

SMITHERS: *(With a sniff)* Yankee bluff done it.

JONES: Ain't a man's talkin' big what makes him big-long as he makes folks believe it? Sho', I talks large when I ain't got nothin' to back it up, but I ain't talkin' wild just de same. I knows I kin fool 'em—I *knows* it—and dat's backin' enough fo' my game. And ain't I got to learn deir lingo and teach some of dem English befo' I kin talk to 'em? Ain't dat wuk? You ain't never learned ary word er it, Smithers, in do ten years you been heah, dough you' knows it's money in yo' pocket tradin' wid 'em if you does. But you'se too shiftless to take de trouble.

SMITHERS: *(Flushing)* Never mind about me. What's this I've 'eard about yer really 'avin' a sil-ver bullet moulded for yourself?

JONES: It's playin' out my bluff. I has de silver bullet inoulded and I tells 'em when do time comes I kills myself wid it. I tells 'em dat's 'cause I'm de on'y man in de world big enuff to git me. No use'n deir tryin'. And dey falls down and bumps deir heads. *(He laughs.)* I does dat so's I kin take a walk in peace widout no jealous nigger gunnin' at me from behind de trees.

SMITHERS: *(Astonished)* Then you 'ad it made —'onest?

JONES: Sho' did. Heah she he. *(He takes out his revolver, breaks it, and takes the silver bullet out of one chamber.)* Five lead an' dis silver baby at de last. Don't she shine pretty? *(He holds it in his hand, looking at it admiringly, as if strangely fascinated.)*

SMITHERS: Let me see. *(Reaches out his hand for it)*

JONES: *(Harshly)* Keep yo' hands whar dey b'long, white man. *(He replaces it in the chamber and puts the revolver back on his hip.)*

SMITHERS: *(Snarling)* Gawd Nimey! Mink I'm a bleedin' thief, you would.

JONES: No, 'tain't dat. I knows you 'se scared to steal from me. On'y I ain't 'lowin' nary body to touch dis baby. She's my rabbit's foot.

SMITHERS: *(Sneering)* A bloomin' charm, wot? *(Venomously)* Well, you'll need all the bloody charms you 'as before long, s' 'elp me!

JONES: *(Judicially)* Oh, I'se good for six months yit 'fore dey gits sick o' my game. Den, when I sees trouble comin', I makes my getaway.

SMITHERS: Ho! You got it all planned, ain't yer?

JONES: I ain't no fool. I knows dis Emperor's time is sho't. Dat why I make hay when de sun shine. Was you thinkin' I'se aimin' to hold down dis job for life? No, suh! What good is gittin' money if you stays back in dis raggedy country? I wants action when I spends. And when I sees dese niggers gittin' up deir nerve to tu'n me out, and I'se got all de money in sight, I resigns on de spot and beats it quick.

SMITHERS: Where to?

JONES: None o' yo' business.

SMITHERS: Not back to the bloody States, I'll lay my oath.

JONES *(Suspiciously)* Why don't I? *(Then with an easy laugh)* You mean 'count of dat story 'bout me breakin' from jail back dere? Dat's all talk.

SMITHERS: *(Skeptically)* Ho, yes!

JONES: *(Sharply)* You ain't 'sinuatin' I'se a liar, is you?

SMITHERS: *(Hastily)* No, Gawd strike me! I was only thinkin' o' the bloody lies you told the blacks 'ere about killin' white men in the States.

JONES: *(Angered)* How come dey're lies?

SMITHERS: You'd 'ave been in jail, if you 'ad, wouldn't yer then? *(With venom)* And from what I've 'eard, it ain't 'ealthy for a black to kill a white man in the States. They burns 'em in oil, don't they?

JONES: *(With cool deadliness)* You mean lynchin' 'd scare me? Well, I tells you, Smithers, maybe I does kill one white man back dere, Maybe I does. And maybe I kills another right heah 'fore long if he don't look out.

SMITHERS: *(Trying to force a laugh)* I was on'y spoofin' yer. Can't yer take a joke? And you was just sayin' you'd never ken in jail.

JONES: *(In the same tone—slightly boastful)* Maybe I goes to jail dere for gettin' in an argument wid razors ovah a crap game. Maybe I gits twenty years when dat colored man die. Maybe I gits in 'nother argument wid de prison guard was overseer ovah us when we're wukin' de roads. Maybe he hits me wid a whip and I splits his head wid a shovel and runs away and files de chain off my leg and gits away safe. Maybe I does all dat an' maybe I don't. It's a story I tells you so's you knows I'se de kind of man dat if you evah repeats one words of it, I ends yo' stealin' on dis yearth mighty damn quick!

SMITHERS: *(Terrified)* Think I'd peach on yer? Not me! Ain't I always been yer friend?

JONES: *(Suddenly relaxing)* Sho' you has—and you better be.

SMITHERS: *(Recovering his composure—and with it his malice)* And just to show yer I'm yer friend, I'll tell yer that bit o' news I was goin' to.

JONES: Go ahead! Shoot de piece. Must be bad news from de happy way you look.

SMITHERS: *(Warningly)* Maybe it's gettin' time for you to resign—with that bloomin' silver bullet, wot? *(He finishes with a mocking grin.)*

JONES: *(Puzzled)* What's dat you say? Talk plain.

SMITHERS: Ain't noticed any of the guards or servants about the place today, I 'aven't.

JONES: *(Carelessly)* Dey're all out in de garden sleepin' under de trees. When I sleeps, dey sneaks a sleep, too, and I pretends I never suspicions it. All I got to do is to ring de bell and dey come flyin', makin' a bluff dey was wukin' all de time.

SMITHERS: *(In the same mocking tone)* Ring the bell now an' you'll bloody well see what I means.

JONES: *(Startled to alertness, but preserving the same careless tone)* Sho' I rings. *(He reaches below the throne and pulls out a big, common dinner bell which is painted the same vivid scarlet as the throne. He rings this vigorously—then stops to listen. Then he goes to both doors, rings again, and looks out.)*

SMITHERS: *(Watching him with malicious satisfaction, after a pause—mockingly)* The bloody ship is sinkin' an' the bleedin' rats 'as slung their 'ooks.

JONES: *(In a sudden fit of anger flings the bell clattering into a corner)* Low-flung, woods' niggers!

(Then catching SMITHERS's *eye on him, he controls himself and suddenly bursts into a low chuckling laugh.)*

JONES: Reckon I overplays my hand dis once! A man can't take de pot on a bob-tailed flush all de time. Was I sayin' I'd sit in six months mo'? Well, I'se changed my mind den. I cashes in and resigns de job of Emperor right dis minute.

SMITHERS: *(With real admiration)* Blimey, but you're a cool bird, and no mistake.

JONES: No use'n fussin'. When I knows de game's up I kisses it goodbye widout no long waits. Dey've all run off to de hills, ain't dey?

SMITHERS: Yes—every bleedin' man jack of 'em.

JONES: Den de revolution is at de post. And de Emperor better git his feet smokin' up de trail. *(He starts for the door in rear.)*

SMITHERS: Goin' out to look for your 'orse? Yer won't find any. They steals the 'orses first thing. Mine was gone when I went for 'im this mornin'. That's wot first give me a suspicion of wot was up.

JONES: *(Alarmed for a second, scratches his head, then philosophically)* Well, den I hoofs it. Feet, do yo' duty! *(He pulls out a gold watch and looks at it.)* Three-thuty. Sundown's at six-thuty or dereabouts. *(Puts his watch back—with cool confidence)* I got plenty o' time to make it easy.

SMITHERS: Don't be so bloomin' sure of it. They'll be after you 'ot and 'eavy. Ole Lem is at the bottom o' this business an' 'e 'ates you like 'ell. 'E'd rather do for you than eat 'is dinner, 'e would!

JONES: *(Scornfully)* Dat fool no-count nigger! Does you think I'se scared o' him? I stands him on his thick head more'n once befo' dis, and I does it again if he come in my way— *(Fiercely)* And dis time I leave him a dead nigger fo' sho'!

SMITHERS: You'll 'ave to cut through the big forest—an' these blacks 'ere can sniff and follow a trail in the dark like 'ounds. You'd 'ave to 'ustle to get through that forest in twelve hours even if you knew all the bloomin' trails like a native.

JONES: *(With indignant scorn)* Look-a-heah, white man! Does you think I'se a natural bo'n fool? Give me credit fo' havih' some sense, fo' Lawd's sake! Don't you s'pose I'se looked ahead and made sho' of all de chances? I'se gone out in dat big forest, pretendin' to hunt, so many times dat I knows it high an' low like a book. I could go through on dem trails wid my eyes shut. *(With great contempt)* Think dese ig'nerent bush niggers dat ain't got brains enuff to know deir own names even can catch Brutus Jones? Huh, I s'pects not! Not on yo' life! why, man, de white men went after me wid bloodhounds where I come from an' I jes' laughs at 'em. It's a shame to fool dese black trash around heah, dey're so easy. You watch me, man'. I'll make dem look sick, I will. I'll be 'cross de plain to de edge of de forest by time dark comes. Once in de woods in de night, dey got a swell chance o' findin' dis baby! Dawn tomorrow I'll be out at de oder side and on de coast whar dat French gunboat is stayin'. She picks me up, take me to the Martinique when she go dar, and dere I is safe wid a mighty big bankroll in my jeans. It's easy as rollin' off a log.

SMITHERS: *(Maliciously)* But s'posin' somethin' 'appens wrong an' they do nab yer?

JONES: *(Decisively)* Dey don't—dat's de answer.

SMITHERS: But, just for argyment's sake—what'd you do?

JONES: *(Frowning)* I'se got five lead bullets in dis gun good enuff fo' common bush niggers—and after dat I got de silver bullet left to cheat 'em out o' gittin' me.

SMITHERS: *(Jeeringly)* Ho, I was fergettin' that silver bullet. You'll bump yourself orf in style, won't yer? Blimey!

JONES: *(Gloomily)* You kin bet yo' whole roll on one thing, white man. Dis baby plays out his string to de end and when he quits, he quits wid a bang de way he ought. Silver bullet ain't none too good for him when he go, dat's a fac' I— *(Then shaking off his nervousness—with a confident laugh)* Sho'! what is I talkin' about? Ain't come to dat yit and I never will—not wid trash niggers like dese yere. *(Boastfully)* Silver bullet bring me luck anyway. I kin outguess, outrun, outfight, an' outplay de whole lot o' dem all ovah de board any time o' de day er night! You watch me!

(From the distant hills comes the faint, steady thump of a tom-tom, low and vibrating. It starts at a rate exactly corresponding to normal pulse beat—72 to the minute—and continues at a gradually accelerated rate from this point uninterruptedly to the very end of the play. JONES starts at the sound. A strange look of apprehension creeps into his face for a moment as he listens. Then he asks, with an attempt to regain his most casual manner.)

JONES: What's dat drum beatin' fo'?

SMITHERS: *(With a mean grin)* For you. That means the bleedin' ceremony 'as started. I've 'eard it before and I knows.

JONES: Cer'mony? What cer'mony?

SMITHERS: The blacks is 'oldin' a bloody meetin', 'avin' a war dance, gettin' their courage worked up b'fore they starts after you.

JONES: Let dem! Dey'll sho' need it!

SMITHERS: And they're there 'oldin' their 'eathen religious service—makin' no end of devil spells and charms to 'elp 'em against your silver bullet. *(He guffaws loudly.)* Blimey, but they're balmy as 'ell!

JONES: *(A tiny bit awed and shaken in spite of himself)* Huh! Takes more'n dat to scare dis chicken!

SMITHERS: *(Scenting the other's feeling—maliciously)* Ternight when it's pitch black in the forest, they'll 'ave their pet devils and ghosts 'oundin' after you. You'll find yer bloody 'air 'll be standin' on end before termorrow mornin'. *(Seriously)* It's a bleedin' queer place, that stinkin' forest, even in daylight. Yer don't know what might 'appen in there, it's that rotten still. Always sends the cold shivers down my back minute I gets in it.

JONES: *(With a contemptuous sniff)* I ain't no chicken-liver like you is. Trees an' me, we' se friends, and dar's a full moon comin' bring me light. And let dem po' niggers make all de fool spells dey'se a min' to. Does yo' s'pect I'se silly, enuff to b'lieve in ghosts an' ha'nts an' all dat ole woman's talk? G'long, white man! You ain't talkin' to me. *(With a chuckle)* Doesn't you know dey's got to do wid a man was member in good standin' o' de Baptist Church? Sho' I was dat when I was porter on de Pullmans, befo' I gits into my little trouble. Let dem try deir heathen tricks. De Baptist Church done pertect me and land dem all in hell. *(Then with more confident satisfaction)* And I'se got little silver bullet o' my own, don't forgits.

SMITHERS: Ho! You 'aven't give much 'eed to your Baptist Church since you been down 'ere. I've 'card myself you 'ad turned yer coat an' was takin' up with their blarsted witch-docters, or whatever the 'ell yer calls the swine.

JONES: *(Vehemently)* I pretends to! Sho' I pretends! Dat's part o' my game from de fust. If I finds out dem niggers believes dat black is white, den I yells it out louder 'n deir loudest. It don't git me nothin' to do missionary work for de Baptist Church. I'se after de coin, an' I lays my Jesus on de shelf for de time hem'. *(Stops abruptly to look at his watch—alertly)* But I ain't got de time to waste no more fool talk wid you. I'se gwine away from heah dis secon'. *(He reaches in under the throne and pulls out an expensive Panama hat with a bright multi-colored band and sets it jauntily on his head.)* So long, white man! *(With a grin)* See you in jail sometime, maybe!

SMITHERS: Not me, you won't. Well, I wouldn't be in yer bloody boots for no bloomin' money, but 'ere's wishin' yer luck just the same.

JONES: *(Contemptuously)* You're de frightenedest man evah I see! I tells you I'se safe's 'f I was in New York City. It takes dem niggers from now to dark to git up de nerve to start somethin'. By dat time, I'se got a head start dey never kotch up wid.

SMITHERS: *(Maliciously)* Give my regards to any ghosts yer meets up with.

JONES: *(Grinning)* If dat ghost got money, I'll tell him never ha'nt you less'n he wants to lose it.

SMITHERS: *(Flattered)* Garn! *(Then curiously)* Ain't yer takin' no luggage with yer?

JONES: I travels light when I wants to move fast. And I got tinned grub buried on de edge o' de forest. *(Boastfully)* Now say dat I don't look ahead an' use my brains! *(With a wide, liberal gesture)* I will all dat's left in de palace to you—and you better grab all you kin sneak away wid befo' dey gits here.

SMITHERS: *(Gratefully)* Righto—and thanks ter yer.

(As JONES walks toward the door in rear—cautioningly)

SMITHERS: Say! Look 'ere, you am't goin' out that way, are yer?

JONES: Does you think I'd slink out de back door like a common nigger? I'se Emperor yit, ain't I? And de Emperor Jones leaves de way he comes, and dat black trash don't dare stop him—not yit, leastways.

(He stops for a moment in the doorway, listening to the far-off but insistent beat of the tom-tom.)

JONES: Listen to dat roll-call, will you? Must be mighty big drum carry dat far. *(Then with a laugh)* Well, if dey ain't no whole brass band to see me off, I sho' got de drum part of it. So long, white man. *(He puts his hands in his pockets and with studied carelessness, whistling a tune, he saunters out of the doorway and off to the left.)*

SMITHERS: *(Looks after him with a puzzled admiration)* 'E's got 'is bloomin' nerve with 'im, s'elp me! *(Then angrily)* Ho-the bleedin' nigger—puttin' an 'is bloody airs! I 'opes they nabs 'im an' gives 'im what's what! *(Then putting business before the pleasure of this thought, looking around him with cupidity)* A bloke ought to find a 'ole lot in this palace that'd go for a bit of cash. Let's take a look, 'Arry, me lad.

(He starts for the doorway on right as the curtain falls.)

Scene Two

(Nightfall)

(The end of the plain where the Great Forest begins. The foreground is sandy, level ground dotted by a few stones and clumps of stunted bushes cowering close against the earth to escape the buffeting of the trade wind. In the rear the forest is a wall of darkness dividing the world. Only when the eye becomes accustomed to the gloom can the outlines of separate trunks of the nearest trees be made out, enormous pillars of deeper blackness. A somber monotone of wind lost in the leaves moans in the air. Yet this sound serves but to intensify the impression of the forest's relentless

immobility, to form a background throwing into relief its brooding, implacable silence. JONES *enters from the left, walking rapidly. He stops as he nears the edge of the forest, looks around him quickly, peering into the dark as if searching for some familiar landmark. Then, apparently satisfied that he is where he ought to be, he throws himself on the ground, dog-tired.)*

JONES: Well, heah I is. In de nick o' time, too! Little mo' an' it'd be blacker'n de ace of spades heah-abouts. *(He pulls a bandana handkerchief from his hip pocket and mops off his perspiring face.)* Sho'! Gimme air! I'se tuckered out sho' 'nuff. Dat soft Emperor job ain't no trainin' for' a long hike ovah dat plain in de brilin' sun. *(Then with a chuckle)* Cheah up, nigger, de worst is yet to come. *(He lifts his head and stares at the forest. His chuckle peters out abruptly. In a tone of awe)* My goodness, look at dem woods, will you? Dat no-count Smithers said dey'd be black an' he sho' called de turn. *(Turning away from them quickly and looking down at his feet, he snatches at a chance to change the subject—solicitously.)* Feet, you is holdin' up yo' end fine an' I sutinly hopes you ain't blisterin' none. It's time you git a rest. *(He takes off his shoes, his eyes studiously avoiding the forest. He feels of the soles of his feet gingerly.)* You is still in de pink—on'y a little mite feverish. Cool yo'selfs. Remember you done got a long journey yit befo' you. *(He sits in a weary attitude, listening to the rhythmic beating of the tom-tom. He grumbles in a loud tone to cover up a growing uneasiness.)* Bush niggers! Wonder dey wouldn' git sick o' beatin' dat drum. Sound louder, seem like. I wonder if dey's startin' after me?*(He scrambles to his feet, looking back across the plain.)* Couldn't see dem now, nohow, if dey was hundred feet away. *(Then shaking himself like a wet dog to get rid of these depressing thoughts)* Sho', dey's miles an' miles behind. What you gittin' fidgetty about? *(But he sits down and begins to lace up his shoes in great haste, all the time muttering reassuringly.)* You know what? Yo' belly is empty, dat's what's de matter wid you. Come time to eat! Wid nothin' but wind on yo' stumach, o' course you feels jiggedy. Well, we eats right heah an' now soon's I gits dese pesky shoes laced up. *(He finishes lacing up his shoes.)* Dere! Now le's see! *(Gets on his hands and knees and searches the ground around him with his eyes)* White stone, white stone, where is you? *(He sees the first white stone and crawls to it—with satisfaction.)* Heah you is! I knowed dis was de right place. Box of grub, come to me. *(He turns over the stone and feels in under it—in a tone of dismay.)* Ain't heah! Gorry, is I in de right place or isn't I? Dere's 'nother stone. Guess dat's it. *(He scrambles to the next stone and turns it over.)* Ain't heah, neither! Grub, whar is you? Ain't heah. Gorry, has I got to go hungry into dem woods—all de night? *(While he is talking he scrambles from one stone to another, turning them over in frantic haste. Finally, he jumps to his feet excitedly.)* Is I lost de place? Must have! But how dat happen when I was followin' de trail across de plain in broad daylight? *(Almost plaintively)* I'se hungry, I is! I gotta git my feed. Whar's my strength gonna come from if I doesn't? Gorry, I gotta find dat grub high an' low somehow! Why it come dark so quick like dat? Can't see nothin'. *(He scratches a match on his trousers and peers about him. The rate of the beat of the far-off tom-tom increases perceptibly as he does so. He mutters in a bewildered voice.)* How come all dese white stones come heah when I only remembers one? *(Suddenly, with a frightened gasp, he flings the match on the ground and stamps on it.)* Nigger, is you gone crazy mad? Is you lightin' matches to show dem whar you is? Fo' Lawd's sake, use yo' haid. Gorry, I'se got to be careful! *(He stares at the plain behind him apprehensively, his hand on his revolver.)* But how come all dese white stones? And whar's dat tin box o' grub I hid all wrapped up in oil cloth?

(While his back is turned, the LITTLE FORMLESS FEARS *creep out from the deeper blackness of the forest. They are black, shapeless, only their glittering little eyes can be seen. If they have any describable form at all it is that of a grubworm about the size of a creeping child. They move noiselessly, but with deliberate, painful effort, striving to raise themselves on end, failing and sinking prone again.* JONES *turns about to face the forest. He stares up at the tops of the trees, seeking vainly to discover his whereabouts by their conformation.)*

JONES: Can't tell nothin' from dem trees! Gorry, nothin' 'round heah look like I evah seed it befo'. I'se done lost de place sho' 'nuff! *(With mournful foreboding)* It's mighty queer! It's mighty queer! *(With sudden forced defiance—in an angry tone)* Woods, is you tryin' to put somethin' ovah on me?

(From the formless creatures on the ground in front of him comes a tiny gale of low mocking laughter like a rustling of leaves. They squirm upward toward him in twisted attitudes. JONES *looks down, leaps backward with a yell of terror, yanking out his revolver as he does join a quavering voice.)*

JONES: What's dat? who's dar? What is you? Git away from me befo' I shoots you up! You don't?

(He fires. There is a flash, a loud report, then silence broken only by the far-off, quickened throb of the tom-tom. The formless creatures have scurried back into the forest. JONES *remains fixed in his position, listening intently. The sound of the shot, the reassuring feel of the revolver in his hand, have somewhat restored his shaken nerve. He addresses himself with renewed confidence.)*

JONES: Dey're gone. Dat shot fix 'em. Dey was only little animals—little wild pigs, I reckon. Dey've maybe rooted out yo' grub an' eat it. Sho', you fool nigger, what you think dey is—ha'nts? *(Excitedly)* Gorry, you give de game away when you fire dat shot. Dem niggers heah dat fo' su'tin! Time you beat it in de woods widout no long waits. *(He starts for the forest—hesitates before the plunge—then urging himself in with manful resolution.)* Git in, nigger! What you skeered at? Ain't nothin' dere but de trees! Git in! *(He plunges boldly into the forest.)*

Scene Three

(Nine o'clock. In the forest. The moon has just risen. Its beams, drifting through the canopy of leaves, make a barely perceptible, suffused, eerie glow. A dense low wall of under-brush and creepers is in the nearer foreground, fencing in a small triangular clearing. Beyond this is the massed blackness of the forest like an encompassing barrier. A path is dimly discerned leading down to the clearing from left, rear, and winding away from it again toward the right. As the scene opens nothing can be distinctly made out. Except for the beating of the tom-tom, which is a trifle louder and quicker than in the previous scene, there is silence, broken every few seconds by a queer, clicking sound. Then gradually the figure of the negro, JEFF, can be discerned crouching on his haunches at the rear of the triangle. He is middle-aged, thin, brown in color, is dressed in a Pullman porter's uniform, cap, etc. He is throwing a pair of dice on the ground before him, picking them up, shaking them, casting them out with the regular, rigid, mechanical movements of an automaton. The heavy, plodding footsteps of someone approaching along the trail from the left are heard and JONES' *voice, pitched in a slightly higher key and strained in a cheering effort to overcome its own tremors.)*

JONES: De moon's rizen. Does you heah dat, nigger? You gits more light from dis out. No mo' buttin' yo' fool head agin' de trunks an' scratchin' de hide off yo' legs in de bushes. Now you sees whar yo'se gwine. So cheer up! From now on you has a snap. *(He steps just to the rear of the triangular clearing and mops off his face on his sleeve. He has lost his Panama hat. His face is scratched, his brilliant uniform shows several large rents.)* what time's it gittin' to be, I wonder? I dassent light no match to find out. Phoo'. It's wa'm an' dats a fac'! *(Wearily)* How long r been makin' tracks in dese woods? Must be hours an' hours. Seems like fo'evah! Yit can't be, when de moon's jes' riz. Dis am a long night fo' yo', yo' Majesty! *(With a mournful chuckle)* Majesty! Der ain't much majesty 'bout dis baby now. *(With attempted cheerfulness)* Never min'. It's all part o' de game. Dis night come to an end like everything else. And when you gits dar safe and has dat bankroll in yo' hands you laughs at all dis. *(He starts to whistle but checks himself abruptly.)* What yo' whistlin' for, you po' dope! Want all de won' to heah you? *(He stops talking to listen.)* Heah dat ole drum! Sho' gits nearer from de sound. Dey're packin' it along wid 'em. Time fo' me to move. *(He takes a step forward, then stops—worriedly.)* What's dat odder queer clicketty sound I heah? Den it is! Sound close! Sound like—sound like—Fo' God sake, sound like some nigger was shootin' crap! *(Frightenedly)* I better beat it quick when I gits dem notions.

(He walks quickly into the clear space—then stands transfixed as he sees JEFF *in a terrified gasp.)*

JONES: Who dar? Who dat? Is dat you, Jeff? *(Starting toward the other, forgetful for a moment of his surroundings and really believing it is a living man that he sees—in a tone of happy relief)* Jeff! I'se sho' mighty glad to see you! Dey tol' me you done died from dat razor cut I gives you. *(Stopping suddenly, bewilderedly)* But how you come to be heah, nigger? *(He stares fascinatedly at the other who continues his mechanical play with the dice.* JONES' *eyes begin to roll wildly. He stutters.)* Ain't you gwine—look up—can't you speak to me? Is you—is you—a ha'nt? *(He jerks out his revolver in a frenzy of terrified rage.)* Nigger, I kills you dead once. Has I got to kill you agin? You take it den.

(He fires. When the smoke clears away JEFF *has disappeared.* JONES *stands trembling—then with a certain reassurance.)*

JONES: He's gone, anyway. Ha'nt or no ha'nt, dat shot fix him.

(The beat of the far-off tom-tom is perceptibly louder and more rapid. JONES *becomes conscious of it—with a start, looking back over his shoulder.)*

JONES: Dey's gittin' near! Dey'se comin' fast! And heah I is shootin' shots to let 'em know jes' whar I is. Oh, Gorry, I'se got to run. *(Forgetting the path he plunges wildly into the underbrush in the rear and disappears in the shadow.)*

Scene Four

(Eleven o'clock. In the forest. A wide dirt road runs diagonally from right, front, to left, rear. Rising sheer on both sides the forest walls it in. The moon is now up. Under its light the road glimmers ghastly and unreal. It is as if the forest had stood aside momentarily to let the road pass through and accomplish its veiled purpose. This done, the forest will fold in upon itself again and the road will be no more. JONES *stumbles in from the forest on the right. His uniform is ragged and torn. He looks about him with numbed surprise when he sees the road, his eyes blinking in the bright moonlight. He flops down exhaustedly and pants heavily for a while. Then with sudden anger)*

JONES: I'm meltin' wid heat! Runnin' an' runnin' an' runnin'! Damn dis heah coat! Like a strait jacket! *(He tears off his coat and flings it away from him., revealing himself stripped to the waist.)* Den! Dat's better! Now I kin breathe! *(Looking down at his feet, the spurs catch his eye.)* And to hell wid dese high-fangled spurs. Dey're what's been a-trippin' me up an' breakin' my neck. *(He unstraps them and flings them away disgustedly.)* Dere! I gits rid o' dem frippety Emperor trappin's an' I travels lighter. Lawd! I'se tired!

(After a pause, listening to the insistent beat of the tom-tom in the distance)

JONES: I must 'a put some distance between myself an' dem—runnin' like dat—and yit—dat damn drum sound jes' de same—nearer, even. Well, I guess I a'most holds my lead anyhow. Dey won't never catch up. *(With a sigh)* If on'y my fool legs stands up. Oh, I'se sorry I evah went in for dis. Dat Emperor job is sho' hard to shake. *(He looks around him suspiciously.)* How'd dis road evah git heah? Good level road, too. I never remembers seein' it befo'. *(Shaking his head apprehensively)* Dese woods is sho' full o' de queerest things at night. *(With a sudden terror)* Lawd God, don't let me see no more o' dem ha'nts! Dey gits my goat! *(Then trying to talk himself into confidence)* Ha'nts! You fool nigger, dey ain't no such things! Don't de Baptist parson tell you dat many time? Is you civilized, or is you like dese ign'rent black niggers heah? Sho'! Dat was all in yo' own head. Wasn't nothin' dere. Wasn't no Jeff! Know what? You jus' get seem' dem things 'cause yo' belly's empty and you's sick wid hunger inside. Hunger 'fects yo' head and yo' eyes. Any fool know dat. *(Then pleading fervently)* But bless God, I don't come across no more o' dem, whatever dey is! *(Then cautiously)* Rest! Don't talk! Rest! You needs it. Den you gits on yo' way again. *(Looking at the moon)* Night's half gone a'most. You hits de coast in de mawning! Den you'se all safe.

(From the right forward a small gang of negroes enter. They are dressed in striped convict suits, their heads are shaven, one leg drags limpingly, shackled to a heavy ball and chain. Some carry picks, the others shovels. They are followed by a white man dressed in the uniform of a prison guard. A Winchester rifle is slung across his shoulders and he carries a heavy whip. At a signal from the GUARD they stop on the road opposite where JONES is sitting. JONES, who has been staring up at the sky, unmindful of their noiseless approach, suddenly looks down and sees them. His eyes pop out, he tries to get to his feet and fly, but sinks back, too numbed by fright to move. His voice catches in a choking prayer.)

JONES: Lawd Jesus!

(The PRISON GUARD cracks his whip—noiselessly—and at that signal all the convicts start to work on the road. They swing their picks, they shovel, but not a sound comes from their labor. Their movements, like those of JEFF in the preceding scene, are those of automatons,—rigid, slow, and mechanical. The PRISON GUARD points sternly at JONES with his whip, motions him to take his place among the other shovellers. JONES gets to his feet in a hypnotized stupor. He mumbles subserviently.)

JONES: Yes, suh! Yes, suh! I'se comin'. *(As he shuffles, dragging one foot, over to his place, he curses under his breath with rage and hatred.)* God damn yo' soul, I gits even wid you yit, sometime.

(As if there were a shovel in his hands he goes through weary, mechanical gestures of digging up dirt, and throwing it to the roadside. Suddenly the GUARD approaches him angrily, threateningly. He raises his whip and lashes JONES viciously across the shoulders with it. JONES winces with pain and cowers abjectly. The GUARD turns his back on him and walks away contemptuously. Instantly JONES straightens up. With arms upraised as if his shovel were a club in his hands he springs murderously at the unsuspecting GUARD. In the act of crashing down his shovel on the white man's skull, JONES suddenly becomes aware that his hands are empty. He cries despairingly.)

JONES: Whar's my shovel? Gimme my shovel 'till I splits his damn head! *(Appealing to his fellow convicts)* Gimme a shovel, one o' you, fo' God's sake!

(They stand fixed in motionless attitudes, their eyes on the ground. The GUARD *seems to wait expectantly, his back turned to the attacker.* JONES *bellows with baffled, terrified rage, tugging frantically at his revolver.)*

JONES: I kills you, you white debil, if it's de last thing I evah does! Ghost or debil, I kill you agin!

(He frees the revolver and fires point blank at the GUARD's *back. Instantly the walls of the forest close in from both sides; the road and the figures of the convict gang are blotted out in an enshrouding darkness. The only sounds are a crashing in the underbrush as* JONES *leaps away in mad flight and the throbbing of the tom-tom, still far distant, but increased in volume of sound and rapidity of beat.)*

Scene Five

(One o'clock. A large circular clearing, enclosed by the serried ranks of gigantic trunks of tall trees whose tops are lost to view. In the center is a big dead stump—worn by time into a curious resemblance to an auction block. The moon floods the clearing with a clear light. JONES *forces his way in through the forest on the left. He looks wildly about the clearing with hunted, fearful glances. His pants are in tatters, his shoes cut and misshapen, flapping about his feet. He slinks cautiously to the stump in the center and sits down in a tense position, ready for instant flight. Then he holds his head in his hands and rocks back and forth, moaning to himself miserably.)*

JONES: Oh Lawd, Lawd! Oh Lawd, Lawd! *(Suddenly he throws himself on his knees and raises his clasped hands to the sky—in a voice of agonized pleading.)* Lawd Jesus, heah my prayer! I'se a po' sinner, a po' sinner! I knows I done wrong, I knows it! When I cotches Jeff cheatin' wid loaded dice my anger overcomes me and I kills him dead! Lawd, I done wrong! When dat guard hits me wid de whip, my anger overcomes me, and I kills him dead. Lawd, I done wrong! And down heah whar dese fool bush niggers raises me up to the seat o' de mighty, I steals all I could grab. Lawd, I done wrong! I knows it! I'se sorry! Forgive me, Lawd! Forgive dis po' sinner! *(Then beseeching terrifiedly)* And keep dem away, Lawd! Keep dem away from me! And stop dat drum soundin' in my ears! Dat begin to sound ha'nted, too. *(He gets to his feet, evidently slightly reassured by his prayer—with attempted confidence.)*

De Lawd'll preserve me from dem ha'nts after dis. *(Sits down on the stump again)* I ain't skeered o' real men. Let dem come. But dem odders *(He shudders—then looks down at his feet, working his toes inside the shoe—with a groan.)* Oh, my po' feet! Dem shoes ain't no use no more 'ceptin' to hurt. I'se better off widout dem. *(He unlaces them and pulls them off—holds the wrecks of the shoes in his hands and regards them mournfully.)* You was real, A-one patin' leather, too. Look at you now. Emperor, you'se gittin' mighty low!

(He sighs dejectedly and remains with bowed shoulders, staring down at the shoes in his hands as if reluctant to throw them away. While his attention is thus occupied, a crowd of figures silently enter the clearing from all sides. All are dressed in Southern costumes of the period of the fifties of the last century. There are middle-aged who are evidently well-to-do planters. There is one spruce, authoritative individual—the AUCTIONEER. *There are a crowd of curious spectators, chiefly young belles and dandies who have come to the slave-market for diversion. All exchange courtly greetings in dumb show and chat silently together. There is something stiff, rigid, unreal, marionettish about their movements. They group themselves about the stump. Finally a batch of slaves are led in from the left by an attendant—three men of different ages, two women, one with a baby in her arms, nursing. They are placed to the left of the stump, beside* JONES. *The white planters look them over appraisingly as if they were cattle, and exchange judgments on each. The dandies point with their fingers and make witty remarks. The belles titter bewitchingly. All this in silence save for the ominous throb of the tom-tom. The* AUCTIONEER *holds up his hand, taking his place at the stump. The groups strain forward attentively. He touches* JONES *on the shoulder peremptorily, motioning for him to stand on the stump—the auction block.* JONES *looks up, sees the figures on all sides, looks wildly for some opening to escape, sees none, screams and leaps madly to the top of the stump to get as far away from them as possible. He stands there, cowering, paralyzed with horror. The* AUCTIONEER *begins his silent spiel. He points to* JONES, *appeals to the planters to see for themselves. Here is a good field hand, sound in wind and limb as they can see. Very strong still in spite of being middle-aged. Look at that back. Look at those shoulders. Look at the muscles in his arms and his sturdy legs. Capable of any amount of hard labor. Moreover, of a good disposition, intelligent and tractable. Will any gentleman start the bidding? The* PLANTERS *raise their fingers, make their bids. They are apparently all eager to possess* JONES. *The bidding is lively, the crowd interested. While this has been going on,* JONES *has been seized by the courage of desperation. He dares to look down, and around him. Over his face abject terror gives way to mystification, to gradual realization—stutteringly.)*

JONES: what you all doin', white folks? What's all dis? what you all lookin' at me fo'? what you doin' wid me, anyhow? *(Suddenly convulsed with raging hatred and fear)* Is dis a auction? Is you sellin' me like dey uster hefo' de war?

(Jerking out his revolver just as the AUCTIONEER *knocks him down to one of the planters—glaring from him to the purchaser)*

JONES: And you sells me? And you buys me? I shows you I'se a free nigger, damn yo' souls!

(He fires at the AUCTIONEER *and at the* PLANTER *with such rapidity that the two shots are almost simultaneous. As if this were a signal the walls of the forest fold in. Only blackness remains and silence broken by* JONES *as he rushes off, crying with fear—and by the quickened, ever louder beat of the tom-tom.)*

Scene Six

(Three o'clock. A cleared space in the forest. The limbs of the trees meet over it forming a low ceiling about five feet from the ground. The interlocked ropes of creepers reaching upward to entwine the tree trunks gives an arched appearance to the sides. The space thus encloses it like the dark, noisome hold of some ancient vessel. The moonlight is almost completely shut out and only a vague, wan light filters through. There is the noise of someone approaching from the left, stumbling and crawling through the undergrowth. JONES' *voice is heard between chattering moans.)*

JONES: Oh, Lawd, what I gwine do now? Ain't got no bullet left on'y de silver one. If mo' o' dem ha'nts come after me, how I gwine skeer dem away? Oh, Lawd, on'j de silver one left—an' I gotta save dat fo' luck. If I shoots dat one I'm a goner sho' I Lawd, it's black heah! Whar's de moon? Oh, Lawd, don't dis night evah come to an end? *(By the sounds, he is feeling his way cautiously forward.)* Dere! Dis feels like a clear space. I gotta lie down an' rest. I don't care if dem niggers does cotch me. I gotta rest.

(He is well forward now where his figure can be dimly made out. His pants have been so torn away that what is left of them is no better than a breech cloth. He flings himself full length, face downward on the ground, panting with exhaustion. Gradually it seems to grow lighter in the enclosed space and two rows of seated figures can be seen behind JONES. *They are sitting in crumpled, despairing attitudes, hunched, facing one another with their backs touching the forest walls as if they were shackled to them. All are negroes, naked save for loin cloths. At first they are silent and motionless. Then they begin to sway slowly forward toward each and back again in unison, as if they were laxly letting themselves follow the long roll of a ship at sea. At the same time, a low, melancholy murmur rises among them, increasing gradually by rhythmic degrees which seem to be directed and controlled by the throb of the tom-tom in the distance, to a long, tremulous wail of despair that reaches a certain pitch, unbearably acute, then falls by slow graduations of tone into silence and is taken up again.* JONES *starts, looks up, sees the figures, and throws himself down again to shut out the sight. A shudder of terror shakes his whole body as the wail rises up about him again. But the next time, his voice, as if under some uncanny compulsion, starts with the others. As their chorus lifts he rises to a sitting posture similar to the others, swaying back and forth. His voice reaches the highest pitch of sorrow, of desolation. The light fades out, the other voices cease, and only*

darkness is left. JONES *can be heard scrambling to his feet and running off, his voice sinking down the scale and receding as he moves farther and farther away in the forest. The tom-tom beats louder, quicker, with a more insistent, triumphant pulsation.)*

Scene Seven

(Five o'clock. The foot of a gigantic tree by the edge of a great river. A rough structure of boulders, like an altar, is by the tree. The raised river bank is in the nearer background. Beyond this the surface of the river spreads out, brilliant and unruffled in the moonlight, blotted out and merged into a veil of bluish mist in the distance. JONES' *voice is heard from the left rising and falling in the long, despairing wail of the chained slaves, to the rhythmic beat of the tom-tom. As his voice sinks into silence, he enters the open space. The expression on his face is fixed and stony, his eyes have an obsessed glare, he moves with a strange deliberation like a sleepwalker or one in a trance. He looks around at the tree, the rough stone altar, the moonlit surface of the river beyond, and passes his hand over his head with a vague gesture of puzzled bewilderment. Then, as if in obedience to some obscure impulse, he sinks into a kneeling, devotional posture before the altar. Then he seems to come to himself partly, to have an uncertain realization of what he is doing, for he straightens up and stares about him horrifiedly—in an incoherent mumble.)*

JONES: What—what is I doin? What is—dis place? Seems like—seems like I know dat tree—an' dem stones—an' de river. I remember—seems like I been heah befo'. *(Tremblingly)* Oh, Gorry, I'se skeered in dis place! I'se skeered! Oh, Lawd, pertect dis sinner!

(Crawling away from the altar, he cowers close to the ground, his face hidden, his shoulders heaving with sobs of hysterical fright. From behind the trunk of the tree, as if he had sprung out of it, the figure of the CONGO WITCH-DOCTOR *appears. He is wizened and old, naked except for the fur of some small animal tied about his waist, its bushy tail hanging down in front. His body is stained all over a bright red. Antelope horns are on each side of his head, branching upward. In one hand he carries a bone rattle, in the other a charm stick with a bunch of white cockatoo feathers tied to the end. A great number of glass beads and bone ornaments are about his neck, ears, wrists, and ankles. He struts noiselessly with a queer prancing step to a position in the clear ground between* JONES *and the altar. Then with a preliminary, summoning stamp of his foot on the earth, he begins to dance and to chant. As if in response to his summons the beating of the tom-tom grows to a fierce, exultant boom whose throbs seem to fill the air with vibrating rhythm.* JONES *looks up, starts to spring to his feet, reaches a half kneeling, half-squatting position and remains rigidly fixed there, paralyzed with awed fascination by this new apparition. The* WITCH-DOCTOR *sways, stamping with his foot, his bone rattle clicking the time. His voice rises and falls in a weird, monotonous croon, without articulate word divisions. Gradually his dance becomes clearly one of a narrative*

in pantomime, his croon is an incantation, a charm to allay the fierceness of some implacable deity demanding sacrifice. He flees, he is pursued by devils, he hides, he flees again. Ever wilder and wilder becomes his flight, nearer and nearer draws the pursuing evil, more and more the spirit of terror gains possession of him. His croon, rising to intensity, is punctuated by shrill cries. JONES *has become completely hypnotized. His voice joins in the incantation, in the cries, he beats time with his hands and sways his body to and fro from the waist. The whole spirit and meaning of the dance has entered into him, has become his spirit. Finally the theme of the pantomime halts on a howl of despair, and is taken up again in a note of savage hope. There is a salvation. The forces of evil demand sacrifice. They must be appeased. The* WITCH-DOCTOR *points with his wand to the sacred tree, to the river beyond, to the altar, and finally to* JONES *with a ferocious command.* JONES *seems to sense the meaning of this. It is he who must offer himself for sacrifice. He beats his forehead abjectly to the ground, moaning hysterically.)*

JONES: Mercy, Oh Lawd! Mercy! Mercy on dis po' sinner.

(The WITCH-DOCTOR *springs to the river bank. He stretches out his arms and calls to some God within its depths. Then he starts backward slowly, his arms remaining out. A huge head of a crocodile appears over the bank and its eyes, glittering greenly, fasten upon* JONES. *He stares into them fascinatedly. The* WITCH-DOCTOR *prances up to him, touches him with his wand, motions with hideous command toward the waiting monster.* JONES *squirms on his belly nearer and nearer, moaning continually.)*

JONES: Mercy, Lawd! Mercy!

(The crocodile heaves more of his enormous hulk onto the land. JONES *squirms toward him. The* WITCH-DOCTOR'S *voice shrills out in furious exultation, the tom-tom beats madly.* JONES *cries out in a fierce, exhausted spasm of anguished pleading.)*

JONES: Lawd, save me! Lawd Jesus, hear my prayer!

(Immediately, in answer to his prayer, comes the thought of the one bullet left him. He snatches at his hip, shouting defiantly.)

JONES: De silver bullet! You don't git me yit!

(He fires at the green eyes in front of him. The head of the crocodile sinks back behind the river bank, the WITCH-DOCTOR *springs behind the sacred tree and disappears.* JONES *lies with his face to the ground, his arms outstretched, whimpering with fear as the throb of the tom-tom fills the silence about him with a somber pulsation, a baffled but revengeful power.)*

Scene Eight

(Dawn. Same as Scene Two, the dividing line of forest and plain. The nearest tree trunks are dimly revealed but the forest behind them is still a mass of glooming shadow. The tom-tom seems on the very spot, so loud and continuously vibrating are its beats. LEM *enters from the left, followed by a small squad of his soldiers, and by the Cockney trader,* SMITHERS. LEM *is a heavy-set, ape-faced old savage of the extreme African type, dressed only in a loin cloth. A revolver and cartridge belt are about his waist. His soldiers are in different degrees of rag-concealed nakedness. All wear broad palm leaf hats. Each one carries a rifle.* SMITHERS *is the same as in Scene One. One of the soldiers, evidently a tracker, is peering about keenly on the ground. He grunts and points to the spot where* JONES *entered the forest.* LEM *and* SMITHERS *come to look.)*

SMITHERS: *(After a glance, turns away in disgust)* That's where 'e went in right enough. Much good it'll do yer. 'E's miles orf by this an' safe to the Coast damn 'S 'ide! I tole yer yer'd lose 'im, didn't I?—wastin' the 'ole bloomin' night beatin' yer bloody drum and castin' yer silly spells! Gawd blimey, wot a pack!

LEM: *(Gutturally)* We cotch him. You see.

(He makes a motion to his soldiers who squat down on their haunches in a semi-circle.)

SMITHERS: *(Exasperatedly)* Well, ain't yer goin 'in an' 'unt 'im in the woods? What the 'ell's the good of waitin'?

LEM: *(Imperturbably—squatting down himself)* We cotch him.

SMITHERS: *(Turning away from him contemptuously)* Aw! Garn! 'E's a better man than the lot o' you put together. I 'ates the sight o' 'im but I'll say that for 'im.

(A sound of snapping twigs comes from the forest. The soldiers jump to their feet, cocking their rifles alertly. LEM *remains sitting with an imperturbable expression, but listening intently. The sound from the woods is repeated.* LEM *makes a quick signal with his hand. His followers creep quickly but noiselessly into the forest, scattering so that each enters at a different spot.)*

SMITHERS: *(In the silence that follows—a contemptuous whisper)* You ain't thinkin' that would be 'im, I 'ope?

LEM: *(Calmly)* We cotch him.

SMITHERS: Blarsted fat 'eads! *(Then after a second's thought—wonderingly)* Still an' all, it 'might 'appen. If 'e lost 'is bloody way in these stinkin' woods 'e'd likely turn in a circle without 'is knowin' it. They all does.

LEM: *(Peremptorily)* Sssh!

(The reports of several rifles sound from the forest, followed a second later by savage, exultant yells. The beating of the tom-tom abruptly ceases. LEM *looks up at the white man with a grin of satisfaction.)*

LEM: We cotch him. Him dead.

SMITHERS: *(With a snarl)* 'Ow d'yer know it's 'im an' 'ow d'yer know 'e's dead?

LEM: My mens dey got 'urn silver bullets. Dey kill him shore.

SMITHERS: *(Astonished)* They got silver bullets?

LEM: Lead bullet no kill him. He got urn strong charm. I cook urn money, make urn silver bullet, make urn strong charm, too.

SMITHERS: *(Light breaking upon him)* So that's wot you was up to all night, wot? You was scared to put after 'im till you'd moulded silver bullets, eh?

LEM: *(Simply stating a fact)* Yes. Him got strong charm. Lead no good.

SMITHERS: *(Slapping his thigh and guffawing)* Haw-haw! If yer don't beat all 'ell! *(Then recovering himself—scornfully)* I'll bet yer it ain't 'im they shot at all, yer bleedin' looney!

LEM: *(Calmly)* Dey come bring him now.

(The soldiers come out of the forest, carrying JONES' *limp body. There is a little reddish purple hole under his left breast. He is dead. They carry him to* LEM *who examines his body with great satisfaction.* SMITHERS *leans over his shoulder— in a tone of frightened awe.)*

SMITHERS: Well, they did for yer fight enough, Jonsey, me lad! Dead as a 'erring! *(Mockingly)* Where's yer 'igh an' mighty airs now, yer bloornin' Majesty? *(Then with a grin)* Silver bullets! Gawd blimey, but yer died in the 'eighth o' style, any'ow!

*(*LEM *makes a motion to the soldiers to carry the body out left.* SMITHERS *speaks to him sneeringly.)*

SMITHERS: And I s'pose you think it's yer bleedin' charms and yer silly beatin' the drum that made 'im run in a circle when 'e'd lost 'imself, don't yer?

(But LEM *makes no reply, does not seem to hear the question, walks out left after his men.* SMITHERS *looks after him with contemptuous scorn.)*

SMITHERS: Stupid as 'ogs, the lot of 'em! Blarsted niggers!

(Curtain falls.)

END OF PLAY

ANNA CHRISTIE

ORIGINAL PRODUCTION

ANNA CHRISTIE opened at the Vanderbilt Theatre on 2 November 1921. It was produced by Arthur Hopkins. The cast and creative contributors were:

JOHNNY-THE-PRIEST	James C Mack
FIRST LONGSHOREMAN	G O Taylor
SECOND LONGSHOREMAN	John Hanley
A POSTMAN	William Augustin
CHRIS CHRISTOPHERSON	George Marion
MARTHY OWEN	Eugenie Blair
ANNA CHRISTOPHERSON	Pauline Lord
MAT BURKE	Frank Shannon
JOHNSON	Ole Anderson
SAILORS	Messers Reilly, Hansen & Kennedy
Director	Arthur Hopkins
Design	Robert Edmond Jones

CHARACTERS & SETTING

JOHNNY-THE-PRIEST
Two LONGSHOREMEN
A POSTMAN
LARRY, *bartender*
CHRIS CHRISTOPHERSON, *captain of the barge* Simeon Winthrop
MARTHY OWEN
ANNA CHRISTOPHERSON, CHRIS's *daughter*
Three MEN *of a steamer's crew*
MAT BURKE, *a stoker*
JOHNSON, *deckhand on the barge*

ACT ONE: *"Johnny-The-Priest's" saloon near the waterfront, New York City*

ACT TWO: *The barge* Simeon Winthrop, *at anchor in the harbor of Provincetown, MA. Ten days later*

ACT THREE: *Cabin of the barge, at dock in Boston. A week later*

ACT FOUR: *The same. Two days later*

ACT ONE

(*"JOHNNY-THE-PRIEST'S" saloon near South Street in New York City. The stage is divided into two sections, showing a small back room on the right. On the left, forward of the barroom, a large window looking out on the street. Beyond it, the main entrance—a double swinging door. Farther back, another window. The bar runs from left to right nearly the whole length of the rear wall. In back of the bar, a small showcase displaying a few bottles of case goods, for which there is evidently little call. The remainder of the rear space in front of the large mirrors is occupied by half-barrels of cheap whisky of the "nickel-a-shot" variety, from which the liquor is drawn by means of spigots. On the right is an open doorway leading to the back room. In the back room are four round wooden tables with five chairs grouped about each. In the rear, a family entrance opening on a side street. It is late afternoon of a day in fall. As the curtain rises,* JOHNNY *is discovered.* "JOHNNY-THE-PRIEST" *deserves his nickname. With his pale, thin, clean-shaven face, mild blue eyes and white hair, a cassock would seem more suited to him than the apron he wears. Neither his voice nor his general manner dispel this illusion which has made him a personage of the water front. They are soft and bland. But beneath all his mildness one senses the man behind the mask—cynical, callous, hard as nails. He is lounging at ease behind the bar, a pair of spectacles on his nose, reading an evening paper. Two* LONGSHOREMEN *enter from the street, wearing their working aprons, the button of the union pinned conspicuously on the caps pulled sideways on their heads at an aggressive angle.*)

FIRST LONGSHOREMAN: (*As they range themselves at the bar*) Gimme a shock. Number Two. (*He tosses a coin on the bar.*)

SECOND LONGSHOREMAN: Same here.

(JOHNNY *sets two glasses of barrel whisky before them.*)

FIRST LONGSHOREMAN: Here's luck!

(*The other nods. They gulp down their whisky.*)

SECOND LONGSHOREMAN: (*Putting money on the bar*) Give us another.

FIRST LONGSHOREMAN: Gimme a scoop this time—lager and porter. I'm dry.

SECOND LONGSHOREMAN: Same here.

(JOHNNY *draws the lager and porter and sets the big, foaming schooners before them. They drink down half the contents and start to talk together hurriedly in low tones. The door on the left is swung open and* LARRY *enters. He is a boyish, red-cheeked, rather good-looking young fellow of twenty or so.*)

LARRY: *(Nodding to* JOHNNY—*cheerily)* Hello, boss.

JOHNNY: Hello, Larry. *(With a glance at his watch)* Just on time.

(LARRY *goes to the right behind the bar, takes off his coat and puts on an apron.)*

FIRST LONGSHOREMAN: *(Abruptly)* Let's drink up and get back to it.

(They finish their drinks and go out left. THE POSTMAN *enters as they leave. He exchanges nods with* JOHNNY *and throws a letter on the bar.)*

THE POSTMAN: Addressed care of you, Johnny. Know him?

(JOHNNY *picks up the letter, adjusting his spectacles.* LARRY *comes and peers over his shoulders.* JOHNNY *reads very slowly.)*

JOHNNY: Christopher Christopherson.

THE POSTMAN: *(Helpfully)* Square-head name.

LARRY: Old Chris—that's who.

JOHNNY: Oh, sure. I was forgetting Chris carried a hell of a name like that. Letters come here for him sometimes before, I remember now. Long time ago, though.

THE POSTMAN: It'll get him all right then?

JOHNNY: Sure thing. He comes here whenever he's in port.

THE POSTMAN: *(Turning to go)* Sailor, eh?

JOHNNY: *(With a grin)* Captain of a coal barge.

THE POSTMAN: *(Laughing)* Some job! Well, s'long.

JOHNNY: S'long. I'll see he gets it.

(THE POSTMAN *goes out.* JOHNNY *scrutinizes the letter.)*

JOHNNY: You got good eyes, Larry. Where's it from?

LARRY: *(After a glance)* Saint Paul. That'll be in Minnesota, I'm thinkin'. Looks like a woman's writing, too, the old divil!

JOHNNY: He's got a daughter somewheres out West, I think he told me once. *(He puts the letter on the cash register.)* Come to think of it, I ain't seen old Chris in a dog's age. *(Putting his overcoat on, he comes around the end of the bar.)* Guess I'll be getting home. See you tomorrow.

LARRY: Good-night to ye, boss.

(As JOHNNY *goes toward the street door, it is pushed open and* CHRISTOPHER CHRISTOPHERSON *enters. He is a short, squat, broad-shouldered man of about fifty, with a round, weather-beaten, red face from which his light blue eyes peer short-sightedly, twinkling with a simple good humor. His large mouth, overhung by a thick, drooping, yellow mustache, is childishly self-willed and weak, of an obstinate kindliness. A thick neck is jammed like a post into the heavy trunk of his body. His*

arms with their big, hairy, freckled hands, and his stumpy legs terminating in large flat feet, are awkwardly short and muscular. He walks with a clumsy, rolling gait. His voice, when not raised in a hollow boom, is toned down to a sly, confidential half-whisper with something vaguely plaintive in its quality. He is dressed in a wrinkled, ill-fitting dark suit of shore clothes, and wears a faded cap of gray cloth over his mop of grizzled, blond hair. Just now his face beams with a too-blissful happiness, and he has evidently been drinking. He reaches his hand out to JOHNNY.)

CHRIS: Hello, Yohnny! Have drink on me. Come on, Larry. Give us drink. Have one yourself. *(Putting his hand in his pocket)* Ay gat money—plenty money....

JOHNNY: *(Shakes* CHRIS *by the hand)* Speak of the devil. We was just talkin' about you.

LARRY: *(Coming to the end of the bar)* Hello, Chris. Put it there.

(They shake hands.)

CHRIS: *(Beaming)* Give us drink.

JOHNNY: *(With a grin)* You got a half-snootful now. Where'd you get it?

CHRIS: *(Grinning)* Oder fallar on oder barge—Irish fallar—he gat bottle vhisky and we drank it, yust us two. Dot vhisky gat kick, by yingo! Ay yust come ashore. Give us drink, Larry. Ay vas little drunk, not much. Yust feel good. *(He laughs and commences to sing in a nasal, high-pitched quaver,)* "My Yosephine, come board de ship. Long time Ay vait for you. De moon, she shi-i-i-ine. She looka yust like you. Tchee-tchee, tchee-tchee, tchee-tchee, tchee-tchee." *(To the accompaniment of this last he waves his hand as if he were conducting an orchestra.)*

JOHNNY: *(With a laugh)* Same old Yosie, eh Chris?

CHRIS: You don' know good song when you hear him. Italian fallar on oder barge, he learn me dat. Give us drink. *(He throws change on the bar.)*

LARRY: *(With a professional air)* What's your pleasure, gentlemen?

JOHNNY: Small beer, Larry.

CHRIS: Vhisky—Number Two.

LARRY: *(As he gets their drinks)* I'll take a cigar on you.

CHRIS: *(Lifting his glass)* Skoal!

JOHNNY: Drink hearty.

CHRIS: *(Immediately)* Have oder drink.

JOHNNY: No. Some other time. Got to go home now. So you've just landed? Where are you in from this time?

CHRIS: Norfolk. Ve make slow voyage—dirty vedder—yust fog, fog, fog, all bloody time!

(There is an insistent ring from the doorbell at the family entrance in the back room. CHRIS *gives a start—hurriedly.)*

CHRIS: Ay go open, Larry. Ay forgat. It vas Marthy. She come with me. *(He goes into the back room.)*

LARRY: *(With a chuckle)* He's still got that same cow livin' with him, the old fool!

JOHNNY: *(With a grin)* A sport, Chris is. Well, I'll beat it home. S'long. *(He goes to the street door.)*

LARRY: So long, boss.

JOHNNY: Oh—don't forget to give him his letter.

LARRY: I won't.

*(*JOHNNY *goes out. In the meantime,* CHRIS *has opened the family entrance door, admitting* MARTHY. *She might be forty or fifty. Her jowly, mottled face, with its thick red nose, is streaked with interlacing purple veins. Her thick, gray hair is piled anyhow in a greasy mop on top of her round head. Her figure is flabby and fat; her breath comes wheezy gasps; she speaks in a loud, mannish voice, punctuated by explosions of hoarse laughter. But there still twinkles in her blood-shot blue eyes a youthful lust for life which hard usage has failed to stifle, a sense of humor mocking, but good tempered. She wears a man's cap, double-breasted man's jacket, and a grimy, calico skirt. Her bare feet are encased in a man's brogans several sizes too large for her, which gives her a shuffling, wobbly gait.)*

MARTHY: *(Grumblingly)* What yab tryin' to do, Dutchy—keep me standin' out there all day? *(She comes forward and sits at the table in the right corner, front.)*

CHRIS: *(Mollifyingly)* Ay'm sorry, Marthy. Ay talk to Yohnny. Ay forgat. What you goin' take for drink?

MARTHY: *(Appeased)* Gimme a scoop of lager an' ale.

CHRIS: Ay go bring him back. *(He returns to the bar.)* Lager and ale for Marthy, Larry. Vhisky for me. *(He throws change on the bar.)*

LARRY: Right you are. *(Then remembering, he takes the letter from in back of the bar.)* Here's a letter for you— from Saint Paul, Minnesota—and a lady's writin'. *(He grins.)*

CHRIS: *(Quickly—taking it)* Oh, den it come from my daughter, Anna. She live dere. *(He turns the letter over in his hands uncertainly.)* Ay don't gat letter from Anna—must be a year.

LARRY: *(Jokingly)* That's a fine fairy tale to be tellin'—your daughter! Sure I'll bet it's some bum.

CHRIS: *(Soberly)* No. Dis come from Anna. *(Engrossed by the letter in his hand—uncertainly)* By golly, Ay tank Ay'm too drunk for read dis letter from Anna. Ay tank Ay sat down a minute. You bring drinks in back room, Larry. *(He goes into the room on right.)*

MARTHY: *(Angrily)* Where's my lager an' ale, yuh big stiff?

CHRIS: *(Preoccupied)* Larry bring him.

(He sits down opposite her. LARRY brings in the drinks and sets them on the table. He and MARTHY exchange nods of recognition. LARRY stands looking at CHRIS curiously. MARTHY takes a long draught of her schooner and heaves a huge sigh of satisfaction, wiping her mouth with the back of her hand. CHRIS stares at the letter for a moment—slowly opens it, and, squinting his eyes, commences to read laboriously, his lips moving as he spells out the words. As he reads his face lights up with an expression of joy and bewilderment.)

LARRY: Good news?

MARTHY: *(Her curiosity also aroused)* What's that yuh got—a letter, fur Gawd's sake?

CHRIS: *(Pauses for a moment, after finishing the letter, as if to let the news sink in—then suddenly pounds his fist on the table with happy excitement)* Py yiminy! Yust tank, Anna say she's comin' here right avay! She gat sick on yob in Saint Paul, she say. It's short letter, don't tal me much more'n dat. *(Beaming)* Py golly, dat's good news all at one time for ole fallar! *(Then turning to MARTHY, rather shamefacedly)* You know, Marthy, Ay've tole you Ay don't see my Anna since she vas little girl in Sveden five year ole.

MARTHY: How old'll she be now?

CHRIS: She must be—lat me see—she must be twenty year ole, py Yo!

LARRY: *(Surprised)* Yon've not seen her in fifteen years?

CHRIS: *(Suddenly growing somber—in a low tone)* No. Ven she ms little gel, Ay vas bo'sun on vindjammer. Ay never gat home only few time dem year. Ay'm fool sailor fallar. My voman—Anna's mother—she gat tired vait all time Sveden for me yen Ay don't never come. She come dis country, bring Anna, dey go out Minnesota, live with her cousins on farm. Den ven her mo'der die ven Ay vas on voyage, Ay tank it's better dem cousins keep Anna. Ay tank it's better Anna live on farm, den she don't know dat ole davil, sea, she don't know fa'der like me.

LARRY: *(With a wink at MARTHY)* This girl, now, 'll be marryin' a sailor herself, likely. It's in the blood.

CHRIS: *(Suddenly springing to his feet and smashing his fist on the table in a rage)* No, py God! She don't do dat!

MARTHY: *(Grasping her schooner hastily—angrily)* Hey, look out, yuh nut! Wanta spill my suds for me?

LARRY: *(Amazed)* Oho, what's up with you? Ain't you a sailor yourself now, and always been?

CHRIS: *(Slowly)* Dat's yust vhy Ay say it. *(Forcing a smile)* Sailor vas all right fallar, but not for marry gel. No. Ay know dat. Anna's mo'der, she know it, too.

LARRY: *(As CHRIS remains sunk in gloomy reflection)* Is your daughter comin'? Soon?

CHRIS: *(Roused)* Py yiminy, Ay forgat. *(Reads through letter hurriedly)* She say she come right avay, dat's all.

LARRY: She'll maybe be comin' here to look for you, I su'pose.

(He returns to the bar, whistling. Left alone with MARTHY, who stares at him with a twinkle of malicious humor in her eyes, CHRIS suddenly becomes desperately ill-at-ease. He fidgets, then gets up hurriedly.)

CHRIS: Ay gat speak with Larry. Ay be right back. *(Mollifyingly)* Ay bring you oder drink.

MARTHY: *(Emptying her glass)* Sure. That's me. *(As he retreats with the glass she guffaws after him derisively.)*

CHRIS: *(To LARRY in an alarmed whisper)* Py yingo, Ay gat gat Marthy shore off barge before Anna come! Anna raise hell if she find dat out. Marthy raise hell, too, for go, py golly!

LARRY: *(With a chuckle)* Serve ye right, ye old divil—havin' a woman at your age!

CHRIS: *(Scratching his head in a quandary)* You tal me lie for tal Marthy, Larry, so's she gat off barge quick.

LARRY: She knows your daughter's comin'. Tell her to get the hell out of it.

CHRIS: No. Ay don't like make her feel bad.

LARRY: You're an old mush! Keep your girl away from the barge then. She'll likely want to stay ashore anyway. *(Curiously)* What does she work at, your Anna?

CHRIS: She stay on dem cousins' farm 'till two year ago. Dan she gat yob nurse gel in Saint Paul. *(Then shaking his head resolutely)* But Ay don't vant for her gat yob now. Ay vant for her stay wit me.

LARRY: *(Scornfully)* On a coal barge! She'll not like that, I'm thinkin'.

MARTHY: *(Shouts from next room)* Don't I get that bucket 'o suds, Dutchy?

CHRIS: *(Startled—in apprehensive confusion)* Yes, Ay come, Marthy.

LARRY: *(Drawing the lager and ale, hands it to* CHRIS—*laughing)* Now you're in for it! You'd better tell her straight to get out!

CHRIS: *(Shaking in his boots)* Py golly.

(He takes her drink in to MARTHY *and sits down at the table. She sips it in silence.* LARRY *moves quietly close to the partition to listen, grinning with expectation.* CHRIS *seems on the verge of speaking, hesitates, gulps down his whisky desperately as if seeking for courage. He attempts to whistle a few bars of "Yosephine" with careless bravado, but the whistle peters out futilely.* MARTHY *stares at him keenly, taking in his embarrassment with a malicious twinkle of amusement in her eye.* CHRIS *clears his throat.)*

CHRIS: Marthy—

MARTHY: *(Aggressively)* Wha's that? *(Then, pretending to fly into a rage, her eyes enjoying* CHRIS's *misery)* I'm wise to what's in back of your nut, Dutchy. Yuh want to git rid o' me, huh?—now she's comin'. Gimme the bum's rush ashore, huh? Lemma tell yuh, Dutchy, there ain't a square-head workin' on a boat man enough to git away with that. Don't start nothin' yuh can't finish!

CHRIS: *(Miserably)* Ay don't start nutting, Marthy.

MARTHY: *(Glares at him for a second—then cannot control a burst of laughter)* Ho-ho! Yuh're a scream, Square-head— an honest-ter-Gawd knockout! Ho-ho! *(She wheezes, panting for breath.)*

CHRIS: *(With childish pique)* Ay don't see nutting for laugh at.

MARTHY: Take a slant in the mirror and yuh'll see. Ho-ho! *(Recovering from her mirth—chuckling, scornfully)* A square-head tryin' to kid Marthy Owen at this late day!—after me campin' with barge men the last twenty years. I'm wise to the game up, down, and sideways. I ain't been born and dragged up on the water front for nothin'. Think I'd make trouble, huh? Not me! I'll pack up me duds an' beat it. I'm quittin' yuh, get me? I'm tellin' yuh I'm sick of stickin' with and I'm leavin' yuh flat, see? There's plenty of other guys on other barges waitin' for me. Always was, I always found.

(She claps the astonished CHRIS *on the back.)*

MARTHY: So cheer up, Dutchy! I'll be offen the barge before she comes. You'll be rid o' me for good—and me o' you—good riddance for both of us. Ho-ho!

CHRIS: *(Seriously)* Ay don' tank dat. You vas good gel, Marthy.

MARTHY: *(Grinning)* Good girl? Aw, can the bull! Well, yuh treated me square, yuhself. So it's fifty-fifty. Nobody's sore at nobody. We're still good frien's, huh?

*(*LARRY *returns to the bar.)*

CHRIS: *(Beaming now that he sees his troubles disappearing)* Yes, py golly.

MARTHY: That's the talkin'! In all my time I tried never to split with a guy with no hard feelin's. But what was yuh so scared about—that I'd kick up a row? That ain't Marthy's way. *(Scornfully)* Think I'd break my heart to lose yuh? Commit suicide, huh? Ho-ho! Gawd! The world's full o' men if that's all I'd worry about! *(Then with a grin, after emptying her glass)* Blow me to another scoop, huh? I'll drink your kid's health for yuh.

CHRIS: *(Eagerly)* Sure tang. Ay go gat him. *(He takes the two glasses into the bar.)* Oder drink. Same for both.

LARRY: *(Getting the drinks and putting them on the bar)* She's not such a bad lot, that one.

CHRIS: *(Jovially)* She's good gel, Ay tal you! Py golly, Ay calabrate now! Give me vhisky here at bar, too.

(He puts down money. LARRY serves him.)

CHRIS: You have drink, Larry.

LARRY: *(Virtuously)* You know I never touch it.

CHRIS: You don't know what you miss. Skoal! *(He drinks—then begins to sing loudly.)* "My Yosephine, come board de ship—" *(He picks up the drinks for MARTHY and himself and walks unsteadily into the back room, singing)* "De moon, she shi-i-i-ine. She looks yust like you. Tchee-tchee, tchee-tchee, tchee-tchee, tchee-tchee."

MARTHY: *(Grinning, hands to ears)* Gawd!

CHRIS: *(Sitting down)* Ay'm good singer, yes? Ve drink, eh? Skoal! Ay calabrate! *(He drinks.)* Ay ealabrate 'cause Anna's coming home. You know, Marthy, Ay never write for her to come, 'cause Ay tank Ay'm no good for her. But all time Ay hope like hell some day she vant for see me and den she come. And dat's vay it happen now, py yiminy! *(His face beaming)* What you tank she look like, Marthy? Ay bet you she's fine, good, strong gel, pooty like hell! Living on farm made her like dat. And Ay bet you some day she marry good, steady land fallar here in East, have home all her own, have kits—and dan Ay'm ole grandfader, py golly! And Ay go visit dem every time Ay gat in port near! *(Bursting with joy)* By yiminy crickens, Ay calabrate dat! *(Shouts)* Bring oder drink, Larry! *(He smashes his fist on the table with a bang.)*

LARRY: *(Coming in from bar—irritably)* Easy there! Don't be breakin' the table, you old goat!

CHRIS: *(By way of reply, grins foolishly and begins to sing)* "My Yosephine, come board de ship—"

MARTHY: *(Touching CHRIS' arm persuasively)* You're soused to the ears, Dutchy. Go out and put a feed into you. It'll sober you up.

(Then as CHRIS *shakes his head obstinately)*

MARTHY: Listen, yuh old nut! Yuh don't know what time your kid's liable to show up. Yuh want to be sober when she comes, don't yuh?

CHRIS: *(Aroused—gets unsteadily to his feet)* Py golly, yes.

LARRY: That's good sense for you. A good beef stew'll fix you. Go round the corner.

CHRIS: All right. Ay be back soon, Marthy. *(He goes through the bar and out the street door.)*

LARRY: He'll come round all right with some grub in him.

MARTHY: Sure.

(LARRY *goes back to the bar and resumes his newspaper.* MARTHY *sips what is left in her schooner reflectively. There is the ring of the family entrance bell.* LARRY *comes to the door and opens it a trifle—then, with a puzzled expression, pulls it wide.* ANNA CHRISTOPHERSON *enters. She is a tall, blond, fully-developed girl of twenty, handsome after a large, Viking-daughter fashion but now run down in health and plainly showing all the outward evidences of belonging to the world's oldest profession. Her youthful face is hard and cynical beneath its layer of make-up. Her clothes are the tawdry finery of peasant stock turned prostitute. She comes and sinks wearily in a chair by the table, left front.)*

ANNA: Gimme a whisky—ginger ale on the side.

(Then, as LARRY *turns to go, forcing a winning smile at him)*

ANNA: And don't be stingy, baby.

LARRY: *(Sarcastically)* Shall I serve it in a pail?

ANNA: *(With a hard laugh)* That suits me down to the ground.

(LARRY *goes into the bar. The two women size each other up with frank stares.* LARRY *comes back with the drink which he sets before* ANNA *and returns to the bar again.* ANNA *downs her drink at a pulp. Then, after a moment, as the alcohol begins to rouse her, she turns to* MARTHY *with a friendly smile.)*

ANNA: Gee, I needed that bad, all right, all right!

MARTHY: *(Nodding her head sympathetically)* Sure—yuh look all in. Been on a bat?

ANNA: No—travelling—day and a half on the train. Had to sit up all night in the dirty coach, too. Gawd, I thought I'd never get here!

MARTHY: *(With a start—looking at her intently)* Where'd yuh come from, huh?

ANNA: Saint Paul—out in Minnesota.

MARTHY: *(Staring at her in amazement—slowly)* So— yuh're— *(She suddenly bursts out into hoarse, ironical laughter.)* Gawd!

ANNA: All the way from Minnesota, sure. *(Flaring up)* What are you laughing at? Me?

MARTHY: *(Hastily)* No, honest, kid. I was thinkin' of somethin' else.

ANNA: *(Mollified—with a smile)* Well, I wouldn't blame you, at that. Guess I do look rotten—yust out of the hospital two weeks. I'm going to have another 'ski. What d'you say? Have something on me?

MARTHY: Sure I will. T'anks. *(She calls.)* Hey, Larry! Little service!

(He comes in.)

ANNA: Same for me.

MARTHY: Same here.

(LARRY takes their glasses and goes out.)

ANNA: Why don't you come sit over here, be sociable. I'm a dead stranger in this burg—and I ain't spoke a word with no one since day before yesterday.

MARTHY: Sure thing.

(She shuffles over to ANNA's table and sits down opposite her. LARRY brings the drinks and ANNA pays him.)

ANNA: Skoal! Here's how! *(She drinks.)*

MARTHY: Here's luck! *(She takes a gulp from her schooner.)*

ANNA: *(Taking a package of Sweet Caporal cigarettes from her bag)* Let you smoke in here, won't they?

MARTHY: *(Doubtfully)* Sure. *(Then with evident anxiety)* On'y trow it away if yuh hear someone comin'.

ANNA: *(Lighting one and taking a deep inhale)* Gee, they're fussy in this dump, ain't they?

(She puffs, staring at the table top. MARTHY looks her over with a new penetrating interest, taking in every detail of her face. ANNA suddenly becomes conscious of this appraising stare—resentfully.)

ANNA: Ain't nothing wrong with me, is there? You're looking hard enough.

MARTHY: *(Irritated by the other's tone—scornfully)* Ain't got to look much. I got your number the minute you stepped in the door.

ANNA: *(Her eyes narrowing)* Ain't you smart! Well, I got yours too, without no trouble. You're me forty years from now. *(She gives a hard little laugh.)*

MARTHY: *(Angrily)* Is that so? Well, I'll tell you straight, that Marthy Owen never— *(She catches herself up short—with a grin.)* What are you and me scrappin' over? Let's cut it out, huh? Me, I don't want no hard feelin's with no one. *(Extending her hand)* Shake and forget it, huh?

ANNA: *(Shakes her hand gladly)* Only too glad to. I ain't looking for trouble. Let's have 'nother. What d'you say?

MARTHY: *(Shaking her head)* Not for mine. I'm full up. And you—Had anythin' to eat lately?

ANNA: Not since this morning on the train.

MARTHY: Then yuh better go easy on it, hadn't yuh?

ANNA: *(After a moment's hesitation)* Guess you're right. I got to meet someone, too. But my nerves is on edge after that rotten trip.

MARTHY: Yuh said yuh was just outa the hospital?

ANNA: Two weeks ago. *(Leaning over to* MARTHY *confidentially)* The joint I was in out in Saint Paul got raided. That was the start. The judge give all us girls thirty days. The others didn't seem to mind being in the cooler much. Some of 'em was used to it. But me, I couldn't stand it. It got my goat right—couldn't eat or sleep or nothing. I never could stand being caged up nowheres. I got good and sick and they had to send me to the hospital. It was nice there. I was sorry to leave it, honest!

MARTHY: *(After a slight pause)* Did yuh say yuh got to meet someone here?

ANNA: Yes. Oh, not what you mean. It's my Old Man I got to meet. Honest! It's funny, too. I ain't seen him since I was a kid—don't even know what he looks like—yust had a letter every now and then. This was always the only address he give me to write him back. He's yanitor of some building here now—used to be a sailor.

MARTHY: *(Astonished)* Janitor!

ANNA: Sure. And I was thinking maybe, seeing he never done a thing for me in my life, he might be stake me to a room and eats—till I get rested up. *(Wearily)* Gee, I sure need that rest! I'm knocked out. *(Then resignedly)* But I ain't expecting much from him. Give you a kick when you're down, that's what all men do. *(With sudden passion)* Men, I hate 'em—all of 'em! And I don't expect he'll turn out no better than the rest. *(Then with sudden interest)* Say, do you hang out around this dump much?

MARTHY: Oh, off and on.

ANNA: Then maybe you know him—my Old Man—or at least seen him?

MARTHY: It ain't old Chris, is it?

ANNA: Old Chris?

MARTHY: Chris Christopherson, his full name is.

ANNA: *(Excitedly)* Yes, that's him! Anna Christopherson—that's my real name—only out there I called myself Anna Christie. So you know him, eh?

MARTHY: *(Evasively)* Seen him about for years.

ANNA: Say, what's he like, tell me, honest?

MARTHY: Oh, he's short and—

ANNA: *(Impatiently)* I don't care what he looks like. What kind is he?

MARTHY: *(Earnestly)* Well, yuh can bet your life, kid, he's as good an old guy as ever walked on two feet.

ANNA: *(Pleased)* I'm glad to hear it. Then you think he'd stake me to that rest cure I'm after?

MARTHY: *(Emphatically)* Surest thing you know. *(Disgustedly)* But where'd yuh get the idea he was a janitor?

ANNA: He wrote me he was himself.

MARTHY: Well, he was lyin'. He ain't. He's captain of a barge— five men under him.

ANNA: *(Disgusted in her turn)* A barge? What kind of a barge?

MARTHY: Coal, mostly.

ANNA: A coal barge! *(With a harsh laugh)* If that ain't a swell job to find your long lost Old Man working at! Gee, I knew something'd be bound to turn out wrong—always does with me. That puts my idea of his giving me a rest on the bum.

MARTHY: What d'yuh mean?

ANNA: I s'pose he lives on the boat, don't he?

MARTHY: Sure. What about it? Can't you live on it too?

ANNA: *(Scornfully)* Me? On a dirty coal barge? What d'you think I am?

MARTHY: *(Resentfully)* What d'yuh know about barges, huh? Bet yuh ain't never seen one. That's what comes of his bringing yuh up inland—away from the old devil sea—where yuh'd be safe—Gawd! *(The irony of it strikes her sense of humor and she laughs hoarsely.)*

ANNA: *(Angrily)* His bringing me up! Is that what he tells people? I like his nerve! He let them cousins of my Old Woman's keep me on their farm and work me to death like a dog.

MARTHY: Well, he's got queer notions on some things. I've heard him say a farm was the best place for a kid.

ANNA: Sure. That's what he'd always answer back—and a lot of crazy stuff about staying away from the sea—stuff I couldn't make head or tail to. I thought be must be nutty.

MARTHY: He is on that one point. *(Casually)* So you didn't fall for life on the farm, huh?

ANNA: I should say not! The old man of the family, his wife, and four sons—I had to slave for all of 'em. I was only a poor relation, and they treated me worse than they dare treat a hired girl. *(After a moment's hesitation—somberly)* It was one of the sons—the youngest—started me—when I was sixteen. After that, I hated 'em so I'd killed 'em all if I stayed. So I run away—to Saint Paul.

MARTHY: *(Who has been listening sympathetically)* I've heard Old Chris talkin' about your bein' a nurse girl out there. Was that a buff yuh put up when yuh wrote him?

ANNA: Not on your life, it wasn't. It was true for two years. I didn't go wrong all at one jump. Being a nurse girl was yust what finished me. Taking care of other people's kids, always listening to their bawling and crying, caged in, when you're onlya kid yourself and want to go out and see things. At last I got the chance—to get into that house. And you bet your life I took it! *(Defiantly)* And I ain't sorry neither. *(After a pause—with bitter hatred)* It was all men's fault—the whole business. It was men on the farm ordering and beating me—and giving me the wrong start. Then when I was a nurse, it was men again hanging around, bothering me, trying to see what they could get. *(She gives a hard laugh.)* And now it's men all the time. Gawd, I hate 'em all, every mother's son of 'em! Don't you?

MARTHY: Oh, I dunno. There's good ones and bad ones. You've just had a run of bad luck with 'em, that's all. Your Old Man now—Old Chris—he's a good one.

ANNA: *(Skeptically)* He'll have to show me.

MARTHY: Yuh kept right on writing him yuh was a nurse girl still even after yuh was in the house, didn't yuh?

ANNA: Sure. *(Cynically)* Not that I think he'd care a darn.

MARTHY: Yuh're all wrong about him, kid. *(Earnestly)* I know Old Chris well for a long time. He's talked to me 'bout you lots o' times. He thinks the world o' you, honest he does.

ANNA: Aw, quit the kiddin'!

MARTHY: Honest! Only, he's a simple old guy, see? He's got nutty notions. But he means well, honest. Listen to me, kid—

(She is interrupted by the opening and shutting of the street door in the bar and by hearing CHRIS's voice.)

MARTHY: Ssshh!

ANNA: What's up?

CHRIS: *(Who has entered the bar. He seems considerably sobered up)* Py golly, Larry, dat grub taste good. Marthy in back?

LARRY: Sure—and another tramp with her.

(CHRIS *starts for the entrance to the back room.*)

MARTHY: *(To* ANNA *in a hurried, nervous whisper)* That's him now. He's comm' in here. Brace up!

ANNA: Who?

(CHRIS *opens the door.*)

MARTHY: *(As if she were greeting him for the first time)* Why hello, Old Chris.

(Then before he can speak, she shuffles hurriedly past him into the bar, beckoning him to follow her.)

MARTHY: Come here. I wanta tell yuh somethin'. *(He goes out to her. She speaks hurriedly in a low voice.)* Listen! I'm goin' to beat it down to the barge—pack up me duds and blow. That's her in there—your Anna—just come—waitin' for yuh. Treat her right, see? She's been sick. Well s'long! *(She goes into the back room—to* ANNA.*)* S'long, kid. I gotta beat it now. See yuh later.

ANNA: *(Nervously)* So long.

(MARTHY *goes quickly out of the family entrance.*)

LARRY: *(Looking at the stupefied* CHRIS *curiously)* Well, what's up now?

CHRIS: *(Vaguely)* Nutting—nutting.

(He stands before the door to the back room in an agony of embarrassed emotion—then he forces himself to a bold decision, pushes open the door and walks in. He stands there, casts a shy glance at ANNA, *whose brilliant clothes, and, to him, high-toned appearance, awe him terribly. He looks about him with pitiful nervousness as if to avoid the appraising look with which she takes in his face, his clothes, etc.— his voice seeming to plead for her forbearance.)*

CHRIS: Anna!

ANNA: *(Acutely embarrassed in her turn)* Hello—father. She told me it was you. I yust got here a little while ago.

CHRIS: *(Goes slowly over to her chair)* It's good—for see you— after all dem years, Anna.

(He bends down over her. After an embarrassed struggle they manage to kiss each other.)

ANNA: *(A trace of genuine feeling in her voice)* It's good to see you, too.

CHRIS: *(Grasps her arms and looks into her face—then overcome by a wave of fierce tenderness)* Anna lilla! Anna lilla! *(Takes her in his arms)*

ANNA: *(Shrinks away from him, half-frightened)* what's that —Swedish? I don't know it. *(Then as if seeking relief from the tension in a voluble chatter)* Gee, I had an awful trip up here. I'm all in. I had to sit up in the dirty coach all night—couldn't get no sleep, hardly—and then I had a hard job finding this place. I never been in New York before, you know, and—

CHRIS: *(Who has been staring down at her face admiringly, and not hearing what she says—impulsively)* You know you vas awful pooty gel, Anna? Ay bet all men see you fall in love with you, py yiminy!

ANNA: *(Repelled—harshly)* Cut it! You talk same as they all do.

CHRIS: *(Hurt—humbly)* Ain't no harm for your fader talk dat vay, Anna.

ANNA: *(Forcing a short laugh)* No—course not. Only—it's funny to see you and not remember nothing. You're like—a stranger.

CHRIS: *(Sadly)* Ay s'pose. Ay never come home only few times ven you vas kit in Sveden. You don't remember dat?

ANNA: No. *(Resentfully)* But why didn't you never come home them days? Why didn't you never come out West to see me?

CHRIS: *(Slowly)* Ay tank, after your mo'der die, ven Ay vas avay on voyage, it's better for you you don't never see me! *(He sinks down in the chair opposite her dejectedly—then turns to her—sadly.)* Ay don't know, Anna, vhy Ay never come home Sveden in ole year. Ay vant come home end of every voyage. Ay vant see your mo'der, your two bro'der before dey vas drowned, you ven you vas born—but—Ay don't go. Ay sign on oder ships—go South America, go Australia, go China, go every port all over world many times— but Ay never go aboard ship sail for Sveden. Ven Ay gat money for pay passage home as passenger den— *(He bows his head guiltily.)* Ay forgat and Ay spend all money. Ven Ay tank again, it's too late. *(He sighs.)* Ay don't know why but dat's vay with most sailor fallar, Anna. Dat ole davil sea make dem crazy fools with her dirty tricks. It's so.

ANNA: *(Who has watched him keenly while he has been speaking—with a trace of scorn in her voice)* Then you think the sea's to blame for everything, eh? Well, you're still workin' on it, ain't you, spite of all you used to write me about hating it. That dame was here told me you was captain of a coal barge—and you wrote me you was yanitor of a building!

CHRIS: *(Embarrassed but lying glibly)* Oh, Ay vork on land long time as yanitor. Yust short time ago Ay got dig yob cause Ay was sick, need open air.

ANNA: *(Skeptically)* Sick? You? You'd never think it.

CHRIS: And, Anna, dis ain't real sailor yob. Dis ain't real boat on sea. She's yust ole tub—like piece of land with house on it dat float. Yob on her ain't sea yob. No. Ay don't gat yob on sea, Anna, if Ay die first. Ay swear dat ven your mo'der die. Ay keep my word, py yingo!

ANNA: *(Perplexed)* Well, I can't see no difference. *(Dismissing the subject)* Speaking of being sick, I been there myself—yust out of the hospital two weeks ago.

CHRIS: *(Immediately all concern)* You, Anna? Py golly! *(Anxiously)* You feel better now, dough, don't you? You look tired, dat's all!

ANNA: *(Wearily)* I am. Tired to death. I need a long rest and I don't see much chance of getting it.

CHRIS: What you mean, Anna?

ANNA: Well, when I made up my mind to come to see you, I thought you was a yanitor—that you'd have a place where, maybe, if you didn't mind having me, I could visit a while and rest up—till I felt able to get back on the job again.

CHRIS: *(Eagerly)* But Ay gat place, Anna—nice place. You rest all you want, py yiminy! You don't never have to vork as nurse gel no more. You stay with me, py golly!

ANNA: *(Surprised and pleased by his eagerness—with a smile)* Then you're really glad to see me—honest?

CHRIS: *(Pressing one of her hands in both of his)* Anna, Ay like see you like hell, Ay tal you! And don't you talk no more about gatting yob. You stay with me. Ay don't see you for long time, you don't forgat dat. *(His voice trembles.)* Ay'm gatting ole. Ay gat no one in vorld but you.

ANNA: *(Touched—embarrassed by this unfamiliar emotion)* Thanks. It sounds good to hear someone—talk to me that way. Say, though—if you're so lonely—it's funny—why ain't you ever married again?

CHRIS: *(Shaking his head emphatically—after a pause)* Ay love your mo'der too much for ever do dat, Anna.

ANNA: *(Impressed—slowly)* I don't remember nothing about her. What was she like? Tell me.

CHRIS: Ay tal you all about everytang—and you tal me all tangs happen to you. But not here now. Dis ain't good for young gel, anyway. Only no good sailor fallar come here for gat drunk. *(He gets to his feet quickly and picks up her bag.)* You come with me, Anna. You need lie down, gat rest.

ANNA: *(Half rises to her feet, then sits down again)* Where're you going?

CHRIS: Come. Ve gat on board.

ANNA: *(Disappointedly)* On board your barge, you mean? *(Dryly)* Nix for mine! *(Then seeing his crestfallen look—forcing a smile)* Do you think that's a good place for a young girl like me—a coal barge?

CHRIS: *(Dully)* Yes, Ay tank. *(He hesitates—then continues more and more pleadingly.)* You don't know how nice it's on barge, Anna. Tug come and ve gat towed out on voyage—yust water all round, and sun, and fresh air, and good grub for make you strong, healthy gel. You see many tangs you don't see before. You gat moonlight at night, maybe; see steamer pass; see schooner make sail—see everytang dat's pooty. You need take rest like dat. You work too hard for young gel already. You need vacation, yes!

ANNA: *(Who has listened to him with a growing interest—with an uncertain laugh)* It sounds good to hear you tell it. I'd sure like a trip on the water, all right. It's the barge idea has me stopped. Well, I'll go down with you and have a look—maybe I'll take a chance. Gee, I'd do anything once.

CHRIS: *(Picks up her bag again)* Ve go, eh?

ANNA: What's the rush? Wait a second. *(Forgetting the situation for a moment, she relapses into the familiar form and flashes one of her winning trade smiles at him)* Gee, I'm thirsty.

CHRIS: *(Sets down her bag immediately—hastily)* Ay'm sorry, Anna. What you tank you like for drink, eh?

ANNA: *(Promptly)* I'll take a— *(Then suddenly reminded—confusedly)* I don't know. What'a they got here?

CHRIS: *(With a grin)* Ay don't tank dey got much fancy for young gel in dis place, Anna. Yinger ale—sas'prilla, maybe.

ANNA: *(Forcing a laugh herself)* Make it sas, then.

CHRIS: *(Coming up to her—with a wink)* Ay tal you, Anna, ve calabrate, yes—dis one time because ve meet after many year. *(In a half whisper, embarrassedly)* Dey gat good port vine, Anna. It's good for you, Ay tank—little bit—for give you appetite. It ain't strong, neider. One glass don't go to your head, Ay promise.

ANNA: *(With a half hysterical laugh)* All right. I'll take port.

CHRIS: Ay go gat him.

(He goes out to the bar. As soon as the door closes, ANNA *starts to her feet.)*

ANNA: *(Picking up her bag—half-aloud—stammeringly)* Gawd, I can't stand this! I better beat it. *(Then she lets her bag drop; stumbles over to her chair again, and covering her face with her hands, begins to sob.)*

LARRY: *(Putting down his paper as* CHRIS *comes up—with a grin)* Well, who's the blond?

CHRIS: *(Proudly)* Dat vas Anna, Larry.

LARRY: *(In amazement)* Your daughter, Anna?

*(*CHRIS *nods.* LARRY *lets a long, low whistle escape him and turns away embarrassedly.)*

CHRIS: Don't you tank she vas pooty gel, Larry?

LARRY: *(Rising to the occasion)* Sure! A peach!

CHRIS: You bet you! Give me drink for take back—one port vine for Anna—she calabrate dis one time with me—and small beer for me.

LARRY: *(As he gets the drinks)* Small beer for you, eh? She's reformin' you already.

CHRIS: *(Pleased)* You bet!

(He takes the drinks. As she hears him coming, ANNA hastily dries her eyes, tries to smile. CHRIS comes in and sets the drinks down on the table—stares at her for a second anxiously—patting her hand.)

CHRIS: You look tired, Anna. Veil, Ay make you take good long rest now. *(Picking up his beer)* Come, you drink vine. It put new life in you.

(She lifts her glass—he grins.)

CHRIS: Skoal, Anna! You know dat Svedish word?

ANNA: Skoal! *(Downing her port at a gulp like a drink of whisky—her lips trembling)* Skoal? Guess I know that word, all right!

(The curtain falls.)

END OF ACT ONE

ACT TWO

(Ten days later. The stern of the deeply-laden barge, Simeon Winthrop, *at anchor in the outer harbor of Provincetown, Mass. It is ten o'clock at night. Dense fog shrouds the barge on all sides, and she floats motionless on a calm. A lantern set up on an immense coil of thick hawser sheds a dull, filtering light on objects near it—the heavy steel bits for making fast the tow lines, etc. In the rear is the cabin, its misty windows glowing wanly with the light of a lamp inside. The chimney of the cabin stove rises a few feet above the roof. The doleful tolling of bells, on Long Point, on ships at anchor, breaks the silence at regular intervals. As the curtain rises* ANNA *is discovered standing near the coil of rope on which the lantern is placed. She looks healthy, transformed, the natural color has come back to her face. She has on a black oilskin coat, but wears no hat. She is staring out into the fog astern with an expression of awed wonder. The cabin door is pushed open and* CHRIS *appears. He is dressed in yellow oilskins—coat, pants, sou'wester—and wears high sea-boots.)*

CHRIS: *(The glare from the cabin still in his eyes, peers blinkingly astern)* Anna! *(Receiving no reply, he calls again, this time with apparent apprehension.)* Anna!

ANNA: *(With a start—making a gesture with her hand as if to impose silence—in a hushed whisper)* Yes, here I am. What d'you want?

CHRIS: *(Walks over to her—solicitously)* Don't you come turn in, Anna? It's late—after four bells. It ain't good for you stay out here in fog, Ay tank.

ANNA: Why not? *(With a trace of strange exultation)* I love this fog! Honest! It's so— *(She hesitates, groping for a word.)* Funny and still. I feel as if I was—out of things altogether.

CHRIS: *(Spitting disgustedly)* Fog's vorst one of her dirty tricks, py yingo!

ANNA: *(With a short laugh)* Beefing about the sea again? I'm getting so's I love it, the little I've seen.

CHRIS: *(Glancing at her moodily)* Dat's foolish talk, Anna. You see her more, you don't talk dat vay. *(Then seeing her irritation, he hastily adopts a more cheerful tone.)* But Ay'm glad you like it on barge. Ay'm glad it makes you feel good again. *(With a placating grin)* You like live like dis alone with ole fa'der, eh?

ANNA: Sure I do. Everything's been so different from anything I ever come across before. And now—this fog—Gee, I wouldn't have missed it for nothing. I never thought living on ships was so different from land. Gee, I'd yust love to work on it, honest I would, if I was a man. I don't wonder you always been a sailor.

CHRIS: *(Vehemently)* Ay ain't sailor, Anna. And dis ain't real sea. You only see nice part. *(Then as she doesn't answer, he continues hopefully.)* Vell, fog lift in morning, Ay tank.

ANNA: *(The exultation again in her voice)* I love it! I don't give a rap if it never lifts!

(CHRIS *fidgets from one foot to the other worriedly.* ANNA *continues slowly, after a pause.)*

ANNA: It makes me feel clean—out here—'s if I'd taken a bath.

CHRIS: *(After a pause)* You better go in cabin read book. Dat put you to sleep.

ANNA: I don't want to sleep. I want to stay out here—and think about things.

CHRIS: *(Walk: away from her toward the cabin—then comes back)* You act funny tonight, Anna.

ANNA: *(Her voice rising angrily)* Say, what're you trying to do—make things rotten? You been kind as kind can be to me and I certainly appreciate it—only don't spoil it all now. *(Then, seeing the hurt expression on her father's face, she forces a smile.)* Let's talk of something else. Come. Sit down here. *(She points to the coil of rope.)*

CHRIS: *(Sits down beside her with a sigh)* It's gatting pooty late in night, Anna. Must be near five bells.

ANNA: *(Interestedly)* Five bells? What time is that?

CHRIS: Half past ten.

ANNA: Funny I don't know nothing about sea talk—but those cousins was always talking crops and that stuff. Gee, wasn't I sick of it—and of them!

CHRIS: You don't like live on farm, Anna?

ANNA: I've told you a hundred times I hated it. *(Decidedly)* I'd rather have one drop of ocean than all the farms in the world! Honest! And you wouldn't like a farm, neither. Here's where you belong. *(She makes a sweeping gesture seaward.)* But not on a coal barge. You belong on a real ship, sailing all over the world.

CHRIS: *(Moodily)* Ay've done dat many year, Anna, when Ay vas damn fool.

ANNA: *(Disgustedly)* Oh, rats! *(After a pause she speaks musingly.)* Was the men in our family always sailors—as far back as you know about?

CHRIS: *(Shortly)* Yes. Damn fools! All men in our village on coast, Sveden, go to sea. Ain't nutting else for dem to do. My fa'der die on board ship in Indian Ocean. He's buried at sea. Ay don't never know him only little bit. Den my tree bro'der, older'n me, dey go on ships. Den Ay go, too. Den my mo'der she's left all 'lone. She die pooty quick after dat—all 'lone. Ve vas all avay on voyage when she die. *(He pauses sadly.)* Two my bro'der dey gat lost on fishing boat same like your bro'ders vas drowned. My oder bro'der, he save money, give up sea, den he die home in bed. He's only one dat ole davil don't kill. *(Defiantly)* But me, Ay bet you Ay die ashore in bed, too!

ANNA: Were all of 'em yust plain sailors?

CHRIS: Able body seaman, most of dem. *(With a certain pride)* Dey vas all smart seaman, too—A one. *(Then after hesitating a moment—shyly)* Ay vas bo'sun.

ANNA: Bo'sun?

CHRIS: Dat's kind of officer.

ANNA: Gee, that was fine. What does he do?

CHRIS: *(After a second's hesitation, plunged into gloom again by his fear of her enthusiasm)* Hard vork all time. It's rotten, Ay tal you, for go to sea. *(Determined to disgust her with sea life—volubly)* Dey're all fool falla; dem fallar in our family. Dey all vork rotten yob on sea for nutting, don't care nutting but yust gat big pay day in pocket, gat drunk, gat robbed, ship avay again on oder voyage. Dey don't come home. Dey don't do anytang like good man do. And dat ole davil, sea, sooner, later she svallow dem up.

ANNA: *(With an excited laugh)* Good sports, I'd call 'em. *(Then hastily)* But say—listen—did all the women of the family marry sailors?

CHRIS: *(Eagerly—seeing a chance to drive home his point)* Yes—and it's bad on dem like hell vorst of all. Dey don't see deir men only once in long while. Dey set and vait all 'lone. And vhen deir boys grows up, go to sea, dey sit and vait some more. *(Vehemently)* Any gel marry sailor, she's crazy fool! Your mo'der she tal you same tang if she vas alive. *(He relapses into an attitude of somber brooding.)*

ANNA: *(After a pause—dreamily)* Funny! I do feel sort of—nutty, tonight. I feel old.

CHRIS: *(Mystified)* Ole?

ANNA: Sure—like I'd been living a long, long time—out here in the fog. *(Frowning perplexedly)* I don't know how to tell you yust what I mean. It's like I'd come home after a visit away some place. It all seems like I'd been here before lots of times—on boats—in this same fog. *(With a short laugh)* You must think I'm off my base.

CHRIS: *(Gruffly)* Anybody feel funny dat vay in fog.

ANNA: *(Persistently)* But why d'you s'pose I feel so—so—like I'd found something I'd missed and been looking for—'s if this was the right place for me to fit in? And I seem to have forgot—everything that's happened—like it didn't matter no more. And I feel clean, somehow—like you feel yust after you've took a bath. And I feel happy for once—yes, honest!— happier than I ever been anywhere before!

(As CHRIS *makes no comment but a heavy sigh, she continues wonderingly.)*

ANNA: It's nutty for me to feel that way, don't you think?

CHRIS: *(A grim foreboding in his voice)* Ay tank Ay'm damn fool for bring you on voyage, Anna.

ANNA: *(Impressed by his tone)* You talk—nutty tonight yourself. You act 's if you was scared something was going to happen.

CHRIS: Only God know dat, Anna.

ANNA: *(Half-mockingly)* Then it'll be Gawd's will, like the preachers say—what does happen.

CHRIS: *(Starts to his feet with fierce protest)* No! Dat ole davil, sea, she ain't God!

(In the pause of silence that comes after his defiance a hail in a man's husky, exhausted voice comes faintly out of the fog to port: "Ahoy!" CHRIS *gives a startled exclamation.)*

ANNA: *(Jumping to her feet)* What's that?

CHRIS: *(Who has regained his composure—sheepishly)* Py golly, dat scare me for minute. It's only some fallar hail, Anna—loose his course in fog. Must be fisherman's power boat. His engine break down, Ay guess.

(The "ahoy" comes again through the wall of fog, sounding much nearer this time. CHRIS *goes over to the port bulwark.)*

CHRIS: Sound from dis side. She come in from open sea. *(He holds his hands to his mouth, megaphone-fashion, and shouts back.)* Ahoy, dere! Vhat's trouble?

THE VOICE: *(This time sounding nearer but up forward toward the bow)* Heave a rope when we come alongside. *(Then, irritably)* Where are ye, ye scut?

CHRIS: Ay hear dem rowing. Dey come up by bow, Ay tank. *(Then shouting out again)* Dis ray!

THE VOICE: Right ye are!

(There is a muffled sound of oars in oar-locks.)

ANNA: *(Half to herself—resentfully)* why don't that guy stay where he belongs?

CHRIS: *(Hurriedly)* Ay go up bow. All hands asleep 'cepting fallar on vatch. Ay gat heave line to dat fallar.

(He picks up a coil of rope and hurries off toward the bow. ANNA *walks back toward the extreme stern as if she wanted to remain as much isolated as possible. She turns*

her back on the proceedings and stares out into the fog. THE VOICE *is heard again shouting "Ahoy" and* CHRIS *answering "Dis vay." Then there is a pause—the murmur of excited voices—then the scuffling of feet.* CHRIS *appears from around the cabin to port. He is supporting the limp form of a man dressed in dungarees, holding one of the man's arms around his neck. The deckhand,* JOHNSON, *a young blond Swede, follows him, helping along another exhausted man in a similar fashion.* ANNA *turns to look at them.* CHRIS *stops for a second—volubly.)*

CHRIS: Anna! You come help, vill you? You find vhisky in cabin. Dese fallars need drink for fix dem. Dey vas near dead.

ANNA: *(Hurrying to him)* Sure—but who are they? What's the trouble?

CHRIS: Sailor fallars. Deir steamer gat wrecked. Dey been five days in open boat—four fallars—only one left able stand up. Come, Anna.

(She precedes him into the cabin, holding the door open while he and JOHNSON *carry in their burdens. The door is shut then opened again as* JOHNSON *comes out.* CHRIS' *voice shouts after him.)*

CHRIS: Go gat oder fallar, Yohnson.

JOHNSON: Yes, sir.

(He goes. The door is closed again. MAT BURKE *stumbles in around the port side of the cabin. He moves slowly, feeling his way uncertainly, keeping hold of the port bulwark with his right hand to steady himself. He is stripped to the waist, has on nothing but a pair of dirty dungaree pants. He is a powerful, broad-chested six-footer, his face handsome in a hard, rough, bold, defiant way. He is about thirty, in the full power of his heavy-muscled, immense strength. His dark eyes are bloodshot and wild from sleeplessness. The muscles of his arms and shoulders are lumped in knots and bunches, the veins of his forearms stand out like blue cords. He finds his way to the coil of hawser and sits down on it facing the cabin, his back bowed, head in his hands, in an attitude of spent weariness.)*

BURKE: *(Talking aloud to himself)* Row, ye divil! Row! *(Then lifting his head and looking about him)* What's this tub? Well, we're safe anyway—with the help of God.

(He makes the sign of the cross mechanically. JOHNSON *comes along the deck to port, supporting the fourth man, who is babbling to himself incoherently.* BURKE *glances at him disdainfully.)*

BURKE: Is it losing the small wits ye iver had, ye are? Deck-scrubbing scut!

(They pass him and go into the cabin, leaving the door open. BURKE *sags forward wearily.)*

BURKE: I'm bate out—bate out entirely.

ANNA: *(Comes out of the cabin with a tumbler quarter-full of whisky in her hand. She gives a start when she sees* BURKE *so near her, the light from the open door falling full on him. Then, overcoming what is evidently a feeling of repulsion, she comes up beside him.)* Here you are. Here's a drink for you. You need it, I guess.

BURKE: *(Lifting his head slowly—confusedly)* Is it dreaming I am?

ANNA: *(Half smiling)* Drink it and you'll find it ain't no dream.

BURKE: To hell with the drink—but I'll take it just the same. *(He tosses it down.)* Ahah! I'm needin' that—and 'tis fine stuff. *(Looking up at her with frank, grinning admiration)* But 'twasn't the booze I meant when I said, was I dreaming. I thought you was some mermaid out of the sea come to torment me. *(He reaches out to feel of her arm.)* Aye, rale flesh and blood, divil a less.

ANNA: *(Coldly. Stepping back from him)* Cut that.

BURKE: But tell me, isn't this a barge I'm on—or isn't it?

ANNA: Sure.

BURKE: And what is a fine handsome woman the like of you doing on this scow?

ANNA: *(Coldly)* Never you mind. *(Then half amused in spite of herself)* Say, you're a great one, honest—starting right in kidding after what you been through.

BURKE: *(Delighted—proudly)* Ah, it was nothing—aisy for a rale man with guts to him, the like of me. *(He laughs.)* All in the day's work, darlin'. *(Then, more seriously but still in a boastful tone, confidentially)* But I won't be denying 'twas a damn narrow squeak. We'd all ought to be with Davy Jones at the bottom of the sea, be rights. And only for me, I'm telling you, and the great strength and guts is in me, we'd be being scoffed by the fishes this minute!

ANNA: *(Contemptuously)* Gee, you hate yourself, don't you? *(Then turning away from him indifferently)* Well, you'd better come in and lie down. You must want to sleep.

BURKE: *(Stung—rising unsteadily to his feet with chest out and head thrown back—resentfully)* Lie down and sleep, is it? Divil a wink I'm after having for two days and nights and divil a bit I'm needing now. Let you not be thinking I'm the like of them three weak scuts come in the boat with me. I could lick the three of them sitting down with one hand tied behind me. They may be bate out, but I'm not—and I've been rowing the boat with them lying in the bottom not able to raise a hand for the last two days we was in it. *(Furiously, as he sees this is making no impression on her)* And I can lick all hands on this tub, wan be wan, tired as I am!

ANNA: *(Sarcastically)* Gee, ain't you a hard guy! *(Then, with a trace of sympathy, as she notices him swaying from weakness)* But never mind that fight talk: I'll take your word for all you've said. Go on and sit down out here, anyway, if I can't get you to come inside.

(He sits down weakly.)

ANNA: You're all in, you might as well own up to it.

BURKE: *(Fiercely)* The hell I am!

ANNA: *(Coldly)* Well, be stubborn then for all I care. And I must say I don't care for your language. The men I know don't pull that rough stuff when ladies are around.

BURKE: *(Getting unsteadily to his feet again—in a rage)* Ladies! Ho-ho! Divil mend you! Let you not be making game of me. What would ladies be doing on this bloody hulk?

(As ANNA attempts to go to the cabin, he lurches into her path.)

BURKE: Aisy, now! You're not the old Squarehead's woman, I suppose you'll be telling me next—living in his cabin with him, no less!

(Seeing the cold, hostile expression on ANNA's face, he suddenly changes his tone to one of boisterous joviality.)

BURKE: But I do be thinking, iver since the first look my eyes took at you, that it's a fool you are to be wasting yourself—a fine, handsome girl—on a stumpy runt of a man like that old Swede. There's too many strapping great lads on the sea would give their heart's blood for one kiss of you.

ANNA: *(Scornfully)* Lads like you, eh?

BURKE: *(Grinning)* Ye take the words out o' my mouth. I'm the proper lad for you, if it's meself do be saying it. *(With a quick movement he puts his arms about her waist.)* Whisht, now, me daisy! Himself's in the cabin. It's wan of your kisses I'm needing to take the tiredness from me bones. Wan kiss, now!

(He presses her to him and attempts to kiss her.)

ANNA: *(Struggling fiercely)* Leggo of me, you big mutt!

(She pushes him away with all her might. BURKE, weak and tottering, is caught off his guard. He is thrown down backward and, in falling, hits his head a hard thump against the bulwark. He lies there still, knocked out for the moment. ANNA stands for a second, looking down at him frightenedly. Then she kneels down beside him and raises his head to her knee, staring into his face anxiously for some sign of life.)

BURKE: *(Stirring a bit—mutteringly)* God stiffen it! *(He opens his eyes and blinks up at her with vague wonder.)*

ANNA: *(Letting his head sink back on the deck, rising to her feet with a sigh of relief)* You're coming to all right, eh? Gee, I was scared for a moment I'd killed you.

BURKE: *(With difficulty rising to a sitting position—scornfully)* Killed, is it? It'd take more than a bit of a blow to crack my thick skull. *(Then looking at her with the most intense admiration)* But, glory be, it's a power of strength is in them two fine arms of yours. There's not a man in the world can say the same as you, that he seen Mat Burke lying at his feet and him dead to the world.

ANNA: *(Rather remorsefully)* Forget it. I'm sorry it happened, see?

(BURKE *rises and sits on bench. Then severely:*)

ANNA: Only you had no right to be getting fresh with me. Listen, now, and don't go getting any more wrong notions. I'm on this barge because I'm making a trip with my father. The captain's my father. Now you know.

BURKE: The old square—the old Swede, I mean?

ANNA: Yes.

BURKE: *(Rising—peering at her face)* Sure I might have known it, if I wasn't a bloody fool from birth. Where else'd you get that fine yellow hair is like a golden crown on your head.

ANNA: *(With an amused laugh)* Say, nothing stops you, does it? *(Then attempting a severe tone again)* But don't you think you ought to be apologizing for what you said and done yust a minute ago, instead of trying to kid me with that mush?

BURKE: *(Indignantly)* Mush! *(Then bending forward toward her with very intense earnestness)* Indade and I will ask your pardon a thousand times—and on my knees, if ye like. I didn't mean a word of what I said or did. *(Resentful again for a second)* But divil a woman in all the ports of the world has iver made a great fool of me that way before!

ANNA: *(With amused sarcasm)* I see. You mean you're a lady-killer and they all fall for you.

BURKE: *(Offended. Passionately)* Leave off your fooling! 'Tis that is after getting my back up at you. *(Earnestly)* 'Tis no lie I'm telling you about the women. *(Ruefully)* Though it's a great jackass I am to be mistaking you, even in anger, for the like of them cows on the waterfront is the only women I've met up with since I was growed to a man.

(As ANNA *shrinks away from him at this, he hurries on pleadingly.*)

BURKE: I'm a hard, rough man and I'm not fit, I'm thinking, to be kissing the shoe-soles of a fine, dacent girl the like of yourself 'Tis only the ignorance of your kind made me see you wrong. So you'll forgive me, for the love of God, and let us be friends from this out. *(Passionately)* I'm thinking I'd rather be friends with you than have my wish for anything else in the world. *(He holds out his hand to her shyly.)*

ANNA: *(Looking queerly at him, perplexed and worried, but moved and pleased in spite of herself—takes his hand uncertainly)* Sure.

BURKE: *(With boyish delight)* God bless you! *(In his excitement he squeezes her hand tight.)*

ANNA: Ouch!

BURKE: *(Hastily dropping her hand—ruefully)* Your pardon, Miss. 'Tis a clumsy ape I am. *(Then simply—glancing down his arm proudly)* It's great power I have in my hand and arm, and I do be forgetting it at times.

ANNA: *(Nursing her crushed hand and glancing at his arm, not without a trace of his own admiration)* Gee, you're some strong, all right.

BURKE: *(Delighted)* It's no lie, and why shouldn't I be, with me shoveling a million tons of coal in the stokeholes of 'ships since I was a lad only. *(He pats the coil of hawser invitingly.)* Let you sit down, now, Miss, and I'll be telling you a bit of myself, and you'll be telling me a bit of yourself, and in an hour we'll be as old friends as if we was born in the same house. *(He pulls at her sleeve shyly.)* Sit down now, if you plaze.

ANNA: *(With a half laugh)* Well— *(She sits down.)* But we won't talk about me, see? You tell me about yourself and about the wreck.

BURKE: *(Flattered)* I'll tell you, surely. But can I be asking you one question, Miss, has my head in a puzzle?

ANNA: *(Guardedly)* Well—I dunno—what is it?

BURKE: What is it you do when you're not taking a trip with the Old Man? For I'm thinking a fine girl the like of you ain't living always on this tub.

ANNA: *(Uneasily)* No—of course I ain't.

(She searches his face suspiciously, afraid there may be some hidden insinuation in his words. Seeing his simple frankness, she goes on confidently.)

ANNA: Well, I'll tell you. I'm a governess, see? I take care of kids for people and learn them things.

BURKE: *(Impressed)* A governess, is it? You must be smart, surely.

ANNA: But let's not talk about me. Tell me about the wreck, like you promised me you would.

BURKE: *(Importantly)* 'Twas this way, Miss. Two weeks out we ran into the divil's own storm, and she sprang wan hell of a leak up for'ard. The skipper was hoping to make Boston before another blow would finish her, but ten days back we met up with another storm the like of the first, only worse. Four days we was in it with green seas raking over her from bow to stern. That was a terrible time, God help us. *(Proudly)* And if 'twasn't for me and my great strength, I'm telling you— and it's God's truth—there'd been mutiny itself in the stokehole. 'Twas me held them to it, with a kick to wan and a clout to another, and they not caring a damn for the engineers any more, but fearing a clout of my right arm more than they'd fear the sea itself. *(He glances at her anxiously, eager for her approval.)*

ANNA: *(Concealing a smile—amused by this boyish boasting of his)* You did some hard work, didn't you?

BURKE: *(Promptly)* I did that! I'm a divil for sticking it out when them that's weak give up. But much good it did anyone! 'Twas a mad, fightin' scramble in the last seconds with each man for himself. I disremember how it come about, but there was the four of us in wan boat and when we was raised high on a great wave I took a look about and divil a sight there was of ship or men on top of the sea.

ANNA: *(In a subdued voice)* Then all the others was drowned?

BURKE: They was, surely.

ANNA: *(With a shudder)* What a terrible end!

BURKE: *(Turns to her)* A terrible end for the like of them swabs does live on land, maybe. But for the like of us does be roaming the seas, a good end, I'm telling you—quick and clane.

ANNA: *(Struck by the word)* Yes, clean. That's yust the word for—all of it—the way it makes me feel.

BURKE: The sea, you mean? *(Interestedly)* I'm thinking you have a bit of it in your blood, too. Your Old Man wasn't only a barge rat—begging your pardon—all his life, by the cut of him.

ANNA: No, he was bo'sun on sailing ships for years. And all the men on both sides of the family have gone to sea as far back as he remembers, he says. All the women have married sailors, too.

BURKE: *(With intense satisfaction)* Did they, now? They had spirit in them. It's only on the sea you'd find rale men with guts is fit to wed with fine, high-tempered girls *(Then he adds half-boldly)* the like of yourself.

ANNA: *(With a laugh)* There you go kiddin' again. *(Then seeing his hurt expression—quickly)* But you was going to tell me about yourself. You're Irish, of course I can tell that.

BURKE: *(Stoutly)* Yes, thank God, though I've not seen a sight of it in fifteen years or more.

ANNA: *(Thoughtfully)* Sailors never do go home hardly, do they? That's what my father was saying.

BURKE: He wasn't telling no lie. *(With sudden melancholy)* It's a hard and lonesome life, the sea is. The only women you'd meet in the ports of the world who'd be willing to speak you a kind word isn't woman at all. You know the kind I mane, and they're a poor, wicked lot, God forgive them. They're looking to steal the money from you only.

ANNA: *(Her face averted—rising to her feet—agitatedly)* I think—I guess I'd better see what's doing inside.

BURKE: *(Afraid he has offended her—beseechingly)* Don't go, I'm saying! Is it I've given you offense with my talk of the like of them? Don't heed it at all! I'm clumsy in my wits when it comes to talking proper with a girl the like of you. And why wouldn't I be? Since the day I left home for to go to sea punching coal this is the first time I've had a word with a rale, dacent woman. So don't turn your back on me now, and we beginning to be friends.

ANNA: *(Turning to him again—forcing a smile)* I'm not sore at you, honest.

BURKE: *(Gratefully)* God bless you!

ANNA: *(Changing the subject abruptly)* But if you honestly think the sea's such a rotten life, why don't you get out of it?

BURKE: *(Surprised)* Work on land, is it?

(She nods. He spits scornfully.)

BURKE: Digging spuds in the muck from dawn to dark, I suppose? *(Vehemently)* I wasn't made for it, Miss.

ANNA: *(With a laugh)* I thought you'd say that.

BURKE: *(Argumentatively)* But there's good jobs and bad jobs at sea, like there'd be on land. I'm thinking if it's in the stokehole of a proper liner I was, I'd be able to have a little house and be home to it wan week out of four. And I'm thinking that maybe then I'd have the luck to find a fine dacent girl—the like of yourself, now—would be willing to wed with me.

ANNA: *(Turning away from him with a short laugh—uneasily)* Why, sure. Why not?

BURKE: *(Edging up close to her—exultantly)* Then you think a girl the like of yourself might maybe not mind the past at all but only be seeing the good herself put in me?

ANNA: *(In the same tone)* Why, sure.

BURKE: *(Passionately)* She'd not be sorry for it, I'd take my oath! 'Tis no more drinking and roving about I'd be doing then, but giving my pay day into her hand and staying at home with her as meek as a lamb each night of the week I'd be in port.

ANNA: *(Moved in spite of herself and troubled by this half-concealed proposal—with a forced laugh)* All you got to do is find the girl.

BURKE: I have found her!

ANNA: *(Half-frightenedly—trying to laugh it off)* You have? When? I thought you was saying—

BURKE: *(Boldly and forcefully)* This night. *(Hanging his head—humbly)* If she'll be having me. *(Then raising his eyes to hers—simply)* 'Tis you' I mean.

ANNA: *(Is held by his eyes for a moment—then shrinks back from him with a strange, broken laugh)* Say—are you—going crazy? Are you trying to kid me? Proposing—to me !—for Gawd's sake !—on such short acquaintance?

(CHRIS *comes out of the cabin and stands staring blinkingly astern. When he makes out* ANNA *in such intimate proximity to this strange sailor, an angry expression comes over his face.*)

BURKE: *(Following her—with fierce, pleading insistence)* I'm telling you there's the will of God in it that brought me safe through the storm and fog to the wan spot in the world where you was! Think of that now, and isn't it queer—

CHRIS: Anna! *(He comes toward them, raging, his fists clenched)* Anna, you gat in cabin, you hear!

ANNA: *(All her emotions immediately transformed into resentment at his bullying tone)* Who d'you think you're talking to—a slave?

CHRIS: *(Hurt—his voice breaking—pleadingly)* You need gat rest, Anna. You gat sleep.

(*She does not move. He turns on* BURKE *furiously.*)

CHRIS: What you doing here, you sailor fallar? You ain't sick like oders. You gat in fo'c's'tle. Dey give you bunk. *(Threateningly)* You hurry, Ay tal you!

ANNA: *(Impulsively)* But he is sick. Look at him. He can hardly stand up.

BURKE: *(Straightening and throwing out his chest—with a bold laugh)* Is it giving me orders ye are, me bucko? Let you look out, then! With wan hand, weak as I am, I can break ye in two and fling the pieces over the side—and your crew after you. *(Stopping abruptly)* I was forgetting. You're her Old Man and I'd not raise a fist to you for the world.

(*His knees sag, he wavers and seems about to fall.* ANNA *utters an exclamation of alarm and hurries to his side.*)

ANNA: *(Taking one of his arms over her shoulder)* Come on in the cabin. You can have my bed if there ain't no other place.

BURKE: *(With jubilant happiness—as they proceed toward the cabin)* Glory be to God, is it holding my arm about your neck you are! Anna! Anna! Sure it's a sweet name is suited to you.

ANNA: *(Guiding him carefully)* Sssh! Sssh!

BURKE: Whisht, is it? Indade, and I'll not. I'll be roaring it out like a fog horn over the sea! You're the girl of the world and we'll be marrying soon and I don't care who knows it!

ANNA: *(As she guides him through the cabin door)* Ssshh! Never mind that talk. You go to sleep.

(They go out of sight in the cabin. CHRIS, who has been listening to BURKE's last words with open-mouthed amazement stands looking after them desperately.)

CHRIS: *(Turns suddenly and shakes his fist out at the sea—with bitter hatred)* Dat's your dirty trick, damn ole davil, you! *(Then in a frenzy of rage)* But, py God, you don't do dat! Not while Ay'm living! No, py God, you don't!

(The curtain falls.)

END OF ACT TWO

ACT THREE

(*The interior of the cabin on the barge,* Simeon Winthrop *[at dock in Boston]*—*a narrow, low-ceilinged compartment the walls of which are painted a light brown with white trimmings. In the rear on the left, a door leading to the sleeping quarters. In the far left corner, a large locker-closet, painted white, on the door of which a mirror hangs on a nail. In the rear wall, two small square windows and a door opening out on the deck toward the stern. In the right wall, two more windows looking out on the port deck. White curtains, clean and stiff, are at the windows. A table with two cane-bottomed chairs stands in the center of the cabin. A dilapidated, wicker rocker, painted brown, is also by the table.*)

(*It is afternoon of a sunny day about a week later. From the harbor and docks outside, muffled by the closed door and windows, comes the sound of steamers' whistles and the puffing snort of the donkey engines of some ship unloading nearby.*)

(*As the curtain rises,* CHRIS *and* ANNA *are discovered.* ANNA *is seated in the rocking-chair by the table, with a newspaper in her hands. She is not reading but staring straight in front of her. She looks unhappy, troubled, frowningly concentrated on her thoughts.* CHRIS *wanders about the room, casting quick, uneasy side glances at her face, then stopping to peer absent-mindedly out of the window. His attitude betrays an overwhelming, gloomy anxiety which has him on tenterhooks. He pretends to be engaged in setting things shipshape, but this occupation is confined to picking up some object, staring at it stupidly for a second, then aimlessly putting it down again. He clears his throat and starts to sing to himself in a low, doleful voice:*)

CHRIS: "My Yosephine, come board de ship. Long time Ay vait for you."

ANNA: (*Turning on him, sarcastically*) I'm glad someone's feeling good. (*Wearily*) Gee, I sure wish we was out of this dump and back in New York.

CHRIS: (*With a sigh*) Ay'm glad vhen ve sail again, too. (*Then, as she makes no comment, he goes on with a ponderous attempt at sarcasm.*) Ay don't see vhy you don't like Boston, dough. You have good time here, Ay tank. You go ashore all time, every day and night veek ve've been here. You go to movies, see show, gat all kinds fun— (*His eyes hard with hatred*) All with that damn Irish fallar!

ANNA: (*With weary scorn*) Oh, for heaven's sake, are you off on that again? Where's the harm in his taking me around? D'you want me to sit all day and night in this cabin with you—and knit? Ain't I got a right to have as good a time as I can?

CHRIS: It ain't right kind of fun—not with that fallar, no.

ANNA: I been back on board every night by eleven, ain't I? *(Then struck by some thought—looks at him with keen suspicion—with rising anger)* Say, look here, what d'you mean by what you yust said?

CHRIS: *(Hastily)* Nutting but what Ay say, Anna.

ANNA: You said "ain't right" and you said it funny. Say, listen here, you ain't trying to insinuate that there's something wrong between us, are you?

CHRIS: *(Horrified)* No, Anna! No, Ay svear to God, Ay never tank dat!

ANNA: *(Mollified by his very evident sincerity—sitting down again)* Well, don't you never think it neither if you want me ever to speak to you again. *(Angrily again)* If I ever dreamt you thought that, I'd get the hell out of this barge so quick you couldn't see me for dust.

CHRIS: *(Soothingly)* Ay wouldn't never dream— *(Then after a second's pause, reprovingly)* You vas gatting learn to svear. Dat ain't nice for young gel, you tank?

ANNA: *(With a faint trace of a smile)* Excuse me. You ain't used to such language, I know. *(Mockingly)* That's what your taking me to sea has done for me.

CHRIS: *(Indignantly)* No, it ain't me. It's dat damn sailor fallar learn you bad tangs.

ANNA: He ain't a sailor. He's a stoker.

CHRIS: *(Forcibly)* Dat vas million times vorse, Ay tal you! Dem fallars dat vork below shoveling coal vas de dirtiest, rough gang of no-good fallars in vorld!

ANNA: I'd hate to hear you say that to Mat.

CHRIS: Oh, Ay tal him same tang. You don't gat it in head Ay'm scared of him yust 'cause he vas stronger'n Ay vas. *(Menacingly)* You don't gat for fight with fists with dem fallars. Dere's oder vay for fix him.

ANNA: *(Glancing at him with sudden alarm)* What d'you mean?

CHRIS: *(Sullenly)* Nutting.

ANNA: You'd better not. I wouldn't start no trouble with him if I was you. He might forget some time that you was old and my father—and then you'd be out of luck.

CHRIS: *(With smoldering hatred)* Veil, yust let him! Ay'm ole bird maybe, but Ay bet Ay show him trick or two.

ANNA: *(Suddenly changing her tone—persuasively)* Aw come on, be good. What's eating you, anyway? Don't you want no one to be nice to me except yourself?

CHRIS: *(Placated—coming to her—eagerly)* Yes, Ay do, Anna—only not fallar on sea. But Ay like for you marry steady fallar got good yob on land. You have little home in country all your own—

ANNA: *(Rising to her feet—brusquely)* Oh, cut it out! *(Scornfully)* Little home in the country! I wish you could have seen the little home in the country where you had me in jail till I was sixteen! *(With rising irritation)* Some day you're going to get me so mad with that talk, I'm going to turn loose on you and tell you—a lot of things that'll open your eyes.

CHRIS: *(Alarmed)* I don't want—

ANNA: I know you don't; but you keep on talking yust the same.

CHRIS: Ay don't talk no more den, Anna.

ANNA: Then promise me you'll cut out saying nasty things about Mat Burke every chance you get.

CHRIS: *(Evasive and suspicious)* Vhy? You like dat fallar—very much, Anna?

ANNA: Yes, I certainly do! He's a regular man, no matter what faults he's got. One of his fingers is worth all the hundreds of men I met out there—inland.

CHRIS: *(His face darkening)* Maybe you tank you love him, den?

ANNA: *(Defiantly)* What of it if I do?

CHRIS: *(Scowling and forcing out the words)* Maybe—you tank you—marry him?

ANNA: *(Shaking her head)* No!

(CHRIS' *face lights up with relief.*)

ANNA: *Continues slowly, a trace of sadness in her voice)* If I'd met him four years ago—or even two years ago—I'd have jumped at the chance, I tell you that straight. And I would now—only he's such a simple guy—a big kid—and I ain't got the heart to fool him. *(She breaks off suddenly.)* But don't never say again he ain't good enough for me. It's me ain't good enough for him.

CHRIS: *(Snorts scornfully)* Py yiminy, you go crazy, Ay tank!

ANNA: *(With a mournful laugh)* Well, I been thinking I was myself the last few days. *(She goes and takes a shawl from a hook near the door and throws it over her shoulders.)* Guess I'll take a walk down to the end of the dock for a minute and see what's doing. I love to watch the ships passing. Mat'll be along before long, I guess. Tell him where I am, will you?

CHRIS: *(Despondently)* All right, Ay tal him.

(ANNA *goes out the doorway on rear.* CHRIS *follows her out and stands on the deck outside for a moment looking after her. Then he comes back inside and shuts the door. He stands looking out of the window—mutters—"Dirty ole davil, you."*)

Then he goes to the table, sets the cloth straight mechanically, picks up the newspaper ANNA *has let fall to the floor and sits down in the rocking-chair. He stares at the paper for a while, then puts it on the table, holds his head in his hands and sighs drearily. The noise of a man's heavy footsteps comes from the deck outside and there is a loud knock on the door.* CHRIS *starts, makes a move as if to get up and go to the door, then thinks better of it and sits still. The knock is repeated— then as no answer comes, the door is flung open and* BURKE *appears.* CHRIS *scowls at the intruder and his hand instinctively goes back to the sheath knife on his hip.* BURKE *is dressed up—wears a cheap blue suit, a striped cotton shirt with a black tie, and black shoes newly shined. His face is beaming with good humor.)*

BURKE: *(As he sees* CHRIS—*in a jovial tone of mockery)* Well, God bless who's here! *(He bends down and squeezes his huge form through the narrow doorway.)* And how is the world treating you this afternoon, Anna's father?

CHRIS: *(Sullenly)* Pooty goot—if it ain't for some fallars.

BURKE: *(With a grin)* Meaning me, do you? *(He laughs.)* Well, if you ain't the funny old crank of a man! *(Then soberly)* Where's herself?

(CHRIS *sits dumb, scowling, his eyes averted.* BURKE *is irritated by this silence.)*

BURKE: Where's Anna, I'm after asking you?

CHRIS: *(Hesitating—then grouchily)* She go down end of dock.

BURKE: I'll be going down to her, then. But first I'm thinking I'll take this chance when we're alone to have a word with you. *(He sits down opposite* CHRIS *at the table and leans over toward him.)* And that word is soon said. I'm marrying your Anna before this day is out, and you might as well make up your mind to it whether you like it or no.

CHRIS: *(Glaring at him with hatred and forcing a scornful laugh)* Ho-ho! Dat's easy for say!

BURKE: You mean I won't? *(Scornfully)* Is it the like of yourself will stop me, are you thinking?

CHRIS: Yes, Ay stop it, if it come to vorst.

BURKE: *(With scornful pity)* God help you!

CHRIS: But ain't no need for me do dat. Anna—

BURKE: *(Smiling confidently)* Is it Anna you think will prevent me?

CHRIS: Yes.

BURKE: And I'm telling you she'll not. She knows I'm loving her, and she loves me the same, and I know it.

CHRIS: Ho-ho! She only have fun. She make big fool of you, dat's all!

BURKE: *(Unshaken—pleasantly)* That's a lie in your throat, divil mend you!

CHRIS: No, it ain't lie. She tal me yust before she go out she never marry fallar like you.

BURKE: I'll not believe it. 'Tis a great old liar you are, and a divil to be making a power of trouble if you had your way. But 'tis not trouble I'm looking for, and me sitting down here. *(Earnestly)* Let us be talking it out now as man to man. You're her father, and wouldn't it be a shame for us to be at each other's throats like a pair of dogs, and I married with Anna. So out with the truth, man alive. What is it you're holding against me at all?

CHRIS: *(A bit placated, in spite of himself, by BURKE's evident sincerity—but puzzled and suspicious)* Vell—Ay don't vant for Anna gat married. Listen, you fallar. Ay'm a ole man. Ay don't see Anna for fifteen year. She ras all Ay gat in vorld. And now ven she come on first trip—you tank Ay vant her leave me 'lone again?

BURKE: *(Heartily)* Let you not be thinking I have no heart at all for the way you'd be feeling.

CHRIS: *(Astonished and encouraged—trying to plead persuasively)* Den you do right tang, eh? You ship avay again, leave Anna alone. *(Cajolingly)* Big fallar like you dat's on sea, he don't need vife. He gat new gel in every port, you know dat.

BURKE: *(Angrily for a second)* God stiffen you! *(Then controlling himself—calmly)* I'll not be giving you the lie on that. But divil take you, there's a time comes to every man, on sea or land, that isn't a born fool, when he's sick of the lot of them cows, and wearing his heart out to meet up with a fine dacent girl, and have a home to call his own and be rearing up children in it. 'Tis small use you're asking me to leave Anna. She's the wan woman of the world for me, and I can't live without her now, I'm thinking.

CHRIS: You forgat all about her in one veek out of port, Ay bet you!

BURKE: You don't know the like I am. Death itself wouldn't make me forget her. So let you not be making talk to me about leaving her. I'll not, and be damned to you! It won't be so bad for you as you'd make out at all. She'll be living here in the States, and her married to me. And you'd be seeing her often so—a sight more often than ever you saw her the fifteen years she was growing up in the West. It's quare you'd be the one to be making great trouble about her leaving you when you never laid eyes on her once in all them years.

CHRIS: *(Guiltily)* Ay taught it vas better Anna stay away, grow up inland where she don't ever know ole davil, sea.

BURKE: *(Scornfully)* Is it blaming the sea for your troubles ye are again, God help you? Well, Anna knows it now. 'Twas in her blood, anyway.

CHRIS: And Ay don't vant she ever know no-good fallar on sea—

BURKE: She knows one now.

CHRIS: *(Banging the table with his fist—furiously)* Dat's yust it! Dat's yust what you are—no-good, sailor failar! You tank Ay lat her life be made sorry by you like her mo'der's vas by me! No, Ay svear! She don't marry you if Ay gat kill you first!

BURKE: *(Looks at him a moment in astonishment—then laughing uproariously)* Ho-ho! Glory be to God, it's bold talk you have for a stumpy runt of a man!

CHRIS: *(Threateningly)* Vell—you see!

BURKE: *(With grinning defiance)* I'll see, surely! I'll see myself and Anna married this day, I'm telling you. *(Then with contemptuous exasperation)* It's quare fool's blather you have about the sea done this and the sea done that. You'd ought to be 'shamed to be saying the like, and you an old sailor yourself. I'm after hearing a lot of it from you and a lot more that Anna's told me you do be saying to her, and I'm thinking it's a poor weak thing you are, and not a man at all!

CHRIS: *(Darkly)* You see if Ay'm man—maybe quicker'n you tank.

BURKE: *(Contemptuously)* Yerra, don't be boasting. I'm thinking 'tis out of your wits you've got with fright of the sea. You'd be wishing Anna married to a farmer, she told me. That'd be a swate match, surely! Would you have a fine girl the like of Anna lying down at nights with a muddy scut stinking of pigs and dung? Or would you have her tied for life to the like of them skinny, shriveled swabs does be working in cities?

CHRIS: Dat's lie, you fool!

BURKE: 'Tis not. 'Tis your own mad notions I'm after telling. But you know the truth in your heart, if great fear of the sea has made you a liar and coward itself. *(Pounding the table)* The sea's the only life for a man with guts in him isn't afraid of his own shadow! 'Tis only on the sea he's free, and him roving the face of the world, seeing all things, and not giving a damn for saving up money, or stealing from his friends, or any of the black tricks that a landlubber'd waste his life on. 'Twas yourself knew it once, and you a bo'sun for years.

CHRIS: *(Sputtering with rage)* You vas crazy fool, Ay tal you!

BURKE: You've swallowed the anchor. The sea gives you a clout once, knocked you down, and you're not man enough to get up for another, but lie there for the rest of your life howling bloody murder. *(Proudly)* Isn't it myself the sea has nearly drowned, and me battered and bate till I was that close to hell I could hear the flames roaring, and never a groan out of me till the sea gave up and it seeing the great strength and guts of a man was in me?

CHRIS: *(Scornfully)* Yes, you vas hell of fallar, hear you tal it!

BURKE: *(Angrily)* You'll be calling me a liar once too often, me old bucko! Wasn't the whole story of it and my picture itself in the newspapers of Boston a week back? *(Looking* CHRIS *up and down belittlingly)* Sure I'd like to see you in the best of your youth do the like of what I done in the storm and after. 'Tis a mad lunatic, screeching with fear, you'd be this minute!

CHRIS: Ho-ho! You vas young fool! In ole years when Ay was on windyammer, Ay vas through hundred storms vorse'n dat! Ships vas ships den—and men dat sail on dem vas real men. And now what you gat on steamers? You gat fallars on deck don't know ship from mudscow. *(With a meaning glance at* BURKE*)* And below deck you gat fallars yust know how for shovel coal—might yust as vell vork on coal vagon ashore!

BURKE: *(Stung, angrily)* Is it casting insults at the men in the stokehole ye are, ye old ape? God stiffen you! Wan of them is worth any ten stock-fish-swilling Square-heads evershipped on a windbag!

CHRIS: *(His face working with rage, his hand going back to the sheath-knife on his hip)* Irish svine, you!

BURKE: *(Tauntingly)* Don't ye like the Irish, ye old baboon? 'Tis that you're needing in your family, I'm telling you—an Irishman and a man of the stokehole—to put guts in it so that you'll not be having grandchildren would be fearful cowards and jackasses the like of yourself!

CHRIS: *(Half rising from his chair—in a voice choked with rage)* You look out!

BURKE: *(Watching him intently— a mocking smile on his lips)* And it's that you'll be having, no matter what you'll do to prevent; for Anna and me'll be married this day, and no old fool the like of you will stop us when I've made up my mind.

CHRIS: *(With a hoarse cry)* You don't!

(He throws himself at BURKE, *knife in hand, knocking his chair over backwards.* BURKE *springs to his feet quickly in time to meet the attack. He laughs with the pure love of battle. The old Swede is like a child in his hands.* BURKE *does not strike or mistreat him in any way, but simply twists his right hand behind his back and forces the knife from his fingers. He throws the knife into a far corner of the room—tauntingly.)*

BURKE: Old men is getting childish shouldn't play with knives.

(Holding the struggling CHRIS *at arm's length——with a sudden rush of anger, drawing back his fist)*

BURKE: I've half a mind to hit you a great clout will put sense in your square head. Kape off me now, I'm warning you!

(He gives CHRIS *a push with the flat of his hand which sends the old Swede staggering back against the cabin wall, where he remains standing, panting heavily,*

his eyes fixed on BURKE *with hatred, as if he were only collecting his strength to rush at him again.)*

BURKE: *(Warningly)* Now don't be coming at me again, I'm saying, or I'll flatten you on the floor with a blow, if 'tis Anna's father you are itself! I've no patience left for you. *(Then with an amused laugh)* Well, 'tis a bold old man you are just the same, and I'd never think it was in you to come tackling me alone.

(A shadow crosses the cabin windows. Both men start. ANNA *appears in the doorway.)*

ANNA: *(With pleased surprise as she sees* BURKE*)* Hello, Mat. Are you here already? I was down— *(She stops, looking from one to the other, sensing immediately that something has happened.)* What's up? *(Then noticing the overturned chair—in alarm)* How'd that chair get knocked over? *(Turning on* BURKE *reproachfully)* You ain't been fighting with him, Mat—after you promised?

BURKE: *(His old self again)* I've not laid a hand on him, Anna. *(He goes and picks up the chair, then turning on the still questioning* ANNA—*with a reassuring smile)* Let you not be worried at all. 'Twas only a bit of an argument we was having to pass the time till you'd come.

ANNA: It must have been some argument when you got to throwing chairs. *(She turns on* CHRIS*)* Why don't you say something? What was it about?

CHRIS: *(Relaxing at last—avoiding her eyes—sheepishly)* Ve vas talking about ships and fallars on sea.

ANNA: *(With a relieved smile)* Oh—the old stuff, eh?

BURKE: *(Suddenly seeming to come to a bold decision—with a defiant grin at* CHRIS*)* He's not after telling you the whole of it. We was arguing about you mostly.

ANNA: *(With a frown)* About me?

BURKE: And we'll be finishing it out right here and now in your presence if you're willing. *(He sits down at the left of table.)*

ANNA: *(Uncertainly—looking from him to her father)* Sure. Tell me what it's all about.

CHRIS: *(Advancing toward the table—protesting to* BURKE*)* No! You don't do dat, you! You tal him you don't vant for hear him talk, Anna.

ANNA: But I do. I want this cleared up.

CHRIS: *(Miserably afraid now)* Vell, not now, anyvay. You vas going ashore, yes? You ain't got time—

ANNA: *(Firmly)* Yes, right here and now. *(She turns to* BURKE*)* You tell me, Mat, since he don't want to.

BURKE: *(Draws a deep breath—then plunges in boldly)* The whole of it's in a few words only. So's he'd make no mistake, and him hating the sight of me, I told him in his teeth I loved you. *(Passionately)* And that's God truth, Anna, and well you know it!

CHRIS: *(Scornfully—forcing a laugh)* Ho-ho! He tal same tang to gel every port he go!

ANNA: *(Shrinking from her father with repulsion—resentfully)* Shut up, can't you? *(Then to* BURKE—*feelingly)* I know it's true, Mat. I don't mind what he says.

BURKE: *(Humbly grateful)* God bless you!

ANNA: And then what?

BURKE: And then— *(Hesitatingly)* And then I said— *(He looks at her pleadingly.)* I said I was sure—I told him I thought you have a bit of love for me, too. *(Passionately)* Say you do, Anna! Let you not destroy me entirely, for the love of God! *(He grasps both her hands in his two.)*

ANNA: *(Deeply moved and troubled—forcing a trembling laugh)* So you told him that, Mat? No wonder he was mad. *(Forcing out the words)* Well, maybe it's true, Mat. Maybe I do. I been thinking and thinking—I didn't want to, Mat, I'll own up to that—I tried to cut it out—but— *(She laughs helplessly.)* I guess I can't help it anyhow. So I guess I do, Mat. *(Then with a sudden joyous defiance)* Sure I do! What's the use of kidding myself different? Sure I love you, Mat!

CHRIS: *(With a cry of pain)* Anna! *(He sits crushed.)*

BURKE: *(With a great depth of sincerity in his humble gratitude)* God be praised!

ANNA: *(Assertively)* And I ain't never loved a man in my life before, you can always believe that—no matter what happens.

BURKE: *(Goes over to her and puts his arms around her)* Sure I do be believing ivery word you iver said or iver will say. And 'tis you and me will be having a grand, beautiful life together to the end of our days! *(He tries to kiss her. At first she turns away her head—then, overcome by a fierce impulse of passionate love, she takes his head in both her hands and holds his face close to hers, staring into his eyes. Then she kisses him full on the lips.)*

ANNA: *(Pushing him away from her—forcing a broken laugh)* Good-by. *(She walks to the doorway in rear—stands with her back toward them, looking out. Her shoulders quiver once or twice as if she were fighting back her sobs.)*

BURKE: *(Too in the seventh heaven of bliss to get any correct interpretation of her words— with a laugh)* Good-by, is it? The divil you say! I'll be coming back at you in a second for more of the same! *(To* CHRIS, *who has quickened to instant attention at his daughter's good-by, and has looked back at her with a stirring of foolish hope in his eyes)* Now, me old bucko, what'll you be saying? You heard the words from her own lips. Confess I've bate you. Own up like a man when you're bate fair and square. And here's my hand to you— *(Holds out his hand)* And let you take it and we'll shake and forget what's over and done, and be friends from this out.

CHRIS: *(With implacable hatred)* Ay don't shake hands with you fallar—not vhile Ay live!

BURKE: *(Offended)* The back of my hand to you then, if that suits you better. *(Growling)* 'Tis a rotten bad loser you are, divil mend you!

CHRIS: Ay don't lose. *(Trying to be scornful and self-convincing)* Anna say she like you little bit but you don't hear her say she marry you, Ay bet.

(At the sound of her name ANNA has turned round to them. Her face is composed and calm again, but it is the dead calm of despair.)

BURKE: *(Scornfully)* No, and I wasn't hearing her say the sun is shining either.

CHRIS: *(Doggedly)* Dat's all right. She don't say it, yust same.

ANNA: *(Quietly—coming forward to them)* No, I didn't say it, Mat.

CHRIS: *(Eagerly)* Dere! You hear!

BURKE: *(Misunderstanding her—with a grin)* You're waiting till you do be asked, you mane? Well, I'm asking you now. And we'll be married this day, with the help of God!

ANNA: *(Gently)* You heard what I said, Mat—after I kissed you?

BURKE: *(Alarmed by something in her manner)* No—I disremember.

ANNA: I said good-by. *(Her voice trembling)* That kiss was for good-by, Mat.

BURKE: *(Terrified)* What d'you mane?

ANNA: I can't marry you, Mat—and we've said good-by. That's all.

CHRIS: *(Unable to hold back his exultation)* Ay know it! Ay know dat vas so!

BURKE: *(Jumping to his feet—unable to believe his ears)* Anna! Is it making game of me you'd be? 'Tis a quare time to joke with me, and don't be doing it, for the love of God.

ANNA: *(Looking him in the eyes—steadily)* D'you think I'd kid you? No, I'm not joking, Mat. I mean what I said.

BURKE: Ye don't! Ye can't! 'Tis mad you are, I'm telling you!

ANNA: *(Fixedly)* No, I'm not.

BURKE: *(Desperately)* But what's come over you so sudden? You was saying you loved me—

ANNA: I'll say that as often as you want me to. It's true.

BURKE: *(Bewilderedly)* Then why—what, in the divil's name— Oh, God help me, I can't make head or tail to it at all!

ANNA: Because it's the best way out I can figure, Mat. *(Her voice catching)* I been thinking it over and thinking it over day and night all week. Don't think it ain't hard on me too, Mat.

BURKE: For the love of God, tell me then, what is it that's preventing you wedding me when the two of us has love? *(Suddenly getting an idea and pointing at* CHRIS—*desperately)* Is it giving heed to the like of that old fool ye are, and him hating me and filling your ears full of bloody lies against me?

CHRIS: *(Getting to his feet—raging triumphantly before* ANNA *has a chance to get in a word)* Yes, Anna believe me, not you! She know her old fa'der don't lie like you.

ANNA: *(Turning on her father angrily)* You sit down, d'you hear? Where do you come in butting in and making things worse? You're like a devil, you are! *(Harshly)* Good Lord, and I was beginning to like you, beginning to forget all I've got held up against you!

CHRIS: *(Crushed feebly)* You ain't got nutting for hold against me, Anna.

ANNA: Ain't I yust! Well, lemme tell you— *(She glances at* BURKE *and stops abruptly)* Say, Mat, I'm s'prised at you. You didn't think anything he'd said—

BURKE: *(Glumly)* Sure, what else would it be?

ANNA: Think I've ever paid any attention to all his crazy bull? Gee, you must take me for a five-year-old kid.

BURKE: *(Puzzled and beginning to be irritated at her too)* I don't know how to take you, with your saying this one minute and that the next.

ANNA: Well, he has nothing to do with it.

BURKE: Then what is it has? Tell me, and don't keep me waiting and sweating blood.

ANNA: *(Resolutely)* I can't tell you—and I won't. I got a good reason— and that's all you need to know. I can't marry you, that's all there is to it. *(Distractedly)* So, for Gawd's sake, let's talk of something else.

BURKE: I'll not! *(Then fearfully)* Is it married to someone else you are— in the West maybe?

ANNA: *(Vehemently)* I should say not.

BURKE: *(Regaining his courage)* To the divil with all other reasons then. They don't matter with me at all. *(He gets to his feet confidently, assuming a masterful tone.)* I'm thinking you're the like of them women can't make up their mind til they're drove to it. Well, then, I'll make up your mind for you bloody quick. *(He takes her by the arms, grinning to soften his serious bullying.)* We've had enough of talk! Let you be going into your room now and be dressing in your best and we'll be going ashore.

CHRIS: *(Aroused—angrily)* No, py God, she don't do that! *(Takes hold of her arm)*

ANNA: *(Who has listened to* BURKE *in astonishment. She draws away from him, instinctively repelled by his tone, but not exactly sure if he is serious or not—a trace of resentment in her voice)* Say, where do you get that stuff?

BURKE: *(Imperiously)* Never mind, now! Let you go get dressed, I'm saying. *(Then turning to* CHRIS*)* We'll be seeing who'll win in the end—me or you.

CHRIS: *(To* ANNA—*also in an authoritative tone)* You stay right here, Anna, you hear!

(ANNA *stands looking from one to the other of them as if she thought they had both gone crazy. Then the expression of her face freezes into the hardened sneer of her experience.*)

BURKE: *(Violently)* She'll not! She'll do what I say! You've had your hold on her long enough. It's my turn now.

ANNA: *(With a hard laugh)* Your turn? Say, what am I, anyway?

BURKE: 'Tis not what you are, 'tis what you're going to be this day—and that's wedded to me before night comes. Hurry up now with your dressing.

CHRIS: *(Commandingly)* You don't do one tang he say, Anna!

(ANNA *laughs mockingly.*)

BURKE: She will, so!

CHRIS: Ay tal you she don't! Ay'm her fa'der.

BURKE: She will in spite of you. She's taking my orders from this out, not yours.

ANNA: *(Laughing again)* Orders is good!

BURKE: *(Turning to her impatiently)* Hurry up now, and shake a leg. We've no time to be wasting. *(Irritated as she doesn't move)* Do you hear what I'm telling you?

CHRIS: You stay dere, Anna!

ANNA: *(At the end of her patience—blazing out at them passionately)* You can go to hell, both of you!

(*There is something in her tone that makes them forget their quarrel and turn to her in a stunned amazement.* ANNA *laughs wildly.*)

ANNA: You're just like all the rest of them—you two! Gawd, you'd think I was a piece of furniture! I'll show you! Sit down now!

(As they hesitate—furiously)

ANNA: Sit down and let me talk for a minute. You're all wrong, see? Listen to me! I'm going to tell you something—and then I'm going to beat it. *(To* BURKE—*with a harsh laugh)* I'm going to tell you a funny story, so pay attention. *(Pointing to* CHRIS*)* I've been meaning to turn it loose on him every time he'd get my goat with his bull about keeping me safe inland. I wasn't going to tell you, but you've forced me into it. What's the dif? It's all wrong anyway, and you might as well get cured that way as any other. *(With hard mocking)* Only don't forget what you said a minute ago about it not mattering to you what other reason I got so long as I wasn't married to no one else.

BURKE: *(Manfully)* That's my word, and I'll stick to it!

ANNA: *(Laughing bitterly)* What a chance! You make me laugh, honest! Want to bet you will? Wait 'n see! *(She stands at the table rear, looking from one to the other of the two men with her hard, mocking smile. Then she begins, fighting to control her emotion and speak calmly.)* First thing is, I want to tell you two guys something. You was going on 's if one of you had got to own me. But nobody owns me, see?—'cepting myself. I'll do what I please and no man, I don't give a hoot who he is, can tell me what to do! I ain't asking either of you for a living. I can make it myself—one way or other. I'm my own boss. So put that in your pipe and smoke it! You and your orders!

BURKE: *(Protestingly)* I wasn't meaning it that way at all and well you know it. You've no call to be raising this rumpus with me. *(Pointing to* CHRIS*)* 'Tis him you've a right—

ANNA: I'm coming to him. But you—you did mean it that way, too. You sounded—yust like all the rest. *(Hysterically)* But, damn it, shut up! Let me talk for a change!

BURKE: 'Tis quare, rough talk, that—for a dacent girl the like of you!

ANNA: *(With a hard laugh)* Decent? Who told you I was?

*(*CHRIS *is sitting with bowed shoulders, his head in his hands. She leans over in exasperation and shakes him violently by the shoulder.)*

ANNA: Don't go to sleep, Old Man! Listen here, I'm talking to you now!

CHRIS: *(Straightening up and looking about as if he were seeking a way to escape—with frightened foreboding in his voice)* Ay don't vant for hear it. You vas going out of head, Ay tank, Anna.

ANNA: *(Violently)* Well, living with you is enough to drive anyone off their nut. Your bunk about the farm being so fine! Didn't I write you year after year how rotten it was and what a dirty slave them cousins made of me? What'd you care? Nothing! Not even enough to come out and see me! That crazy bull about wanting to keep me away from the sea don't go down with me! You yust didn't want to be bothered with me! You're like all the rest of 'em!

CHRIS: *(Feebly)* Anna! It ain't so—

ANNA: *(Not heeding his interruption—vengefully)* But one thing I never wrote you. It was one of them cousins that you think is such nice people—the youngest son—Paul—that started me wrong. *(Loudly)* It wasn't none of my fault. I hated him worse'n hell and he knew it. But he was big and strong— *(Pointing to* BURKE*)* —like you!

BURKE: *(Half springing to his feet—his fists clenched)* God blarst it! *(He sinks slowly back in his chair again, the knuckles showing white on his clenched hands, his face tense with the effort to suppress his grief and rage.)*

CHRIS: *(In a cry of horrified pain)* Anna!

ANNA: *(To him—seeming not to have heard their interruptions)* That was why I run away from the farm. That was what made me get a yob as nurse girl in Saint Paul. *(With a hard, mocking laugh)* And you think that was a nice yob for a girl, too, don't you? *(Sarcastically)* With all them nice inland fellers yust looking for a chance to marry me, I s'pose. Marry me? What a chance! They wasn't looking for marrying.

(As BURKE *lets a groan of fury escape him—desperately)* I'm owning up to everything fair and square. I was caged in, I tell you—yust like in yail—taking care of other people's kids—listening to 'em bawling and crying day and night— when I wanted to be out—and I was lonesome—lonesome as hell! *(With a sudden weariness in her voice)* So I give up finally. What was the use?

(She stops and looks at the two men. Both are motionless and silent. CHRIS *seems in a stupor of despair, his house of cards fallen about him.* BURKE's *face is livid with the rage that is eating him up but he is too stunned and bewildered yet to find a vent for it. The condemnation she feels in their silence goads* ANNA *into a harsh, strident defiance.)*

ANNA: You don't say nothing—either of you—but I know what you're thinking. You're like all the rest! *(To* CHRIS—*furiously)* And who's to blame for it, me or you? If you'd even acted like a man—if you'd even had been a regular father and had me with you—maybe things would be different!

CHRIS: *(In agony)* Don't talk dat vay, Anna! Ay go crazy! Ay von't listen! *(Puts his hands over his ears)*

ANNA: *(Infuriated by his action—stridently)* You will too listen! *(She leans over and pulls his hands from his ears— with hysterical rage.)* You—keeping me safe inland—I wasn't no nurse girl the last two years—I lied when I wrote you— I was in a house, that's what!—yes, that kind of a house— the kind sailors like you and Mat goes to in port—and your nice inland men, too—and all men, God damn 'em! I hate 'em! Hate 'em!

(She breaks into hysterical sobbing, throwing herself into the chair and hiding her face in her hands on the table. The two men have sprung to their feet.)

CHRIS: *(Whimpering like a child)* Anna! Anna! It's a lie! It's a lie! *(He stands wringing his hands together and begins to weep.)*

BURKE: *(His whole great body tense like a spring—dully and gropingly)* So that's what's in it!

ANNA: *(Raising her head at the sound of his voice—with extreme mocking bitterness)* I s'pose you remember your promise, Mat? No other reason was to count with you so long as I wasn't married already. So I s'pose you want me to get dressed and go ashore, don't you? *(She laughs.)* Yes, you do!

BURKE: *(On the verge of his outbreak—stammeringly)* God stiffen you!

ANNA: *(Trying to keep up her hard, bitter tone, but gradually letting a note of pitiful pleading creep in)* I s'pose if I tried to tell you I wasn't—that—no more you'd believe me, wouldn't you? Yes, you would! And if I told you that yust getting out in this barge and being on the sea had changed me and made me feel different about things, 's if all I'd been through wasn't me and didn't count and was yust like it never happened—you'd laugh, wouldn't you? And you'd die laughing sure if I said that meeting you that funny way that night in the fog and afterwards seeing that you was straight goods stuck on me, had got me to thinking for the first time, and I sized you up as a different kind of man—a sea man as different from the ones on land as water is from mud—and that was why I got stuck on you, too. I wanted to marry you and fool you, but I couldn't. Don't you see how I've changed? I couldn't marry you with you believing a lie—and I was shamed to tell you the truth—till the both of you forced my hand, and I seen you was the same as all the rest. And now, give me a bawling out and beat it, like I can tell you're going to.

(She stops, looking at BURKE. He is silent, his face averted, his features beginning to work with fury. She pleads passionately.)

ANNA: Will you believe it if I tell you that loving you has made me—clean? It's the straight goods, honest! *(Then as he doesn't reply—bitterly)* Like hell you will! You're like all the rest!

BURKE: *(Blazing out—turning on her in a perfect frenzy of rage—his voice trembling with passion)* The rest, is it? God's curse on you! Clane, is it? You slut, you, I'll be killing you now!

(He picks up the chair on which he has been sitting and, swinging it high over his shoulder, springs toward her. CHRIS rushes forward with a cry of alarm, trying to ward off the blow from his daughter. ANNA looks up into BURKE's eyes with the fearlessness of despair. BURKE checks himself, the chair held in the air.)

CHRIS: *(Wildly)* Stop, you crazy fool! You vant for murder her!

ANNA: *(Pushing her father away brusquely, her eyes still holding* BURKE's*)* Keep out of this, you! *(To* BURKE—*dully)* Well, ain't you got the nerve to do it? Go ahead! I'll be thankful to you, honest. I'm sick of the whole game.

BURKE: *(Throwing the chair away into a corner of the room—helplessly)* I can't do it, God help me, and your two eyes looking at me. *(Furiously)* Though I do be thinking I'd have a good right to smash your skull like a rotten egg. Was there iver a woman in the world had the rottenness in her that you have, and was there iver a man the like of me was made the fool of the world, and me thinking thoughts about you, and having great love for you, and dreaming dreams of the fine life we'd have when we'd be wedded! *(His voice high pitched in a lamentation that is like a keen)* Yerra, God help me! I'm destroyed entirely and my heart is broken in bits! I'm asking God Himself, was it for this He'd have me roaming the earth since I was a lad only, to come to black shame in the end, where I'd be giving a power of love to a woman is the same as others you'd meet in any hooker-shanty in port, with red gowns on them and paint on their grinning mugs, would be sleeping with any man for a dollar or two!

ANNA: *(In a scream)* Don't, Mat! For Gawd's sake! *(Then raging and pounding on the table with her hands)* Get out of here! Leave me alone! Get out of here!

BURKE: *(His anger rushing back on him)* I'll be going, surely! And I'll be drinking sloos of whisky will wash that black kiss of yours off my lips; and I'll be getting dead rotten drunk so I'll not remember if 'twas iver born you was at all; and I'll be shipping away on some boat will take me to the other end of the world where I'll never see your face again! *(He turns toward the door.)*

CHRIS: *(Who has been standing in a stupor—suddenly grasping* BURKE *by the arm—stupidly)* No, you don't go. Ay tank maybe it's better Anna marry you now.

BURKE: *(Shaking* CHRIS *off—furiously)* Lave go of me, ye old ape! Marry her, is it? I'd see her roasting in hell first! I'm shipping away out of this, I'm telling you! *(Pointing to* ANNA—*passionately)* And my curse on you and the curse of Almighty God and all the Saints! You've destroyed me this day and may you lie awake in the long nights, tormented with thoughts of Mat Burke and the great wrong you've done him!

ANNA: *(In anguish)* Mat!

(But he turns without another word and strides out of the doorway. ANNA *looks after him wildly, starts to run after him, then hides her face in her outstretched arms, sobbing.* CHRIS *stands in a stupor, staring at the floor.)*

CHRIS: *(After a pause, dully)* Ay tank Ay go ashore, too.

ANNA: *(Looking up, wildly)* Not after him! Let him go! Don't you dare—

CHRIS: *(Somberly)* Ay go for gat drink.

ANNA: *(With a harsh laugh)* So I'm driving you to drink, too, eh? I s'pose you want to get drunk so's you can forget like him?

CHRIS: *(Bursting out angrily)* Yes, Ay vant! You tank Ay like hear dem tangs. *(Breaking down—weeping)* Ay tank you vasn't dat kind of gel, Anna.

ANNA: *(Mockingly)* And I s'pose you want me to beat it, don't you? You don't want me here disgracing you, I s'pose?

CHRIS: No, you stay here! *(Goes over and pats her on the shoulder, the tears running down his face)* Ain't your fault, Anna, Ay know dat. *(She looks up at him, softened. He bursts into rage.)* It's dat ole davil, sea, do this to me! *(He shakes his fist at the door.)* It's her dirty tricks! It vas all right on barge with yust you and me. Den she bring dat Irish fallar in fog, she make you like him, she make you fight with me all time! If dat Irish fallar don't never come, you don't never tal me dem tangs, Ay don't never know, and everytang's all right. *(He shakes his fist again.)* Dirty ole davil!

ANNA: *(With spent weariness)* Oh, what's the use? Go on ashore and get drunk.

CHRIS: *(Goes into room on left and gets his cap. He goes to the door, silent and stupid—then turns.)* You vait here, Anna?

ANNA: *(Dully)* Maybe and maybe not. Maybe I'll get drunk, too. Maybe I'll— But what the hell do you care what I do? Go on and beat it.

(CHRIS *turns stupidly and goes out.* ANNA *sits at the table, staring straight in front of her.)*

(The curtain falls.)

END OF ACT THREE

ACT FOUR

(Same as ACT THREE, about nine o'clock of a foggy night two days later. The whistles of steamers in the harbor can be heard. The cabin is lighted by a small ramp on the table. A suit case stands in the middle of the floor. ANNA is sitting in the rocking-chair. She wears a hat, is all dressed up as in ACT ONE. Her face is pale, looks terribly tired and worn, as if the two days just past had been ones of suffering and sleepless nights. She stares before her despondently, her chin in her hands. There is a timid knock on the door in rear. ANNA jumps to her feet with a startled exclamation and looks toward the door with an expression of mingled hope and fear.)

ANNA: *(Faintly)* Come in. *(Then summoning her courage—more resolutely)* Come in.

(The door is opened and CHRIS appears in the doorway. He is in a very bleary, bedraggled condition, suffering from the after-effects of his drunk. A tin pail full of foaming beer is in his hand. He comes forward, his eyes avoiding ANNA's. He mutters stupidly.)

CHRIS: It's foggy.

ANNA: *(Looking him over with contempt)* So you come back at last, did you? You're a fine looking sight! *(Then jeeringly)* I thought you'd beaten it for good on account of the disgrace I'd brought on you.

CHRIS: *(Wincing—faintly)* Don't say dat, Anna, please! *(He sits in a chair by the table, setting down the can of beer, holding his head in his hands.)*

ANNA: *(Looks at him with a certain sympathy)* What's the trouble? Feeling sick?

CHRIS: *(Dully)* Inside my head feel sick.

ANNA: Well, what d'you expect after being soused for two days? *(Resentfully)* It serves you right. A fine thing—you leaving me alone on this barge all that time!

CHRIS: *(Humbly)* Ay'm sorry, Anna.

ANNA: *(Scornfully)* Sorry!

CHRIS: But Ay'm not sick inside head vay you mean. Ay'm sick from tank too much about you, about me.

ANNA: And how about me? D'you suppose I ain't been thinking, too?

CHRIS: Ay'm sorry, Anna. *(He sees her bag and gives a start.)* You pack your bag, Anna? You vas going—?

ANNA: *(Forcibly)* Yes, I was going right back to what you think.

CHRIS: Anna!

ANNA: I went ashore to get a train for New York. I'd been waiting and waiting 'till I was sick of it. Then I changed my mind and decided not to go today. But I'm going first thing tomorrow, so it'll all be the same in the end.

CHRIS: *(Raising his head—pleadingly)* No, you never do dat, Anna!

ANNA: *(With a sneer)* Why not, I'd like to know?

CHRIS: You don't never gat to do—dat vay—no more, Ay tal you. Ay fix dat up all right.

ANNA: *(Suspiciously)* Fix what up?

CHRIS: *(Not seeming to have heard her question—sadly)* You vas vaiting, you say? You vasn't vaiting for me, Ay bet.

ANNA: *(Callously)* You'd win.

CHRIS: For dat Irish fallar?

ANNA: *(Defiantly)* Yes—if you want to know! *(Then with a forlorn laugh)* If he did come back it'd only be 'cause he wanted to beat me up or kill me, I suppose. But even if he did, I'd rather have him come than not show up at all. I wouldn't care what he did.

CHRIS: Ay guess it's true you vas in love with him all right.

ANNA: You guess!

CHRIS: *(Turning to her earnestly)* And Ay'm sorry for you like hell he don't come, Anna!

ANNA: *(Softened)* Seems to me you've changed your tune a lot.

CHRIS: Ay've been tanking, and Ay guess it vas all my fault—all bad tangs dat happen to you. *(Pleadingly)* You try for not hate me, Anna. Ay'm crazy ole fool, dat's all.

ANNA: Who said I hated you?

CHRIS: Ay'm sorry for everytang Ay do wrong for you, Anna. Ay vant for you be happy all rest of your life for make up! It make you happy marry dat Irish fallar, Ay vant it, too.

ANNA: *(Dully)* Well, there ain't no chance. But I'm glad you think different about it, anyway.

CHRIS: *(Supplicatingly)* And you tank—maybe—you forgive me sometime?

ANNA: *(With a wan smile)* I'll forgive you right now.

CHRIS: *(Seizing her hand and kissing it—brokenly)* Anna lilla! Anna lilla!

ANNA: *(Touched but a bit embarrassed)* Don't bawl about it. There ain't nothing to forgive, anyway. It ain't your fault, and it ain't mine, and it ain't his neither. We're all poor nuts, and things happen, and we yust get mixed in wrong, that's all.

CHRIS: *(Eagerly)* You say right tang, Anna, py golly! It ain't nobody's fault! *(Shaking his fist)* It's dat ole davil, sea!

ANNA: *(With an exasperated laugh)* Gee, won't you ever can that stuff?

(CHRIS *relapses into injured silence. After a pause* ANNA *continues curiously.*)

ANNA: You said a minute ago you'd fixed something up about me. What was it?

CHRIS: *(After a hesitating pause)* Ay'm shipping avay on sea again, Anna.

ANNA: *(Astounded)* You're what?

CHRIS: Ay sign on steamer sail tomorrow. Ay gat my ole yob—bo'sun.

(ANNA *stares at him. As he goes on, a bitter smile comes over her face.*)

CHRIS: Ay tank dat's best tang for you. Ay only bring you bad luck, Ay tank. Ay make your mo'der's life sorry. Ay don't vant make yours dat way, but Ay do yust same. Dat ole davil, sea, she make me Yonah man ain't no good for nobody. And Ay tank now it ain't no use fight with sea. No man dat live going to beat her, py yingo!

ANNA: *(With a laugh of helpless bitterness)* So that's how you've fixed me, is it?

CHRIS: Yes, Ay tank if dat ole davil gat me back she leave you alone den.

ANNA: *(Bitterly)* But, for Gawd's sake, don't you see you're doing the same thing you've always done? Don't you see—?

(But she sees the look of obsessed stubbornness on her father's face and gives it up helplessly.)

ANNA: But what's the use of talking? You ain't right, that's what. I'll never blame you for nothing no more. But how you could figure out that was fixing me—!

CHRIS: Dat ain't all. Ay gat dem fallars in steamship office to pay you all money coming to me every month vhile Ay'm avay.

ANNA: *(With a hard laugh)* Thanks. But I guess I won't be hard up for no small change.

CHRIS: *(Hurt—humbly)* It ain't much, Ay know, but it's plenty for keep you so you never gat go back—

ANNA: *(Shortly)* Shut up, will you? We'll talk about it later, see?

CHRIS: *(After a pause—ingratiatingly)* You like Ay go ashore look for dat Irish fallar, Anna?

ANNA: *(Angrily)* Not much! Think I want to drag him back?

CHRIS: *(After a pause—uncomfortably)* Py golly, dat booze don't go vell. Give me fever, Ay tank. Ay feel hot like hell. *(He takes off his coat and lets it drop on the floor. There is a loud thud.)*

ANNA: *(With a start)* What you got in your pocket, for Pete's sake—a ton of lead? *(She reaches down, takes the coat and pulls out a revolver—looks from it to him in amazement.)* A gun? What were you doing with this?

CHRIS: *(Sheepishly)* Ay forget. Ain't nothing. Ain't loaded, anyvay.

ANNA: *(Breaking it open to make sure—then closing it again—looking at him suspiciously)* That ain't telling me why you got it?

CHRIS: Ay'm ole fool. Ay got it when Ay go ashore first. Ay tank den it's all fault of dat Irish fallar.

ANNA: *(With a shudder)* Say, you're crazier than I thought. I never dreamt you'd go that far.

CHRIS: *(Quickly)* Ay don't. Ay gat better sense right avay. Ay don't never buy bullets even. It ain't his fault, Ay know.

ANNA: *(Still suspicious of him)* Well, I'll take care of this for a while, loaded or not. *(She puts it in the drawer of table and closes the drawer.)*

CHRIS: *(Placatingly)* Throw it overboard if you vant. Ay don't care. *(Then after a pause)* Py golly, Ay tank Ay go lie down. Ay feel sick.

(ANNA takes a magazine from the table. CHRIS hesitates by her chair.)

CHRIS: Ve talk again before Ay go, yes?

ANNA: *(Dully)* Where's this ship going to?

CHRIS: Cape Town. Dat's in South Africa. She's British steamer called Londonderry. *(He stands hesitatingly—finally blurts out.)* Anna—you forgive me sure?

ANNA: *(Wearily)* Sure I do. You ain't to blame. You're yust—what you are—like me.

CHRIS: *(Pleadingly)* Den—you lat me kiss you again once?

ANNA: *(Raising her face—forcing a wan smile)* Sure. No hard feelings.

CHRIS: *(Kisses her brokenly)* Anna lilla! Ay *(He fights for words to express himself, but finds none—miserably—with a sob.)* Ay can't say it. Good-night, Anna.

ANNA: Good-night.

(He picks up the can of beer and goes slowly into the room on left, his shoulders bowed, his head sunk forward dejectedly. He closes the door after him. ANNA turns over the pages of the magazine, trying desperately to banish her thoughts by looking

at the pictures. This fails to distract her, and flinging the magazine back on the table, she springs to her feet and walks about the cabin distractedly, clenching and unclenching her hands. She speaks aloud to herself in a tense, trembling voice.)

ANNA: Gawd, I can't stand this much longer! What am I waiting for anyway?—like a damn fool! *(She laughs helplessly, then checks herself abruptly as she hears the sound of heavy footsteps on the deck outside. She appears to recognize these and her face lights up with joy. She gasps.)* Mat!

(A strange terror seems suddenly to seize her. She rushes to the table, takes the revolver out of drawer and crouches down in the corner, left, behind the cupboard. A moment later the door is flung open and BURKE *appears in the doorway. He is in bad shape—his clothes torn and dirty, covered with sawdust as if he had been grovelling or sleeping on barroom floors. There is a red bruise on his forehead over one of his eyes, another over one cheekbone, his knuckles are skinned and raw—plain evidence of the fighting he has been through on his "bat." His eyes are bloodshot and heavy-lidded, his face has a bloated look. But beyond these appearances—the results of heavy drinking—there is an expression in his eyes of wild mental turmoil, of impotent animal rage baffled by its own abject misery.)*

BURKE: *(Peers blinkingly about the cabin—hoarsely)* Let you not be hiding from me, whoever's here—though 'tis well you know. I'd have a right to come back and murder you. *(He stops to listen. Hearing no sound, he closes the door behind him and comes forward to the table. He throws himself into the rocking-chair—despondently.)* There's no one here, I'm thinking, and 'tis a great fool I am to be coming. *(With a sort of dumb, uncomprehending anguish)* Yerra, Mat Burke, 'tis a great jackass you've become and what's got into you at all, at all? She's gone out of this long ago, I'm telling you, and you'll never see her face again.

*(*ANNA *stands up, hesitating, struggling between joy and fear.* BURKE'*s eyes fall on* ANNA'*s bag. He leans over to examine it.)*

BURKE: What's this? *(Joyfully)* It's hers. She's not gone! But where is she? Ashore? *(Darkly)* What would she be doing ashore on this rotten night? *(His face suddenly convulsed with grief and rage)* 'Tis that, is it? Oh, God's curse on her! *(Raging)* I'll wait 'ti she comes and choke her dirty life out.

*(*ANNA *starts, her face grows hard. She steps into the room, the revolver in her right hand by her side.)*

ANNA: *(In a cold, hard tone)* What are you doing here?

BURKE: *(Wheeling about with a terrified gasp)* Glory be to God!

(They remain motionless and silent for a moment, holding each other's eyes.)

ANNA: *(In the same hard voice)* Well, can't you talk?

BURKE: *(Trying to fall into an easy, careless tone)* You've a year's growth scared out of me, coming at me so sudden and me thinking I was alone.

ANNA: You've got your nerve butting in here without knocking or nothing. What d'you want?

BURKE: *(Airily)* Oh, nothing much. I was wanting to have a last word with you, that's all. *(He moves a step toward her.)*

ANNA: *(Sharply—raising the revolver in her hand)* Careful now! Don't try getting too close. I heard what you said you'd do to me.

BURKE: *(Noticing the revolver for the first time)* Is it murdering me you'd be now, God forgive you? *(Then with a contemptuous laugh)* Or is it thinking I'd be frightened by that old tin whistle? *(He walks straight for her.)*

ANNA: *(Wildly)* Look out, I tell you!

BURKE: *(Who has come so close that the revolver is almost touching his chest)* Let you shoot, then! *(Then with sudden wild grief)* Let you shoot I'm saying, and be done with it! Let you end me with a shot and I'll be thanking you, for it's a rotten dog's life I've lived the past two days since I've known what you are, 'til I'm after wishing I was never born at all!

ANNA: *(Overcome—letting the revolver drop to the floor, as if her fingers had no strength to hold it—hysterically)* What d'you want coming here? Why don't you beat it? Go on! *(She passes him and sinks down in the rocking-chair.)*

BURKE: *(Following her—mournfully)* 'Tis right you'd be asking why did I come. *(Then angrily)* 'Tis because 'tis a great weak fool of the world I am, and me tormented with the wickedness you'd told of yourself, and drinking oceans of booze that'd make me forget. Forget? Divil a word I'd forget, and your face grinning always in front of my eyes, awake or asleep 'til I do be thinking a madhouse is the proper place for me.

ANNA: *(Glancing at his hands and face—scornfully)* You look like you ought to be put away some place. Wonder you wasn't pulled in. You been scrapping, too, ain't you?

BURKE: I have—with every scut would take off his coat to me! *(Fiercely)* And each time I'd be hitting one a clout in the mug, it wasn't his face I'd be seeing at all, but yours, and me wanting to drive you a blow would knock you out of this world where I wouldn't be seeing or thinking more of you.

ANNA: *(Her lips trembling pitifully)* Thanks!

BURKE: *(Walking up and down—distractedly)* That's right, make game of me! Oh, I'm a great coward surely, to be coming back to speak with you at all. You've a right to laugh at me.

ANNA: I ain't laughing at you, Mat.

BURKE: *(Unheeding)* You to be what you are, and me to be Mat Burke, and me to be drove back te look at you again! 'Tis black shame is on me!

ANNA: *(Resentfully)* Then get out. No one's holding you!

BURKE: *(Bewilderedly)* And me to listen to that talk from a woman like you and be frightened to close her mouth with a slap! Oh, God help me, I'm a yellow coward for all men to spit at! *(Then furiously)* But I'll not be getting out of this 'till I've had me word. *(Raising his fist threateningly)* And let you look out how you'd drive me! *(Letting his fist fall helplessly)* Don't be angry now! I'm raving like a real lunatic, I'm thinking, and the sorrow you put on me has my brains drownded in grief. *(Suddenly bending down to her and grasping her arm intensely)* Tell me it's a lie, I'm saying! That's what I'm after coming to hear you say.

ANNA: *(Dully)* A lie? What?

BURKE: *(With passionate entreaty)* All the badness you told me two days back. Sure it must be a lie! You was only making game of me, wasn't' you? Tell me 'twas a lie, Anna, and I'll be saying prayers of thanks on my two knees to the Almighty God!

ANNA: *(Terribly shaken—faintly)* I can't, Mat. *(As he turns away—imploringly)* Oh, Mat, won't you see that no matter what I was I ain't that any more? Why, listen! I packed up my bag this afternoon and went ashore. I'd been waiting here all alone for two days, thinking maybe you'd come back— thinking maybe you'd think over all I'd said—and maybe—oh, I don't know what I was hoping! But I was afraid to even go out of the cabin for a second, honest—afraid you might come and not find me here. Then I gave up hope when you didn't show up and I went to the railroad station. I was going to New York. I was going back—

BURKE: *(Hoarsely)* God's curse on you!

ANNA: Listen, Mat! You hadn't come, and I'd gave up hope. But—in the station—I couldn't go. I'd bought my ticket and everything. *(She takes the ticket from her dress and tries to hold it before his eyes.)* But I got to thinking about you— and I couldn't take the train—I couldn't! So I come back here—to wait some more. Oh, Mat, don't you see I've changed? Can't you forgive what's dead and gone—and forget it?

BURKE: *(Turning on her—overcome by rage again)* Forget, is it? I'll not forget 'til my dying day, I'm telling you, and me tormented with thoughts. *(In a frenzy)* Oh, I'm wishing I had wan of them fornenst me this minute and I'd beat him with my fists 'til he'd be a bloody corpse! I'm wishing the whole lot of them will roast in hell 'til the Judgment Day— and yourself along with them, for you're as bad as they are.

ANNA: *(Shuddering)* Mat! *(Then after a pause—in a voice of dead, stony calm)* Well, you've had your say. Now you better beat it.

BURKE: *(Starts slowly for the door—hesitates—then after a pause)* And what'll you be doing?

ANNA: What difference does it make to you?

BURKE: I'm asking you!

ANNA: *(In the same tone)* My bag's packed and I got my ticket. I'll go to New York tomorrow.

BURKE: *(Helplessly)* You mean—you'll be doing the same again?

ANNA: *(Stonily)* Yes.

BURKE: *(In anguish)* You'll not! Don't torment me with that talk! 'Tis a she-divil you are sent to drive me mad entirely!

ANNA: *(Her voice breaking)* Oh, for Gawd's sake, Mat, leave me alone! Go away! Don't you see I'm licked? Why d'you want to keep on kicking me?

BURKE: *(Indignantly)* And don't you deserve the worst I'd say, God forgive you?

ANNA: All right. Maybe I do. But don't rub it in. Why ain't you done what you said you was going to? Why ain't you got that ship was going to take you to the other side of the earth where you'd never see me again?

BURKE: I have.

ANNA: *(Startled)* What—then you're going—honest?

BURKE: I signed on today at noon, drunk as I was—and—she's sailing tomorrow.

ANNA: And where's she going to?

BURKE: Cape Town.

ANNA: *(The memory of having heard that name a little while before coming to her—with a start, confusedly)* Cape Town? Where's that? Far away?

BURKE: 'Tis at the end of Africa. That's far for you.

ANNA: *(Forcing a laugh)* You're keeping your word all right, ain't you? *(After a slight pause—curiously)* What's the boat's name?

BURKE: *The Londonderry.*

ANNA: *(It suddenly comes to her that this is the same ship her father is sailing on.)* The Londonderry! It's the same— Oh, this is too much! *(With wild, ironical laughter)* Ha-ha-ha!

BURKE: What's up with you now?

ANNA: Ha-ha-ha! It's funny, funny! I'll die laughing!

BURKE: *(Irritated)* Laughing at what?

ANNA: It's a secret. You'll know soon enough. It's funny. *(Controlling herself—after a pause—cynically)* What kind of a place is this Cape Town? Plenty of dames there, I suppose?

BURKE: To hell with them! That I may never see another woman to my dying hour!

ANNA: That's what you say now, but I'll bet by the time you get there you'll have forgot all about me and start in talking the same old bull you talked to me to the first one you meet.

BURKE: *(Offended)* I'll not, then! God mend you, is it making me out to be the like of yourself you are, and you taking up with this one and that all the years of your life?

ANNA: *(Angrily assertive)* Yes, that's yust what I do mean! You been doing the same thing all your life, picking up a new girl in every port. How're you any better than I was?

BURKE: *(Thoroughly exasperated)* Is it no shame you have at all? I'm a fool to be wasting talk on you and you hardened in badness. I'll go out of this and lave you alone forever. *(He starts for the door—then stops to turn on her furiously.)* And I suppose 'tis the same lies you told them all before that you told to me?

ANNA: *(Indignantly)* That's a lie! I never did!

BURKE: *(Miserably)* You'd be saying that, anyway.

ANNA: *(Forcibly, with growing intensity)* Are you trying to accuse me—of being in love—really in love—with them?

BURKE: I'm thinking you were, surely.

ANNA: *(Furiously, as if this were the last insult—advancing on him threateningly)* You mutt, you! I've stood enough from you. Don't you dare. *(With scornful bitterness)* Love 'em! Oh, my Gawd! You damn thick-head! Love 'em? *(Savagely)* I hated 'em, I tell you! Hated 'em, hated 'em, hated 'em! And may Gawd strike me dead this minute and my mother, too, if she was alive, if I ain't telling you the honest truth!

BURKE: *(Immensely pleased by her vehemence—a light beginning to break over his face—but still uncertain, torn between doubt and the desire to believe—helplessly)* If I could only be believing you now!

ANNA: *(Distractedly)* Oh, what's the use? What's the use of me talking? what's the use of anything? *(Pleadingly)* Oh, Mat, you mustn't think that for a second! You mustn't think all the other bad about me you want to, and I won't kick, 'cause you've a right to. But don't think that! *(On the point of tears)* I couldn't bear it! It'd be yust too much to know you was going away where I'd never see you again—thinking that about me!

BURKE: *(After an inward struggle—tensely—forcing out the words with difficulty)* If I was believing—that you'd never had love for any other man in the world but me—I could be forgetting the rest, maybe.

ANNA: *(With a cry of joy)* Mat!

BURKE: *(Slyly)* If 'tis truth you're after telling, I'd have a right, maybe, to believe you'd changed—and that I'd changed you myself 'til the thing you'd been all your life wouldn't be you any more at all.

ANNA: *(Hanging on his words—breathlessly)* Oh, Mat! That's what I been trying to tell you all along!

BURKE: *(Simply)* For I've a power of strength in me, to lead men the way I want, and women, too, maybe, and I'm thinking I'd change you to a new woman entirely, so I'd never know, or you either, what kind of woman you'd been in the past at all.

ANNA: Yes, you could, Mat! I know you could!

BURKE: And I'm thinking 'twasn't your fault maybe, but having that old ape for a father that left you to grow up alone, made you what you was. And if I could be believing 'tis only me you—

ANNA: *(Distractedly)* You got to believe it, Mat! What can I do? I'll do anything, anything you want to prove I'm not lying!

BURKE: *(Suddenly seems to have a solution. He feels in the pocket of his coat and grasps something—solemnly)* Would you be willing to swear an oath, now— a terrible, fearful oath would send your soul to the divils in hell if you was lying?

ANNA: *(Eagerly)* Sure, I'll swear, Mat—on anything!

BURKE: *(Takes a small, cheap old crucifix from his pocket and holds it up for her to see)* Will you swear on this?

ANNA: *(Reaching out for it)* Yes. Sure I will. Give it to me.

BURKE: *(Holding it away)* 'Tis a cross was given me by my mother, God rest her soul. *(He makes the sign of the cross mechanically.)* I was a lad only, and she told me to keep it by me if I'd be waking or sleeping and never lose it and it'd bring me luck. She died soon after. But I'm after keeping it with me from that day to this, and I'm telling you there's great power in it and 'tis great bad luck it's saved me from and me roaming the seas, and I having it tied round my neck when my last ship sunk, and it bringing me safe to land when the others went to their death. *(Very earnestly)* And I'm warning you now, if you'd swear an oath on this, 'tis my old woman herself will be looking down from Hivin above, and praying Almighty God and the Saints to put a great curse on you if she'd hear you swearing a lie!

ANNA: *(Awed by his manner—superstitiously)* I wouldn't have the nerve—honest—if it was a lie. But it's the truth and I ain't scared to swear. Give it to me.

BURKE: *(Handing it to her—almost frightenedly, as if he feared for her safety)* Be careful what you'd swear, I'm saying.

ANNA: *(Holding the cross gingerly)* Well—what do you want me to swear? You say it.

BURKE: Swear I'm the only man in the world ivir you felt love for.

ANNA: *(Looking into his eyes steadily)* I swear it.

BURKE: And that you'll be forgetting from this day all the badness you've done and never do the like of it again.

ANNA: *(Forcibly)* I swear it! I swear it by God!

BURKE: And may the blackest curse of God strike you if you're lying. Say it now!

ANNA: And may the blackest curse of God strike me if I'm lying!

BURKE: *(With a stupendous sigh)* Oh, glory be to God, I'm after believing you now! *(He takes the cross from her hand, his face beaming with joy, and puts it back in his pocket. He puts his arm about her waist and is about to kiss her when he stops, appalled by some terrible doubt.)*

ANNA: *(Alarmed)* What's the matter with you?

BURKE: *(With sudden fierce questioning)* Is it Catholic ye are?

ANNA: *(Confused)* No. Why?

BURKE: *(Filled with a sort of bewildered foreboding)* Oh, God, help me! *(With a dark glance of suspicion at her)* There's some divil's trickery in it, to be swearing an oath on a Catholic cross and you wan of the others.

ANNA: *(Distractedly)* Oh, Mat, don't you believe me?

BURKE: *(Miserably)* If it isn't a Catholic you are—

ANNA: I ain't nothing. What's the difference? Didn't you hear me swear?

BURKE: *(Passionately)* Oh, I'd a right to stay away from you—but I couldn't! I was loving you in spite of it all and wanting to be with you, God forgive me, no matter what you are. I'd go mad if I'd not have you! I'd be killing the world— *(He seizes her in his arms and kisses her fiercely.)*

ANNA: *(With a gasp of joy)* Mat!

BURKE: *(Suddenly holding her away from him and staring into her eyes as if to probe into her soul—slowly)* If your oath is no proper oath at all, I'll have to be taking your naked word for it and have you anyway, I'm thinking— I'm needing you that bad!

ANNA: *(Hurt—reproachfully)* Mat! I swore, didn't I?

BURKE: *(Defiantly, as if challenging fate)* Oath or no oath, 'tis no matter. We'll be wedded in the morning, with the help of God. *(Still more defiantly)* We'll be happy now, the two of us, in spite of the divil!

(He crushes her to him and kisses her again. The door on the left is pushed open and CHRIS appears in the doorway. He stands blinking at them. At first the old expression of hatred of BURKE comes into his eyes instinctively. Then a look of resignation and relief takes its place. His face lights up with a sudden happy thought. He turns back into the bedroom—reappears immediately with the tin can of beer in his hand—grinning)

CHRIS: Ve have drink on this, py golly!

(They break away from each other with startled exclamations.)

BURKE: *(Explosively)* God stiffen it! *(He takes a step toward CHRIS threateningly.)*

ANNA: *(Happily—to her father)* That's the way to talk! *(With a laugh)* And say, It's about time for you and Mat to kiss and make up. You're going to be shipmates on the Londonderry, did you know it?

BURKE: *(Astounded)* Shipmates—Has himself—

CHRIS: *(Equally astounded)* Ay vas bo'sun on her.

BURKE: The divil! *(Then angrily)* You'd be going back to sea and leaving her alone, would you?

ANNA: *(Quickly)* It's all right, that's where he belongs, and I want him to go. You got to go, too; we'll need the money. *(With a laugh, as she gets the glasses)* And as for me being alone, that runs in the family, and I'll get used to it. *(Pouring out their glasses)* I'll get a little house somewhere and I'll make a regular place for you two to come back to—wait and see. And now you drink up and be friends.

BURKE: *(Happily—but still a bit resentful against the old man)* Sure! *(Clinking his glass against CHRIS's)* Here's luck to you! *(He drinks.)*

CHRIS: *(Subdued—his face melancholy)* Skoal. *(He drinks.)*

BURKE: *(To ANNA, with a wink)* You'll not be lonesome long. I'll see to that, with the help of God. 'Tis himself here will be having a grandchild to ride on his foot, I'm telling you!

ANNA: *(Turning away in embarrassment)* Quit the kidding now.

(She picks up her bag and goes into the room on left. As soon as she is gone, BURKE relapses into an attitude of gloomy thought. CHRIS stares at his beer absent-mindedly. Finally BURKE turns on him.)

BURKE: Is it any religion at all you have, you and your Anna?

CHRIS: *(Surprised)* Vhy yes. Ve vas Lutheran in ole country.

BURKE: *(Horrified)* Luthers, is it? *(Then with a grim resignation, slowly, aloud to himself)* Well, I'm damned then surely. Yerra, what's the difference? 'Tis the will of God, anyway.

(Moodily preoccupied with his own thoughts—speaks with somber premonition as ANNA *reenters from the left)*

CHRIS: It's funny. It's queer, yes—you and me shipping on same boat dat ray. It ain't right. Ay don't know—it's dat funny vay ole davil sea do her vorst dirty tricks, yes. It's so. *(He gets up and goes back and, opening the door, stares out into the darkness.)*

BURKE: *(Nodding his head in gloomy acquiescence—with a great sigh)* I'm fearing maybe you have the right of it for once, divil take you.

ANNA: *(Forcing a laugh)* Gee, Mat, you ain't agreeing with him, are you? *(She comes forward and puts her arm about his shoulder—with a determined gayety.)* Aw say, what's the matter? Cut out the gloom. We're all fixed now, ain't we, me and you? *(Pours out more beer into his glass and fills one for herself—slaps him on the back)* Come on! Here's to the sea, no matter what! Be a game sport and drink to that! Come on!

(She gulps down her glass. BURKE *banishes his superstitious premonitions with a defiant jerk of his head, grins up at her, and drinks to her toast)*

CHRIS: *(Looking out into the night—lost in his somber preoccupation—shakes his head and mutters)* Fog, fog, fog, all bloody time. You can't see vhere you vas going, no. Only dat ole davil, sea—she knows!

(The two stare at him. From the harbor comes the muffled, mournful wail of steamers' whistles)

(The curtain falls.)

END OF PLAY

www.ingramcontent.com/pod-product-compliance
Lightning Source LLC
Chambersburg PA
CBHW070756100426
42742CB00012B/2154